*Everything
you always
wanted
to know about
sex . . .*

Everything you always wanted to know about sex*

EXPLAINED BY DAVID R. REUBEN, M.D.

* *but were afraid to ask*

W. H. Allen *London & New York* 1970

© David R. Reuben, M.D., *1969*
First British edition, 1970
Printed and bound in Great Britain by
Butler & Tanner Ltd, Frome and London,
for the publishers
W. H. Allen & Co Ltd,
43 Essex Street, London WC 2R 3JG

SBN *0 491 00056 1*

ACKNOWLEDGMENTS

Obviously this book is not based solely on my personal experiences. It is to a certain extent a reflection of the combined experiences of several thousand patients who have entrusted me with the responsibility of treating their emotional difficulties. With this in mind I have taken elaborate precautions to preserve their anonymity in every sense of the word.

I would like to thank two of my distinguished medical colleagues, Dr. Joseph Kwint and Dr. Louis Schlom, for reading and commenting on certain material. Miss Melicia Cranny of the San Diego County Medical Society Library and the staff of the library were very helpful in obtaining reference material. The librarians at the Bio-Medical Library of the University of California at San Diego also provided assistance. In addition, the staff at the Spring Valley Branch of the San Diego County Library cooperated in many ways.

More than a dozen patients currently in treatment contributed valuable comments after reading segments of the manuscript related to their specific areas; I would like to thank them collectively here. My agent, Mr. Don Congdon, merits my deep appreciation for his expert guidance through the literary maze. I am grateful to my editor, Mrs. Eleanor Rawson, whose tact and sensitivity helped the book take its final form.

Vivienne Miller, my loyal medical assistant, controlled my office with a steady hand and thereby preserved intact many of the hours necessary to produce this book. John Pridinoff aggressively and enthusiastically typed a portion of the manuscript. My wife, Barbara, with her unlimited patience, not only typed the remainder of the manuscript but made numerous valuable suggestions regarding the content and format of the book itself. Only her modesty prevents me from naming her as co-author.

Finally, my son David contributed to the book by graciously giving up some of the hours he would have preferred to spend playing with his father. For a two-year-old it was a significant sacrifice, though the debt has since been repaid.

Rancho Los Gatos
Spring Valley, California

CONTENTS

ix

PUBLISHER'S NOTE

The author of this book, Dr. David Reuben, is an American psychiatrist who practises in southern California. Many of the specific episodes as well as some of the terminology and statistics reflect American expressions of sexuality. Similarly, the chapters on homosexuality, abortion, and venereal disease reflect the contrast in legal procedures between Britain and the United States. However, the basic aspects of human sexual behaviour are universal and it has not been considered necessary to edit the original work for the British edition.

1

BEYOND THE BIRDS AND BEES

As a psychiatrist I am constantly impressed with one outstanding paradox. In virtually every patient, I see a person living in the Space Age who has left his (or her) sexual organs in the Stone Age. The cumulative effect of thousands of years of education, culture, and refinement have not had much impact on our knowledge about the genitals. Despite all the frank, "for adults only," films and books today, most people still are abysmally ignorant about sex. A jet pilot propels his airliner through space at 600 miles an hour—he cannot propel his own penis seven inches into a vagina. During the day a woman physicist explores the mysteries of nuclear particles. At night she is left to ponder the mystery of her own homosexuality. Most of us are in the uncomfortable position of knowing more about what occurs 238,000 miles away on the surface of the moon than what happens six inches below our own navels.

Something else has happened. In a mysterious, barely comprehensible way the members of our society who are least qualified scientifically and emotionally have taken control of sex. Anthony Comstock, the psychotic legislator, was responsible for a myriad of bizarre sexual laws that remain on the books today. The Reverend Bowdler, a sick man, systematically went through classical works of literature and expunged the remotest sexual reference. "Bowdlerized" even today is a synonym for literary rape.

Sexual behaviour is often judged by clergymen whose qualifications include their solemn renunciation of sexual intercourse. Tragically, those who undertake to control our sexual destinies are often sexually sick themselves. The decency leagues dedicated to abridging sexual behaviour—except on their terms—are simply trying to deprive others of the reasonable use of their sexual organs.

Every one of us has made that seven-inch journey through the penis into the vagina to meet the other half of our future protoplasm, and has then settled in the uterus for the 280-day wait. There is no reason now to be ashamed of how we travelled and where we grew—there is no more suitable place.

These are the reasons I chose to write this book. The first step in bringing knowledge of our sexual behaviour up to the same standard as, for example, our knowledge of pigs' sexual behaviour, is simply to make available all the facts on the subject. There are at least a dozen well-written, honest books on swine-breeding—they tell the *whole* story, directly, scientifically, and sometimes even entertainingly. There should be at least one book about us—human beings—that does it the same way.

Previously published books in this area generally approach sex from one of several directions. One popular theme is the technical manual which should be entitled *How to Copulate Efficiently*, or euphemistically, *Sexual Pleasure in Marriage*, *Sex Without Guilt*, etc. Such books tell how to "do it" in a nice, socially acceptable way. They ignore the almost unlimited range of human sexual behaviour which occurs from sunset to sunrise each twenty-four hours. What do the whores do? What do the freaks do? What do the nice girls do that they didn't find in the marriage manuals?

The other category of book widely circulated is the How-It-

Feels book: *How It Feels to Be a Homosexual, How It Feels to Be a Prostitute, How It Feels to Be a Homosexual Prostitute.* The range and combinations are only limited by the ingenuity of the author and the ingenuousness of the reader. Generally the basic theme of these books is: "I did it and it felt wonderful but I felt horrible and I kept on doing it and then wrote this so no one else will be tempted to make the same mistake I did." Even an unsophisticated reader recognizes the basic insincerity of this type of book. Furthermore, it rarely sheds any light on the particular sexual aberration he (or she) is guiltily indulging in.

Another group of books on the subject of sex are those written by alleged crusaders. These can be lumped under the general title, "*Why Can't We Do Anything We Want?*" On the very day they are published they have an antiquated aroma, because they overlook the fact that right now we are doing anything we want—at least sexually. We are feeling plenty guilty about it and often aren't quite sure what we're doing—but we are doing it just the same.

Most people have more sexual freedom than they know how to handle. In our sophisticated society it is usually a simple matter to find a willing partner, a quiet place, and get down to business. Knowing what you're doing is another story.

One problem among others is to make an individual aware of the capabilities and potentials of his sexual organs so he can utilize them to their fullest capacity. The average person has not even begun to experience the range of sexual gratification of which he is capable. Or as one patient jokingly put it, "Sexually, the surface hasn't even been scratched yet."

The purpose of this book is to tell the reader what he wants to know and what he *needs* to know to achieve the greatest possible degree of sexual satisfaction. It is designed to answer questions that have never been answered except in obscure medical books.

What we refer to as modern sex education is laughable. Over great resistance we have finally advanced to the point of telling school children that the penis somehow comes in contact with the vagina and other vague sorts of things happen. It is becoming more and more apparent that pupils in these classes, especially in secondary school, are very considerate of their elders . . . by not laughing out loud. More and more, they are cramming a wider range of sex into one weekend than their menopausal teacher experienced in a lifetime . . . not to say that they understand what they are doing.

In spite of the shrill denials of the professional moralists, it is obvious that human beings were designed by their Creator to copulate. An active and rewarding sexual life, at a mature level, is indispensable if one is to achieve his full potential as a member of the human race. Those whose sexual behaviour is shrouded in ignorance and circumscribed with fear have little chance of finding happiness in their short years on this planet. The goal of this book is to replace ignorance with knowledge and replace fear with confidence by telling, honestly and directly, EVERYTHING YOU ALWAYS WANTED TO KNOW ABOUT SEX—BUT WERE AFRAID TO ASK.

2

MALE SEXUAL ORGANS

How big is the normal penis?

That is the question of the century. Every male, virtually from the
moment he is aware of this marvellous organ, is plagued by this
question. Rarely does one encounter a gentleman who is satisfied
with the size of his phallus. Even those endowed with obviously
outsize organs yearn for more—"It could be just a little bit
longer . . ."

This preoccupation with size leads to some unusual behaviour.
Whenever two nude men encounter each other for the first time,
in a public shower, a country club locker room, a YMCA swimming pool, their eyes go first to each other's penises. Rapidly,
sometimes almost imperceptibly, they measure the organ, compare
it with their own, then continue with the matter at hand. Even in
public washrooms, standing at the urinal, eyes dart swiftly to
organs, the mental micrometer steps off the distance and makes the
comparative calculation. In more than one private club the
management has thoughtfully installed large magnifying mirrors
over the urinals so that each gentleman who avails himself of their

facilities can feast his eyes on the reflection of a phallus which would do credit to a bull elephant.

Unfortunately these penile Olympics are a no-win proposition. Those who spy larger organs than their own are chagrined: their fears are confirmed. A man whose penis is the longest in the locker room *that day* receives scant consolation. With each new contest he will be up against new and unmeasured competition.

Perhaps one of the reasons behind this forlorn quest is the enormous disparity between the penises of father and child. At the age of three or four the parent's phallus seems immense by comparison. Not until many years later at puberty does the son's organ begin to catch up. By then the damage is done. Most men are never really sure that their penis has finally caught up to daddy's. Some students of this problem have even gone so far as to suggest that the real reason behind much male modesty is simply a desire to conceal the penis that every man is afraid is much too small.

But how long should a penis be?

According to the story, someone once asked Abraham Lincoln how long a man's legs should be. After a moment of contemplation, Mr. Lincoln replied, "I would say, just about long enough to reach from his body to the ground." From a realistic point of view, the normal size for a penis is long enough to reach from a man's body into the vagina. As long as the sperm can be delivered without spilling, reproduction is facilitated. Since penile size is a hereditary characteristic, transmitted genetically, any man whose penis is too short to reach the vagina will have difficulty reproducing; truly a short-penised race would have died out half a million years ago.

There is no relation whatsoever between the size of the penis—length, diameter, or any other measurement—and the ability to produce sexual orgasm in the female. Almost every aspect of orgiastic sensation in women is concentrated in the accessible genital structures, that is, the clitoris, labia, and related areas. This includes the lower one-third of the vagina, in easy reach of nearly every post-adolescent penis. In sexual intercourse, as in every artistic endeavour, it is quality not quantity that counts.

Notwithstanding, elaborate scientific studies of phallic length have been undertaken. The average erect penis sizes out at six inches. The range extends from four and a half to eight inches. The unofficial world record is held by a man whose erect organ was fourteen inches long and three inches in diameter. No information is available concerning where this contest was held.

What is the angle of the penis during erection?

Normally it varies between twenty and forty degrees to the vertical which, by one of those wonders of nature which we take for granted, exactly corresponds with the angle of the vagina.

The exception is a rare condition (fortunately) known as Peyronies Disease; the medical nickname is "bent-nail syndrome." In this malady the penis is literally bent out of shape. For some unknown reason, scar tissue gradually infiltrates the shaft of the penis. When erection occurs, the shaft of the penis may point northwest while the head of the organ looks southeast. At this stage, sexual intercourse becomes, if not impossible, very confusing.

Treatment is complicated and of questionable value, but fortunately the condition is very rare.

What happens during ejaculation?

Ejaculation consists of a complex sequence of events co-ordinated with split-second timing. It is roughly comparable to a missile launching into outer space. Actually it is a missile launched into "inner space." It makes the most complicated man-made mechanisms look like a game of marbles.

Once erection has taken place (a minor miracle in itself), and the penis is in place in the vagina, the circuits begin to hum. Sensory receptors within the skin of the penis lock into the electrical system. They measure the heat of the vagina, friction against the penis, pressure of the vaginal wall against the penile shaft, amount of vaginal lubrication present, etc. These "situation reports" are constantly relayed to the sexual centres in the spinal cord and brain. In response, the centres direct more blood to the penis, increase the sensitivity of the touch receptors in the organ, and build up nervous energy in the lower segment of the spinal cord.

As intercourse progresses, a constant flow of nerve impulses races between the sexual organs and the central nervous system, building up and reinforcing itself. All other stimuli are integrated into the system. Looking at the sexual partner, touching her, being touched by her, contribute to the rapidly building tension. It is comparable, in one sense, to blowing up a balloon. The pressure gets higher and higher and higher until it is finally released by an explosion.

Finally the critical point is reached, and, in sexual intercourse, ejaculation is the explosion, a tremendous nervous explosion that sets off a chain reaction. Then things start to happen *fast*.

The urethra is sealed off so urine will not be expelled accidentally. Secretions from the prostate gland, seminal vesicles, and testicles are mixed on the spot. The man's pelvic muscles contract to hurl the penis deeper into the vagina: simultaneously involuntary arching of the back drives the entire body forward. At this point consciousness is obliterated and the man loses all contact with the world—except for those few cubic inches of vagina surrounding his penis.

A powerful internal pump swings into action squirting a quarter-ounce of seminal fluid into the vagina in about six consecutive jets. Ten seconds later it is all over—until the next time.

How many sperm are in each ejaculation?

On the average there are about 500,000,000 sperm swimming in each quarter-ounce of semen, or two and a half times the population of the United States. The average man propels about eighteen quarts of seminal fluid in his lifetime, or nearly one and a half *trillion* sperm. Therefore he is able, *theoretically*, to father about 500 times the number of people now living on this planet. Fortunately only one out of 288 acts of intercourse results in impregnation, usually involving one ovum and one sperm.

What about erection?

If ejaculation can be compared to firing a missile, erection corresponds to manufacturing the missile, it has to be done virtually from scratch each time intercourse occurs.

Just under the skin of the penis is a series of small reservoirs resembling rubber balloons. Each reservoir is fed by a group of veins and has two sets of valves, one for filling, another for emptying. The operation of the blood vessels and valves is controlled by a network of nerves running directly to the spinal cord and brain. This genital "Communications Central" carries impulses in both directions; from penis to brain and spinal cord *and* from the central nervous system to the penis.

Why is that important?

It is vital in determining when erection occurs and when it does not. Direct stimulation, *gentle* stimulation, of the skin of the penis almost always results in erection. This is a reflex and can occur if the man is asleep, under anaesthesia, or even paralysed. No nerve connections with the brain are required; the message goes from penis to spinal cord and back to penis.

Erection can also come about without any physical contact whatsoever, as the publishers of girlie magazines are well aware.

In that case, the image of a naked woman in a magazine is perceived by the brain, a nerve impulse goes to the penis via the spinal cord, and erection results.

How does erection actually happen?

Assuming that all other systems are "go," nervous signals cause the filling valves of each penile reservoir to open; blood pours into these distensible chambers. Since these chambers are fixed in place by connective tissue, as they distend the penis becomes stiff and hard. A delicate system of pressure detectors keeps the pressure in balance at all times so the erection is not too hard and not too soft—just right.

What happens after intercourse?

After intercourse the erection usually disappears promptly. Sometimes, however, for some unknown reason, the erection lingers for five minutes or so. The rest is simply a matter of gravity—"Whatever goes up, must come down." The emptying valves open, the blood drains back into the vessels, and the penis settles down to await its next summons.

Though the demolition phase seems automatic and uncomplicated, occasionally something goes wrong and a sexual nightmare ensues: *Priapism.*

Priapism? What's priapism?

Briefly, priapism is too much of a good thing. It refers to an intense, prolonged, persistent erection. It is all the more grotesque in that it often strikes men who have previously had difficulty getting *any* erection at all.

For the first few minutes the unfortunate man feels as King Midas must have felt when first he knew the golden touch. The poor fellow can have intercourse two, three, four times effortlessly. The erection seems to get stronger with each sally. (As a matter of fact, because of the irritation, it does.) The third or fourth times around the victim gets suspicious. Ejaculation becomes impossible—there is nothing more to ejaculate. The ecstasy or orgasm is replaced by pain and pressure. Even the thought of intercourse becomes unbearable. Everything centres around the tense, rigid, aching penis. A touch of impotence would be most welcome at that moment.

What causes priapism?

It is a cruel physical joke played by the body on itself. Usually it is a symptom of a serious disease affecting the entire body which results in irritation of the spinal cord and nerves controlling erection. Sometimes abnormalities of the related blood vessels can bring it on. One thing is for sure—after the first time, no one ever wishes for it again.

What's the cure?

Usually the patient tries to cure it himself by repeated intercourse or masturbation. After this fails he calls the doctor. Rarely, rest and sedation demolish the abnormal erection. More commonly, incisions must be made along the side of the penis; the blood drains out of the reservoirs letting the penis and the victim get some rest.

What does impotence mean?

Impotence is a general term describing any form of male sexual inadequacy. Actually there are three major categories of impotence.

The most disabling and fortunately least common type is absolute impotence. In these cases erection simply does not occur. The show is over before it starts, or more concisely, there *is* no show. Zero. A tantalizing variation of this condition allows the man to have an erection any time there is no possibility of using it. For example, he may have a powerful and embarrassingly obvious erection at a church meeting or in the bus on the way home from work. But let him approach a vagina and everything fizzles out.

The second form of impotence lets the sufferer proceed one step further: he produces a strong erection, inserts the rigid penis into the vagina, and the organ promptly collapses. Usually, so does its owner.

The third type of impotence does not even exist—at least according to some "experts." To those afflicted, however, it is the most exasperating situation imaginable. It goes something like this: everything proceeds smoothly—a firm erection, faultless entry into the vagina, good thrusting action begins and ends *immediately* in ejaculation. Among prostitutes this affliction is known as "Slam-Bam-Thank-You-Ma'am!" For obvious reasons, *they* like it. No one else does.

To a normal woman, it is the ultimate in frustration. Just as her sexual feelings begin to intensify, everything stops. "That's all folks!" The effect is something like being ravenously hungry, sitting down to an appetizing meal, and after the first bite having everything thrown away.

To the man the experience is humiliating. At the same time that it deprives him of a substantial part of the enjoyment of sex, it stamps him as an undesirable sexual partner.

He ruins his own sexual pleasure as well as limiting his future sexual opportunities. No normal woman is going to wait around for an encore.

Some people say this condition doesn't exist?

There are some writers in the field of psychology who insist that this condition, known as "premature ejaculation," is normal. Others even consider it desirable. They say the faster a man ejaculates the *more* normal he is. Wonder what the wives say?

Is there any other form of impotence?

There is a fourth category, very rare. People who suffer from premature ejaculation sometimes think they would rather have this condition. Once in a while they get it; they change their minds immediately.

It takes the form of complete inability to ejaculate in spite of prolonged intercourse. Sometimes the proceedings drag on for an hour or more with no prospect of orgasm for the male. Finally in pain, boredom, and desperation, everyone gives up. Incidentally, nobody claims *this* is normal.

What percentage of men suffer from impotence?

The figure hovers around 100 per cent, depending on the precise definition. Every man, at one time or another in his life, has had some malfunction of his sexual apparatus. Considering the mechanical complexity of the reproductive system and the emotional stresses sometimes involved, an occasional breakdown can be anticipated.

Chronic or repeated impotence probably affects about 30 to 40 per cent of men at any given time. For obvious reasons these gentlemen are among the most miserable of human beings.

Don't the testicles have something to do with potency?

Yes, in an indirect way. These glands have two primary functions. By means of a complex process, they manufacture sperm which they make available to the sexual propulsive system for delivery to the vagina. Just as important, they produce testosterone, the male sex hormone. It is this hormone that makes all male sexual functioning possible. Under the influence of this chemical, at puberty, the penis enlarges, pubic hair appears, and all the other changes associated with sexual maturity occur. Without the testicles and the hormone they produce, none of the sexual events would take place.

What happens if a man loses his testicles?

It depends *when* he loses them. If castration occurs before puberty, before the effect of the male hormone is manifested, that's it right there. The unfortunate lad is finished before he starts. He is a eunuch. No sexual development whatsoever can be expected. The penis will be undersized, the body relatively hairless, the voice high-pitched. His physical appearance will be distorted, since testosterone also influences general body development. He will grow up to be tall, thin, pale, and mean. The mean part is understandable. In the Middle East, eunuchs were used to guard the harems. That made them even meaner.

A certain number of boys were also castrated before puberty to maintain their voices in the soprano range. This was especially popular during the Middle Ages, but the practice was in use as recently as the last part of the nineteenth century. No one ever asked the male sopranos if it was worth it.

What if the testicles are lost after full sexual development?

The results are interesting and somewhat variable. This problem was studied in detail during World War II, thanks to the twisted mind of an unknown engineer.

During the latter part of the war, the Germans developed what came to be called a "castration mine." It was a type of land mine with a dual explosive charge. When an unfortunate infantryman stepped on it, the first charge exploded and hurled the mine to just below waist level. Then the second charge blew up and so did the testicles. The weapon was a modest tactical success; soldiers were understandably reluctant to march through a field sown with these weapons.

In those cases where the testicles were completely destroyed but the penis was relatively undamaged, some men made it all right; they were capable of normal intercourse. In about half the cases where the testicles were obliterated, the victims rapidly showed the effects of castration. The penis decreased in size, body hair diminished, sexual potency disappeared, and of course sterility was absolute. Sexual intercourse was impossible: no erection, no sperm, no orgasm, and no ejaculation.

Mental changes occurred too, but considering the circumstances it was difficult to tell whether the depression and lethargy were a result of a hormone deficiency or a reaction to the complete loss of sexual ability.

What about the half who retained their potency?

That was hard to understand at first. In some cases the erection was not quite as strong and frequency of intercourse was lessened, but they continued sexually potent, though sterile. Erection, orgasm, ejaculation, all went off on schedule.

Their doctors were at a loss to explain the difference. It was like a car running without petrol—no testicles—and yet they continued to function sexually. As the study proceeded, it seemed that those men with understanding wives and sweethearts did best. Reassurance and encouragement probably enabled them to succeed where others had failed. There is no doubt that this was a factor in their recovery. However, there was something else. They were obviously getting testosterone from some other source.

Where else could they be getting it?

That, of course, was the problem. Soon it was discovered that the adrenal glands, two small masses of tissue perched atop the kidneys, were an additional source of the male sex hormone. In about half the cases, these glands produced enough male hormone to allow sexual activity to continue. The rest of the boys weren't quite so lucky. However, in the long run everyone profited.

As a result of this and other related discoveries, all the men were given injections and tablets of testosterone. The results were dramatic.

Those who had been sexual zeroes were astonished to see their penises grow, their voices deepen, their muscles harden, and almost forgotten urges begin to rumble again. Much to their amazement and delight, erections, orgasms, and ejaculations were back, sometimes in spectacular fashion. Even the men who were receiving some help from their own adrenal glands benefited from extra hormone injections. What the German mines had taken away, an injection (every week) put back to stay.

If injections of testosterone cure impotence in these cases, why not give it to all men with impotence?

That's what the doctors said to each other. After all, it seemed so obvious. If the hormone produces normal sexual functioning, then lack of normal sexual functioning can be cured by administering the hormone. Unfortunately it doesn't work that way. After a lot of men got a lot of injections with hardly any results at all, the scientists took a closer look at the whole question. They found out some important things.

First of all, there is a third gland in the human body affecting male sex hormone production. Most of the testosterone is manufactured in the testicles, with a lesser amount coming from the adrenal gland. However, the distributor is the pituitary, located at the base of the brain. If the two producing glands put out too much hormone, the pituitary slows or stops hormone production. If they secrete too little hormone, it tries to increase the output. As a practical matter, it is much easier for the pituitary to stop production than to speed it up.

This is where the trouble begins. If the patient has a deficiency of hormones because his glands are producing a small but inadequate amount of hormone, injection of testosterone into the bloodstream triggers the pituitary to *stop* the testicles and adrenals from working. The body becomes completely dependent on the shots and the glands atrophy. Understandably, the man is upset when he notices his testicles shrinking day by day. As if that weren't bad enough, the artificial hormone doesn't really do the same job as the natural substance, and other problems develop.

The biggest objection to hormone injections for impotence is more basic: they really don't work. The underlying cause of sexual impotence in the male is primarily psychological. As long as the testicles are producing a minimum amount of secretion, the real weakness lies in the brain.

Don't the testicles have something to do with potency?

Unfortunately not. They simply produce the raw material for further processing by the rest of the reproductive system. Once they manufacture their daily quota of hormone and sperm, their job is done.

Nature hasn't made it easy for the testicles. These two vital masses of tissue, which have the responsibility for the continuation of the human race, are hanging right outside in the way of everything. When our ancestors were running on all fours, the testicles were as far back as possible and could be backed out of harm's way when danger threatened, against a tree or the wall of a cave, for example. Nowadays they are vulnerable to every passing hazard, including atomic radiation.

Thousands of years ago there were strong muscles in the skin of the scrotum that hauled the contents up into the abdomen with lightning speed when the need arose. All that is left today are puny remnants of these once mighty defenders, barely enough to cause a few wrinkles on a cold morning.

Then the testicles are always in the scrotum?

No. Before birth they lie up inside the abdominal cavity like their counterparts, the ovaries. Shortly before birth they descend into the scrotum where they *usually* remain. Occasionally they become *migratory*; then they slide up and down from the scrotum into the abdominal cavity like a sort of genital yo-yo.

Testicles that fail to descend at all leave a man with an empty feeling. Sometimes they can be coaxed down with hormone injections (not testosterone this time, but an extract of the anterior pituitary). Otherwise they must be pulled down and anchored surgically.

Why do the testicles have to be pulled down into the scrotum? Why not leave them up in the abdomen where they will be safer?

It sounds like a good idea, but it seems there was a reason after all for putting these organs in the scrotum where they can catch the cooling breezes. The body temperature of 98·6 degrees is just a little too warm for sperm production. Formation of sperm tends to go down as the temperature goes up, and fertility shows a sharp drop. Some primitive tribes take advantage of this information (no one knows where they learned it) and encourage the men of the tribe to soak their testicles in hot water for several days before intercourse as a sort of contraception by climate control. While not as elegant as the pill, it is cheaper, safer, and does work to a certain extent.

Scrotal temperature is about three to four degrees cooler and the organs function better. A second and more ominous factor is that cancer of the testicles is a far greater risk if they reside upstairs in the abdomen.

All other things being equal, isn't a man with big testicles more potent than a fellow with small testicles?

No. It is performance, not size, that counts. In Africa there are many unfortunates afflicted with a parasitic infection which causes "elephantiasis." In this dreadful condition the testicles enlarge to the size of beach balls and *larger*. The victims must wheel their genitals around in wheelbarrows. None has ever been known to set a record for sexual vitality.

Is there any treatment for impotence?

There are dozens. Most of them don't produce any effect at all. However, some of the more ingenious approaches are worth mentioning, if only to illustrate that desperate problems produce desperate solutions.

For thousands of years men (and some women too) have yearned for a magic elixir to prod the reluctant penis into action. Almost the entire range of foods and chemicals known to man have been summoned; only a very few produced responses (see Chapter 5, Aphrodisiacs). However, with the coming of the Industrial Revolution, attention turned to mechanical devices. One gadget developed at that time is still in use. Its original name was the "Vacuum Masculinizer." A small glass bell, similar (appropriately) to the type used for serving food under glass, is placed over the unco-operative organ. By means of a hand-operated vacuum pump (the pump is electric in the de luxe model), the air pressure within the glass jar is reduced. When the pressure falls sufficiently, blood rushes into the penis and produces an erection. Unfortunately there is an additional problem. Like the folks who bought a grand piano—it looks great on the front porch, but how do you get it into the house?

Isn't there something to keep the penis hard all during intercourse?

Yes, there is, and it illustrates some of the obstacles in the path of inventors of potency products. Every new invention in the field solves part of the problem; unfortunately it usually leaves the other part just hanging there.

The problem with the "Vacuum Masculinizer" is that the penis falls down again as soon as it is removed from the glass tank. Unless the entire sexual act can be performed under a big jar, this method doesn't offer much hope.

A subsequent innovation consists of a hollow plastic tube about the size and shape of an erect penis. The flaccid organ is stuffed into it much like stuffing a sausage. The sensation is about what could be expected from a sausage.

There is a variation which consists of a cage-like apparatus made of short hinged corset stays which encircle the unwilling phallus. This version comes also in a folding model, presumably for the man who travels. Obviously this equipment is designed merely to deposit the penis in the vagina. What happens once it gets there is another question.

What about something that lets an impotent man have real intercourse?

Amazingly enough, *something* like that does exist. Through the wonders of electronics and Japanese engineering it is now possible for virtually any man to engage in sexual intercourse regardless of impotence. In spite of its effectiveness, for some reason it just hasn't caught on. The device is simple and fool-proof. There is a small black box about the size of a transistor radio with two wires, each attached to an electrode. One electrode is fastened to the base of the penis; the other (specially designed) is inserted into the rectum. When the current is turned on, high-frequency impulses surge through the nerves controlling the sexual reflexes, producing an immediate, powerful erection. As long as the power is on, the power is in. As intercourse progresses, ejaculation may be hastened by increasing the frequency of intensity of the pulses.

Drawbacks? As one disappointed user says, "I don't even have to wait until my wife gets home!"

Even this, the ultimate in electronic copulation, is no match for good old-fashioned feelings. Clearly there is more to sex than mere mechanical manipulation.

Is there any cure for impotence?

The only treatment that has yielded any results is the one directed at the most important sexual organ of all—the brain. The mind exerts ultimate control over the pelvis. Ask anyone who has been jolted by a jangling telephone at the critical moment in intercourse. Sometimes when the baby wakes up, the sexual organs go to sleep.

Sigmund Freud put it more concisely. It was during the period of psychology when the "experts" were obsessed with the concept of "penis inferiority." One evening at a party Dr. Freud was confronted by a belligerent student who demanded, "Isn't it true, Dr. Freud, that the way a man feels about himself depends on the size of his penis?" Freud reflected a moment, puffed on his ever-present cigar, and replied, "I would prefer to think that the size of the penis depends on the way a man feels about himself."

Then psychiatrists can cure impotence?

Only if they can cure the underlying disease. Inability to perform sexual intercourse adequately is only a symptom. Every sick penis is attached to a sick man. Cure the man and the penis gets well by itself. To put it another way, if the mind works right, the penis works right.

3

FEMALE SEXUAL ORGANS

Is it really true that the clitoris is simply a miniature penis?

Many experts consider the clitoris to be a penis that just didn't grow. They describe the entire female genitalia as male organs that never matured. Understandably, all the scholars who feel this way are men. Women experts look at it another way. According to them, the penis is nothing more than an overgrown clitoris. They consider the male organ a primitive version of the more "refined" female sexual apparatus.

Who's right?

As usual, everybody is about half right. At an early stage in development, the human embryo has both male and female sexual organs. They exist in the form of anlage, a German word for primitive tissue that later differentiates into a specialized organ.

The embryo has a bisexual phallus; in those destined to be male it differentiates into a penis. Future girls will end up with a clitoris. According to the chromosomal decision made at the microsecond of conception, the tiny being may evolve one day into either a topless dancer or a well-muscled lifeguard. For the moment, however, the future chorus girl is as well equipped as the men who will, twenty years from now, whistle and stamp their feet in appreciation of her feminine charms. Likewise, the future lifeguard has, potentially, all the pelvic endowments of the bikini-clad lovelies who will one day swarm around him.

Fortunately for those concerned, long before birth, the sexual structures of the suppressed sex atrophy and all but disappear. At the time of delivery the normal infant has clear-cut and distinctive sexual features. The obstetrician has no trouble telling the excited parents whether it's a boy or girl. But if he were completely honest, he would say: "Congratulations, you are the proud parents of a six-pound (98 per cent) girl!"

Why only 98 per cent?

Because at least two per cent of the sexual organs of the male and female really belong in the other sex. Boys are two per cent girls and girls are two per cent boys. This is the proportion in normal people—in abnormal cases the percentage can be a lot higher. For example, the testicles are nothing more than female ovaries which have found a new home in the scrotum. (Some experts prefer to consider the ovaries merely testicles which did not descend. The point of view usually depends on whether the expert has testicles or ovaries.)

If the embryo is going to be a boy, the future testicles will drop through the pelvic cavity into the labia majora and expand them into a scrotum. The undifferentiated phallus increases dramatically in size and in the process is pierced by the urethra to become the penis.

If the embryo is to follow the female path, there are fewer changes required. The ovaries stay where they are. The labia majora also remain essentially unchanged. Only a few minor alterations are required to produce uncomplicated structures like the vagina and labia minora.

Does that mean if the original sexual organs don't develop, the embryo will be female?

Not exactly. At the earliest stages, the embryo has little more than gonads—future ovaries or testicles; genital swellings—future labia majora or scrotum; and phallus—future penis or clitoris. If the child is going to be sexually distinctive as male or female, development must occur in one direction or the other. In the male this development is fairly complicated. The female has a much shorter distance to travel.

This has led some researchers, all of them women, to suggest that *every* embryo is originally female. About half of them (the unlucky ones according to these ladies) develop into males.

Is that true?

Probably not. There is however one element of female superiority that is undeniable.

In relatively primitive animals such as chickens, urination, defecation, and reproduction are all conducted at one common orifice known as the cloaca. (Literal-minded scholars coined the term—in Latin *cloaca* means sewer.)

On moving up the evolutionary scale, the functions of the various openings become increasingly specialized. At what we like to consider the top of the tree, human beings, the male has progressed to the point of developing a separate orifice for defecation. He is still committed however to time-sharing for urination and reproduction; the urethra serves both purposes.

The female meanwhile has reached the top. She is a de luxe model, anatomically speaking, with complete segregation of structure and function; three jobs, three orifices. Male superiority? Well, men like to *think* so anyway.

Do all the female sexual organs have a counterpart in the male?

Yes. Since the genitalia originally were identical, there must be at least a remnant of each female organ in the male and of each male organ in the female.

Then do men have a vagina?

Every man carries with him a little souvenir of the time when his masculinity was not so obvious. In the anatomy books it is called vagina masculina, or male vagina. Once upon a time it was destined to become a real vagina, but that never worked out. It is simply a tiny tag of tissue tacked on to the edge of the bladder. Men even have an equivalent of the hymen. Virgin or not, this tiny memento remains permanently intact in every adult male. It is called the "seminal colliculus"—*colliculus* is Latin for little hill. Not nearly as informative as the female hymen, it is simply a little hill of tissue next to the prostate gland, a leftover of the sex that might have been.

If there is a hymen in men, is there a prostate gland in women?

Yes, there is, or at least the equivalent. In women the prostate gland turns out to be Skenes glands, two tiny openings on either side of the urethra. Aside from becoming badly infected in ladies with gonorrhoea, they have long ago lost any function.

Bartholins glands, which get the credit (without doing the work) for supplying vaginal lubrication during intercourse, have developed into structures known as the bulbo-urethral glands in the male.

The bulbo-urethrals don't do much but when they do it, it counts. They rarely supply more than one tiny drop of secretion during intercourse, but it is a mighty important drop.

Yes. This is the way it can happen. The scene is a doctor's office. An attractive twenty-two-year-old girl, Lois, sits across from the doctor who has just finished examining her. She is *very* upset.

"But doctor, I couldn't be! I mean, there's no way! I just don't see how!" The mascara begins to flow down her cheeks, propelled by a gush of tears.

"I'm sorry, but there just isn't any question about it—you are six weeks pregnant."

"But I never did anything. He wanted to but I wouldn't let him because I didn't want to get——" Another flood of tears.

"Why don't you tell me exactly what you *did* let him do, so we can figure out what happened?"

Quickly Lois touched up her eye makeup. "Well, we were over at my place and we got to, you know, fooling around, and so he wanted to put it in me but I was afraid. So I said, 'No, you can just play around outside but you can't, you know . . .' "

"Then what happened?"

"Well, then he did. But he started getting excited and I thought he was going to uhm, you know, all over me, so I pushed him away."

That first treacherous drop claimed another victim. The initial secretion originating at the bulbo-urethral glands appears shortly after erection. No more than an expectant drop at the end of the penis, it can contain as many as 50,000 sperm. If these are wiped against the vulva by an aggressive penis, only one of the kicking, squirming swimmers needs to snake its way up the vagina into the cervix. Then we have a case like Lois: all the consequences without any of the compensations.

What are the chances of something like that really happening?

Because of the long distance involved—from the labia to the cervix, the chances are against being impregnated this way. On the other hand, girls are more likely to play this game instead of fully-fledged intercourse, because of the false sense of security it gives them. Since the odds are directly proportional to the number of exposures, it gets riskier each time. A bigger gamble is the common practice of inserting the penis, starting pelvic thrusts, and disengaging before ejaculation. A bad way to have sex and a good way to get pregnant.

What about the breasts?

This is another example of rudimentary organs present in both sexes. In this case they remain undeveloped until needed. In the male this means they never develop (under normal conditions); in the female they are quiescent until puberty.

The only exception is the first few days of life. Then both male and female breasts produce a clear secretion called colostrum, or "witches milk." This is a product of the milk-producing glands brought on by the large amount of sex hormones present in the infants' body at birth. In a few days the hormones subside and the "milk" disappears.

The breasts themselves are actually *sweat glands* which have increased in size and become specialized in function. Milk is a specialized form of sweat, enriched with proteins from the mother's blood. Fortunately this unromantic fact is buried deep in the textbooks of Embryology. Imagine the effect on the millions of red-blooded men tantalized by gorgeous globular breasts if they learned they were romantically involved with gigantic sweat glands.

Why do women have only two breasts?

This is the type of question that no mere human being can answer with authority. It obviously was decided that way by some higher power. However, we can guess at some possible reasons: Humans usually have only one offspring at a time; two breasts still leave one in reserve. Only human beings, primates, and elephants have a single set of breasts at the nipple line. Other species are more amply endowed, with six or more pairs of mammary glands.

About one out of every 200 women has extra nipples. They usually extend downward over the abdomen from the regular nipples to the pubic area. In rare cases a woman may have an extra set of breasts located just below the original pair. In a culture with such admiration for breasts, it is a wonder that these ladies are not in greater demand.

What about the hymen?

The hymen is a structure that gets attention all out of proportion to its function, which is—*nothing*. For centuries it has been regarded as a barometer of chastity—guardian of purity—sentinel at the gates of Venus. Nothing could be further from the truth.

It is possible for a woman to have sexual intercourse twenty times a day, give birth to a dozen children, and still have that flag of virtue, the hymen, waving at the vaginal portal. It all depends on the kind of hymen she is born with.

How does it work?

To understand the hymen's relative position in the genital area, it helps to have a model. If one makes a circle with the thumb and first finger, the enclosed space represents the vaginal opening. The webbing between the thumb and finger is the hymen in its usual position. *Ordinarily*, during the first sexual act, the penis pushes through the hymen, tearing it in several places. Repeated intercourse continues to erode the membrane, leaving only a few shreds to mark its former position of glory. In some cases the hymen is flexible, and instead of breaking before the penile assault, it merely bends. It is forced down toward the vaginal floor and allows the penis to glide over it. At childbirth the same thing happens in reverse. The child's head pushes the hymen outward without tearing it.

In the Western world, the hymen is a big deal. It is considered the symbol of virginity, and for some yet unexplained reason most normal males want to make it with a virgin. A prostitute with a stretchable hymen, if she plays her cards right, can make a fortune by surrendering her maiden state several times a night, at premium prices.

Certain of the more swinging establishments in European cities make the ceremony into quite a production. It requires a gent (not a regular customer) with a penchant for virgins. The lady of the houses chooses her specialist—the one with the flexible hymen—and arranges for the two to meet—at triple the going rate. The lucky couple occupies a room fitted with a dozen peepholes—admission is charged. The performance is always a sell-out to the men (and ladies) who enjoy this kind of thing. Accompanied by appropriate shrieks and squeals, the ravisher has his way. Virginity loses again. Thirty minutes later, after a hot bath and a little massage, the hymen is back in position ready to do its bit keeping its mistress in the upper tax brackets.

Isn't there always bleeding when the hymen is really broken?

Yes, but professional virgins also bleed. Careful analysis might reveal that an hour earlier the blood flowed in the veins of a chicken, but then most customers are not interested in probing *that* deeply.

Then an intact hymen is not a reliable indicator of virginity?

Correct. And a tattered or absent hymen doesn't mean the young lady has dispensed her favours freely. Some women just don't have much of a hymen. Others lose what they had by vigorous exercise. Sliding down poles and climbing trees are not exactly designed to keep a tiny tab of delicate tissue in place. Another old enemy of the vaginal gatekeeper is masturbation. Introducing a finger into the vagina is tough on any hymen.

A relatively recent innovation, the vaginal tampon to absorb menstrual flow, is also an easy way to say goodbye to this fragile membrane. The only reliable sign of a virgin vagina is what the doctors call an imperforate hymen, and they are rarely seen by anyone *but* doctors.

How come?

This type of hymen closes off the vaginal entrance completely. It is rarely noticed until menstruation begins—or more precisely, does not begin.

Usually if a girl does not start to menstruate by the age of sixteen or so, her mother becomes anxious and takes her to the doctor. After a quick glance at the vaginal orifice he makes the diagnosis. The opening is completely sealed off by a bulging hymen. Actual menstruation may have begun six months ago but instead of draining to the outside, the fluid has backed up into the vagina. A few nicks with the scalpel and the problem disappears. So does the hymen.

At what age does menstruation normally start?

It varies. Every girl operates according to her own biological timetable, so there is no normal age for the onset of menstruation. The range is from six to eighteen years with most girls beginning between ten and fourteen years old.

What actually is menstruation?

Menstruation is the final event in a long series of complex manœuvres executed by the body with split-second timing. The whole process unfolds according to a detailed script prepared by an internal computer. The plan is reviewed constantly, moment by moment, and up-dated monthly. In spite of the advances of science, our knowledge in this area is still rudimentary.

Controlling the menstrual cycle is roughly equivalent to launching a space vehicle, the egg, at the same time the launching pad is being built. Simultaneously a gigantic landing facility, the uterus, must be prepared in case the little traveller through inner space should come back in a new form—fertilized. Concurrently, preparations must be made to tear down everything that has been built up in order to start again from scratch each month. It is almost like demolishing Cape Kennedy the first of every month and rebuilding it by the fifteenth.

As the menstrual period finishes, the ovary begins pouring one of the primary female sex hormones, oestrogen, into the bloodstream. The presence of oestrogen is reported to the Central Control Area, the pituitary gland at the base of the brain. In response, Central Control directs the release of a supporting hormone, FSH. FSH restimulates increased production of oestrogen. Oestrogen acts on every reproductive organ but specifically causes rapid growth of the inner lining of the uterus.

At the surface of the ovary, the egg scheduled for launch that month is already straining at its moorings. Now secretion of the other female sex hormone, progesterone, begins. When the presence of progesterone is detected by the pituitary, it responds with counter hormone, LH.

Most of the progesterone is funnelled to the uterus where it intensifies the preparations already under way. Central Control is constantly monitoring hormone levels at all areas of the body. When the ratio of FSH to LH reaches the critical point, a rapid count-down begins, and the ovum is hurled into the abdominal cavity.

Into the abdominal cavity? Doesn't it go into the Fallopian tubes?

Hopefully. But it goes into the abdomen first. As the egg bursts from the surface of the ovary it travels freely into the vast emptiness of the pelvis. At the upper end of the Fallopian tubes, two enormous funnels with grasping fingers clutch eagerly at the tiny egg. Most eggs slide willingly into the friendly grasp.

Meanwhile, back at the uterus, big things are happening. The lining has enlarged dramatically. Each individual cell is bursting at the seams. The blood vessels have become immense and are pulsating rhythmically. Day after day the build-up continues as the detection systems remain constantly alert for information about the fate of the recently launched egg.

If the egg is *not* fertilized, Central Control reluctantly pushes the button marked DESTRUCT and everything comes crashing down. Ruthlessly the blood supply to the uterine lining is choked off. Cells on the surface are left to starve and die. They will soon slough off by the millions. Menstruation is under way.

For the next three to seven days, all that remains of the ambitious undertaking of the past three weeks goes down the drain. Appropriately, menstruation has been called "the weeping of a disappointed uterus." The body is perpetually optimistic; the entire project will begin again next month.

What does the menstrual flow consist of?

The cupful or so of thin red fluid which trickles out of the vagina during each menstrual period is about fifty per cent blood mixed with varying amounts of mucus and "clots." These so-called "clots" are actually pieces of the uterine lining which have broken away. Menstrual blood itself does not clot.

Why not?

The reason eluded researchers for years: menstrual blood cannot clot because it has *already* clotted. As blood pours out of the uterine wall, it coagulates quickly. As always, a short time after coagulating blood liquefies and once again flows freely.

Is that all there is to menstruation?

Not quite. Some unanswered questions remain:

1. Why does the menstrual tide, like the ocean tide, ebb and flow with the cycle of the moon?
2. Why do nosebleeds frequently accompany the menstrual flow?
3. Why do many women feel inexplicably depressed during menstruation? (Most crimes of violence committed by women occur during menstrual periods.)

The whole subject of menstruation has fascinated mankind for thousands of years. Even the earlier portions of the Bible refer to it. In Leviticus 15:19, "And if a woman have an issue, and her issue in her flesh be blood, she shall be put apart seven days: and whosoever touches her shall be unclean until the even."

What does that mean?

Like any Bible quotation, it is open to an unlimited number of interpretations. However, a few rapid calculations are revealing.

Let us assume the start of menstruation is considered the first day. The flow continues say, seven days. If the woman is "unclean," that is, not approachable for sexual intercourse for the next seven days, the first available moment after the onset of the menstrual period will be fourteen days later. Interestingly enough, that corresponds to the most likely day of ovulation. Intercourse on that day has an excellent chance of returning a fertilized ovum to the waiting uterus.

What guarantee is there that a woman will have intercourse on that specific day?

There is no guarantee of course. However, if she has been waiting impatiently for two weeks and her husband has likewise been counting the hours until his wife is available again, they will probably take advantage of the first opportunity. Synchronizing the lowering of the monthly sexual barriers with the day of greatest fertility was a stroke of genius on the part of the ancient Hebrews. Maybe that is the real meaning of I Chronicles 27:23: "... the Lord said he would increase Israel like to the stars of the heavens."

Why does menstruation stop during pregnancy?

It doesn't always. In a small number of cases monthly bleeding continues throughout pregnancy. Not quite so rare is a menstrual flow during the first month or two. Usually the increase in maternal hormone levels during pregnancy, bolstered by the hormones from the newly formed placenta, are adequate to keep the uterine lining from decomposing. Lactation may further delay the return of the period.

How come?

Another hard question. Lactation itself is not well understood. At birth both breasts are generally prepared to supply abundant milk. If the child begins to nurse, nervous impulses go from the nipples to Central Control in the pituitary gland. This produces still another hormone, lactogenic hormone, which starts the milk flowing and keeps it available until nursing stops. Almost like magic, when the sucking stops, the milk stops. At the same time menstruation is suppressed.

Then the woman can't become pregnant if she isn't menstruating?

Not exactly. Pregnancy is less likely during lactation (reason unknown), but in reproduction anything is possible. Fertilization can occur before, after, or during menstruation. Lots of chaps who pay child support will testify to that.

How do the female genitalia change in preparation for intercourse?

Erection of the penis is relatively simple compared to what must take place before girls are ready for copulation. Let's begin at the bottom and work up.

First, the blood vessels supplying the vulva dilate and bring on the feminine equivalent of a penile erection. The spongy tissues around the labia minora as well as the labia themselves swell and grow turgid. The clitoris becomes erect and peeps from under its diminutive foreskin. The labia majora increase in size and Bartholins glands, the two sentinels located astride the vaginal opening, do—nothing. Once considered the prime source of lubrication—"lover's liniment"—they have been demoted as medical research has discovered a new and fascinating source of these essential juices. The walls of the vagina themselves ooze a super-slippery substance that smoothes the way for eager couples. In the research lab, by means of a special camera in the form of a transparent, optically correct penis, the glistening drops can be observed gently forming on the vaginal wall.

In the meantime, engorgement of the vulva has formed a sort of sexual ante-room in front of the vagina. This increases the effective length of the vaginal canal and thus increases the size of the penis it can accommodate. More important, it brings the sexually sensitive structures—clitoris and labia minora—into closer contact with the penis.

The vagina is also changing. In cross section the relaxed vagina looks like the letter H; the roof is in contact with the floor. During sexual excitement it swiftly assumes the shape of a cylinder to receive an energetic piston, the penis.

What is the function of the clitoris?

The clitoris is the centre of sexual sensation in women. Though it is tiny in comparison to the penis, it has at least the same number of nerve cells and fibres crowded into its miniature proportions. It is a sexual time bomb with a short fuse. Actually, a pair of fuses. The labia minora, looking like misplaced rooster's combs, are attached to the hood or prepuce of the clitoris. Pulling on them applies a gentle tug on the clitoris itself. As the labia are alternately pulled and released, the prepuce slides back and forth over the head of the clitoris. As the gentle friction continues the clitoris swells even more, making each tug even more exquisite.

How do the labia get pulled?

If the vagina can be considered a cylinder and the penis a piston, the labia minora is a crankshaft. With each stroke of the penis into the vagina, the ends of the labia are pulled toward the vagina, drawing down on the prepuce and clitoris. As the penis is withdrawn, the labia are released and the prepuce slides back over the clitoris. At the same time the penis is massaging the labia, the vagina, and the related structures. If everything goes right the result is orgasm.

What happens during orgasm?

Everything. All the transmission lines and circuits of the entire body are suddenly and deliciously overloaded. The wires get red-hot, the fuses blow, the bells chime—and then it's all over until the next time.

As a woman approaches orgasm the whole pace of her body accelerates. The heart rate zooms up to 160 or more. Respiration gives way to panting and groaning. Blood pressure can double. In the meantime the pelvis is going wild. All the veins of the pelvic area are at the point of bursting. The vulva is throbbing rhythmically almost to the point of grabbing at the surging penis. The sensory nerves are at their peak, soaking up each tiny drop of sensation. So much current is drawn by the sexual structures that the lights in the cerebrum begin to dim. The girl loses track of her surroundings and all attention is focussed on that vital five per cent of her body.

Suddenly the master switch is flipped and it happens! Indescribable sensations race from the vulva, vagina, and clitoris throughout the nervous system. The primitive areas of the brain seize control. The back arches, the pelvis lunges forward, the muscles surrounding the vulva expand and contract and send waves of feeling racing over the entire body. The pelvic veins empty rapidly, droplets of sweat burst out on the skin, and a sense of relaxation flows through the entire body.

How many orgasms can a woman have?

Nobody really knows. Recent investigators stopped the experiments after fifty or so consecutive climaxes. The experimental technique itself was rather ingenious. Under carefully controlled conditions, with trained observers, movie lights, tape recorders, and a 16-mm movie camera grinding away, a female volunteer engaged in sexual intercourse with a male volunteer. They copulated until she reached orgasm, duly recorded by electrodes taped to various parts of her body, as well as the camera and tape recorders. The gentleman immediately withdrew from the scene and was replaced by another more or less eager volunteer. This process continued until two score and ten intrepid spirits had given their best for Science. The lady was still more or less willing but the experimenters were hungry for dinner, the recorders were running out of tape, the cameras were running out of film, and anxious wives were beginning to telephone their husbands at the laboratory.

Wasn't the female subject tired?

The official records describe her as: "... tired but happy." One wonders how many more orgasms she might have had without the lights, cameras, recorders, and eager observers.

Actually there are several varieties of orgasm in the female. Male orgasms tend to be of the all-or-nothing variety—a tremendous build-up of tension followed by an explosive release. Women have this type of orgasm too, but they are also capable of "skimming."

This is a series of sexual climaxes which consist of a rapid increase in tension with an equally rapid release, rising immediately to another peak. The effect is something like a flat pebble skimming over the surface of the waves. The peaks are never as high and the valleys are never as deep as a full-scale orgasm, but it is said to be an exquisitely gratifying experience just the same. Most of the female multiple orgasms are of the "skimming" variety.

How can a woman continue to reach climax after climax when a man is finished after the first time around?

The answer depends on their different sexual structure and functioning. Erection in the male is dependent on engorgement of the veins of the penis. When sexual tension subsides, after the first orgasm, the erection droops as the blood begins to drain from the organ. Even if sexual stimulation continues, once the erection fades the organ must go through the full cycle of relaxation, rest, and re-erection. Sometimes this cycle can be speeded up, but the stages must proceed in that order.

The female has no such limitation. Large veins deep in the pelvic area as well as those in the sexual organs themselves never need to empty completely after orgasm. The blood can ebb and flow according to the degree of sexual excitement. Immediately after orgasm, sexual stimulation usually diminishes and the message goes out from the brain and spinal cord to open the drainage valves. If sexual activity should resume, the order is countermanded and the internal and external genitalia become engorged with blood once again.

Then orgasm is caused by blood flowing in the sexual organs?

Not exactly. There are three components to the orgasmic experience; if any of them are missing, orgasm does not take place.

First and most important is the nervous element. Sensations are fed to a cluster of nerves in the spinal cord, sort of an Orgasm Central Control, from every part of the body. Before intercourse, as her partner caresses her breasts, the sensations are fed into the spinal nerve plexus. When she places her hand on his penis, those sensations are routed via the brain to Orgasm Central. Any sexually stimulating sounds or words are also picked up and relayed to the spinal centres. As the man mounts her and begins to slide his penis into her vagina, the number of nervous messages increases a hundred times. The sensation of his skin against hers, the odour of his body, the pressure of his chest upon her breasts, the throbbing of his penis against her labia minora and vaginal entrance; these are all picked up by the appropriate sensing mechanisms and raced to Orgasm Central.

At about that stage the mechanism becomes self-feeding. Nervous impulses are now going in both directions, to the spinal centre and from it. This is what builds up to orgasm.

The impulses from the vagina, clitoris, labia, and even the internal pelvic structures, increase a thousandfold as the penis thrusts in and out. Finally the critical stage is reached, no more sensations can be tolerated, and Orgasm Central gives the command.

Then the second component of orgasm enters the picture. Nerve impulses from the spinal centres cause vigorous muscular contraction. The network of muscles which form a circular tunnel around the vagina clamp down, let go, clamp down, again and again. Even the uterus contracts under the intense nervous stimulation.

This brings on the third element in orgasm—vascular. The vigorous muscular contractions pump all the blood out of the veins—the resulting vacuum drains the tissues of the vulva and sexual tension swiftly declines. That, for the moment, is that.

What part does the uterus play in sexual intercourse?

Sexual feeling is confined, almost entirely, to the clitoris, labia minora, and the outer thirty per cent of the vagina. The rest of the vagina has little sensation and the cervix or lower end of the uterus can hardly feel anything at all. During medical exams the cervix is often held with a sharp-toothed instrument; the patient is rarely aware that anything is happening. This is notable, since most men put a lot of emphasis on the length of the penis (women know better) as an indicator of sexual prowess. Most of the real accomplishments occur in the first three inches of the female reproductive apparatus—it is a rare man who cannot stand up to that.

There is one exception. A certain number of women react sexually to deep pelvic pressure. It is more common among those who have had several children; they may have developed an awareness of the uterus and cervix during pregnancy and labour. These women experience an intensification of pleasure during intercourse and specifically during orgasm if the penis penetrates deeply into the vagina and presses against the cervix. But even here a long penis is not required. By shifting her body and flexing her legs the woman can effectively change the length of her vagina and get the result she wants.

If a woman can have so many more orgasms than a man, why is it some women can't have any orgasms at all?

There is a big difference between having the *potential* to achieve an orgasm and achieving it. The only thing that stands between any woman and an unlimited number of orgasmic experiences is about two pounds of tissue—the brain. The decision to have a sexual climax is not made in the vagina—it occurs at the other end of the body. Nature does not require sexual enjoyment for reproduction—once sperm is deposited in the vagina, she makes no further demands. Enjoyment of sexual intercourse is the individual responsibility of the participants.

Is there any way a man can tell if a woman has really had an orgasm?

Since most women know what men want to hear, especially in the department of sex, they are always willing to acknowledge an orgasm, even if they haven't had one. It doesn't cost them anything and goes a long way toward inflating the male ego. A great number of men in our society feel their manhood enhanced if their partners experience orgasm. Rarely do they inquire too deeply—if she says "yes," that's that. It makes it easier—at least for the moment. However, if he really wants to know, there are two accurate indicators.

Immediately after orgasm a certain number of women experience what is called a sexual flush. This is a measles-like rash over the entire chest. It comes on suddenly, last a few minutes. and then gradually fades away. Not every woman experiences this but they all exhibit the other sign.

Erection of the nipples always follows orgasm in the female. In spite of heaving hips, lunging pelvis, passionate groans—no nipple erection, no orgasm. It is an accurate mammary lie detector —for those who insist on the truth.

What's the difference between a vaginal orgasm and a clitoral orgasm?

Nothing. Many years ago Sigmund Freud theorized that women experienced two distinct types of orgasm, vaginal and clitoral. The clitoral orgasm was presumably based on masturbation in childhood and was considered childish and immature. Vaginal orgasm was related to adult sexual organs, and Dr. Freud considered it mature. The vaginal variety was said to be a more intense, more fulfilling experience. Based on this theory, which was essentially an untested philosophical concept, psychiatric thinking hardened like so much psychic cement. Few psychiatrists thought to ask the women, who were the only ones having clitoral or vaginal orgasms in the first place, what they really felt.

If direct experiments and observations had been possible in Freud's time, he probably would have been a pioneer in that area, too. But since a scientific look at human sexuality has had to wait until recently, Freud's ideas must be revised accordingly. They must make way for an Orgasmic Bill of Rights.

Orgasmic Bill of Rights?

Yes. All orgasms are created equal. Years of careful observation and analysis involving hundreds of men and women who copulated, masturbated, and engaged in nearly every variation thereof, right in the scientific laboratory, have yielded some important answers about female orgasm.

Unless the clitoris participates, orgasm does not take place. This diminutive structure is the centre of every sexual climax. *All* sexual feeling begins and ends here.

What if the vagina is stimulated without exciting the clitoris?

It can't be done. Any object large enough to stimulate the vagina also stimulates the clitoris by pulling down on the labia. Furthermore, nerves from the clitoris extend downward over the entire vulva into the walls of the vagina itself. The penis in the vagina pressing against the vaginal walls is still titillating the clitoris.

If a woman were to lose her clitoris, say in an operation, could she still have orgasms?

Certainly. Many women have had such surgery, because of cancer, for example. Nerves and blood vessels extend from the clitoris to every part of the vulva. Even if the organ itself is removed, the remaining nervous connections are more than adequate for orgasm.

What difference does it make, vaginal or clitoral orgasm?

It makes a lot of difference—to men and to women. As far as men are concerned they can forget all that nonsense in the marriage manuals (women never believed it anyhow) about overcoming frigidity by bringing the penis into contact with the clitoris. Virtually every book on sex technique insists on rubbing the penis and clitoris together during intercourse. Detailed instructions are usually given concerning placing the penis high up toward the front of the vagina so as to massage the penis against the clitoris with each pelvic thrust. Some of the manœuvres require the agility of an acrobat.

Not only is this uncomfortable and strained (as anyone who has ever tried it is aware), but it doesn't work. It doesn't work because it ignores the problem. All attempts to increase sexual excitement by rubbing the penis, head or shaft, against the clitoris are superfluous since in the usual course of copulation the clitoris is getting all the stimulation it can handle. As one old gynaecologist said, "If the clitoris had been intended to come in contact with the penis, it would've grown below the vagina instead of on top."

The Orgasmic Bill of Rights is good news to women because they can stop worrying about not being normal. An orgasm is an orgasm. Orgasms may vary in frequency and intensity but they all begin and end at the same place—the clitoris. Feelings of guilt about immaturity instilled by well-meaning psychiatrists can be cast aside. Every orgasm resulting from penis–vagina intercourse is, by definition, mature.

4

SEXUAL INTERCOURSE

How many kinds of sexual intercourse are there?

Sexual intercourse actually involves three distinct experiences masquerading as one. Sometimes the three events occur simultaneously, sometimes in succession, and often separately.

What do they consist of?

The first type of sexual intercourse is reproductive. It is simple, straightforward, easily understood, and relatively speaking, unpopular. In the average person's lifetime, reproductive sex (or reprosex) occurs on about ten occasions or less. All the requirements of this form of sexuality can be managed nicely in three or four minutes and probably could be done better by a disinterested third party—as it is occasionally in artificial insemination. Reprosex is merely a means of introducing Mr. Sperm to Miss Egg—what they do after that is up to them.

Sex for the sake of reproduction has the approval and endorsement of ministers of the gospel, moral leaders, and maiden aunts. Though they may not engage in it (presumably they have some kind of sexual outlet), they do recommend it for the masses.

Reprosex is uniformly unpopular with teen-agers, unmarried lovers, gay young bachelors, single girls, and ladies with ten children. Major world governments endorse or discourage this variety of sexual intercourse depending on the population supply at the moment.

What is the second form of sex?

Sex can also be a means of expressing love. When all the words have been said, the deep emotional bond that flows from the dramatic fusion of two bodies and two spirits can be the most profound way of saying, "I love you." It can exist among men and women at any stage of their lives, tends to be perishable if not carefully preserved, and those who have experienced it say it tends to grow stronger with the passage of time. Marriage is not a prerequisite, and some cynics even say that marriage takes the love out of sex. Everybody is in favour of love-sex, especially writers of popular songs, though not everyone has the chance to be exposed to it.

How about the third form of sex?

The third kind of sexual intercourse has acquired a bad name over the years. Most Western religions are against it, moral educators unanimously condemn it, parents are (apparently) against it, and everyone wants to do it. This is sex for fun, for the sheer physical and emotional exhilaration of feeling all the good feelings that come from a complete sexual experience. This is recreational sex at its best. Almost everyone under the age of twenty-five is for it openly, and nearly everyone else seeks it actively, if secretly. There is nothing wrong with funsex. Human beings—and for that matter, all mammals—are provided with penis or vagina and an overwhelming compulsion to use them. There is no reason why they shouldn't, and specifically in a way that will bring them the maximum pleasure.

Whole libraries have been devoted to amassing arguments against the sensible enjoyment of sex. Even after centuries of this insidious form of brainwashing, most human beings remain basically unconvinced. But there is a major obstacle to getting the full pleasure from sex.

What's that?

Obtaining the maximum enjoyment from sexual intercourse requires knowledge. Our modern society is careful to teach people how to run their automobiles but deliberately avoids teaching them how to run their sexual organs. What passes for sex education is like the old French joke:

"What's the definition of flirtation?"

"That is when the hand is in the thing-a-ma-jig and the thing-a-ma-jig is in the hand, but the thing-a-ma-jig is never in the thing-a-ma-jig."

After the usual course in sex education, the sixth former emerges with the amazing knowledge that two thing-a-ma-jigs somehow fit together. That, too, is a joke, but a grimmer one. If the schools wasted less time on the physiology of reproduction with all the beautiful diagrams of frantically swimming sperm (which nobody cares about anyhow) and spent more time on the physiology of orgasm (which everybody cares about), this might be a happier world.

Where do people in other societies learn about sex?

Many other cultures have on-the-job training. At puberty the older women of certain tribes take the young boys individually and introduce them to sexual intercourse with all its variations and implications. Older men do the same for the young girls. Imparting extensive knowledge about this most vital of human functions is considered a serious responsibility and is treated in a solemn fashion. The teachers are the wisest and most respected members of the tribe.

The only equivalent in our society is the father who takes his teen-age son to visit his favourite prostitute. It is not quite the same.

What can a person do to increase his enjoyment of sex?

First of all, people must decide what type of sex they are interested in. If they want reprosex, there are few difficulties involved. Generally most individuals who desire this type of sexual activity are already married and having intercourse. If impregnation occurs, that is that. If it doesn't, they seek medical help to arrive at a successful conclusion. Very few people, however, complain about being unable to reproduce—if anything, most of them would like to be less capable in that area.

Enjoying sex as an expression of love is somewhat more complex but also tends to take care of itself. The strong emotional bond and the intense feeling of identification that exists between lovers act as catalysts and accelerate most sexual responses. This makes the early attempts at intercourse emotionally satisfying, even if there is something lacking from a physiological point of view. Closeness of the bodies combined with the symbolic feeding of and being fed at the moment of ejaculation provides strong emotional gratification at this stage.

Recreational sex, however, is more demanding. Here the primary goal is pleasure, and often there is not the same depth of emotion available to compensate for any lapses in sexual function. The accent is on performance—and performance begins with the individual.

How can the individual prepare himself (or herself) for this?

Most important, he (or she) can see recreational sex as it really is; the most enjoyable diversion available to human beings. Unfortunately this goes against everything the child has learned over the years. Children are taught, "Anything enjoyable is forbidden or at least allowed only under the most rigid restrictions." This applies to eating sweets, going swimming, staying up late, and most of all, sex. If we are to believe some of the sex experts of international rank, the only way to have sex is with your wife or husband, once before each pregnancy, and as quickly as possible. Presumably the rest of one's life is spent clenching fists and gritting teeth. It is almost like the patient who asked the doctor what he could eat. The doctor replied, "If you like it, it's not on your diet." The goal of recreational sex is somewhat different. It is designed to obtain the maximum pleasure from sexual activity without doing damage to anyone.

What kind of sexual activity does damage?

Rape and child molesting are certainly damaging. Intercourse with someone else's husband or wife can cause damage. Homosexuality extracts a high emotional price from the participants. But that still leaves a wide range of sexual activities to occupy the average person.

How does one go about it?

The next step is communication, both internal and external. The genitals are specialized receptors which send a wide variety of information to the most important sexual organ of all, the brain. There the information is integrated and processed; further messages are sent to other parts of the body. When the wife caresses her husband's penis, he actually experiences the sensation in the brain. As he stokes the shaft of her clitoris though she "feels" the tingling in that organ, the true feeling exists only in the brain cells. This is the critical bit of information for the real enjoyment of sex. By understanding this, every person can gain maximum sexual enjoyment. No one has to be a "second-class sexual citizen." Since all sexual feelings are gathered and organized by the brain, gaining even a little control over this organ can make everyone capable of abundant gratification.

But aren't some people undersexed?

Nothing could be further from the truth. With very rare exceptions (less than one per cent) everybody has the capacity for full sexual enjoyment. "Oversexed" and "undersexed" are merely labels slapped onto people who have achieved or missed the sexual potential available to everyone. Donna is an example:

"Doctor, I'm twenty-five now and I didn't even know what sex was like until about a year and a half ago. I went through school wondering what other girls were getting so excited about. They were always rushing around with boys and talking about sex—I thought I was above all that." Donna laughed.

"Not only was I dumb, I was smug—I thought I had all the answers. When I started working, I began to date about once a month—but no necking. I suppose my parents had trained me to follow in their footsteps—they probably make it once a year on Christmas Eve in front of the Christmas tree.

"Then I met Carl. I never knew what turned-on meant until he came along. Whenever I went out with him I felt electrified, like a motor was running in my body. After we started necking and petting I just couldn't wait to get him inside me. Sometimes even that wasn't enough. I'd go home and masturbate afterward. In those days I really felt guilty about it but I just couldn't help myself—I wanted him so much. We've been married a year now and it's still the same. All I can say is thank goodness he came along when he did—I never would have known what I was missing."

The "experts" would have classified Donna as undersexed at the age of twenty-three and oversexed a month after she met Carl. They would have been wrong both times. After she met Carl she was simply beginning to fulfil her sexual potential—the same potential available to everyone.

How is that done?

In most sexual activity, the centre of focus for the man is the penis and for the woman, the vagina, clitoris, and related structures. As impulses from these areas reach the brain, they build up, intensify, and hopefully result in the massive neuro-vascular discharge known as orgasm. Like all nervous impulses of this type, sexual sensations are additive. The more sensations that are received at one time, the greater the total effect. For example, an orgasm resulting from penis and vagina contact and nothing else may be pleasant. However, an orgasm resulting from total sexual stimulation will be sensational. And each succeeding orgasm that follows in the same way can be even more exciting.

What is total sexual stimulation?

This is a means of intensifying sexual pleasure by utilizing all the available erotic pathways to reinforce and add to the cumulative gratification of the sexual experience. Every available sensory pathway is recruited, first consciously, later almost automatically, to enhance sexual success.

The first sense to concentrate on is the most obvious (and sometimes neglected) sense of touch. There are two sides to every tactile experience—touching and being touched. If understood, they can reinforce each other. For example, when a man caresses a woman's clitoris with the tip of his index finger, she feels the gentle stroking of the fingertip against the skin of her organ. She also feels the hard-to-describe tingling and throbbing that results. At the same time the man feels the extremely smooth, extremely soft skin of the clitoris against his finger and the pulsation of the organ as it reacts to his touch. This stimulates him sexually and he responds by intensifying his stimulation of the area.

If then the woman pushes her entire genital area against his hand, her stimulation is increased and obviously so is his. So far, only one sensory modality has been involved. Now if she whispers into his ear, a new element has been introduced. As the sense of hearing is brought into action, the man becomes more excited and as a result strives to excite the woman even more.

By gradually rising from one level to another of sensory stimulation, it is possible for everyone to reach the same elevated degree of sexual enjoyment.

Looking and seeing is of paramount importance to the full enjoyment of sex. Viewing the sexual organs is in itself exciting. So is being aware of the changes they undergo as sexual activity proceeds. Seeing the naked human body in motion during intercourse adds to the intensity of the experience; most particularly, a man's sexual excitement is significantly intensified simply by the sight of a naked woman ready to engage in intercourse with him.

What about the other senses?

The sexual life of every mammalian creature except man is dominated by the sense of smell. Man has concentrated on sanitizing and deodorizing his body until there is nothing left to smell —almost. Fortunately the body does not give up so easily. The odour-detection apparatus of the body is a direct extension of the brain; the olfactory bulb is a part of the brain that comes down to almost the upper part of the nose.

Though the sexual puritans would like to eliminate taste and smell from the world of sex (and probably everything else), fortunately both senses are here to stay. We might as well use them, since in sexual activity, they work together. In kissing, the smell of the lips, their slightly salty taste, the smell of the nearby skin (perhaps mixed with perfume or after-shave lotion), all contribute their share to the rising sexual excitement. As a man kisses a woman's breast the smell of her skin, the taste of the nipple all do their part to facilitate sexual arousal. The more of these senses that can be combined in one activity, the more intense the gratification. There is one stage of intercourse where nearly every sense comes into play.

What is that?

When the mouth is used to stimulate the sexual organs, the flow of sensory impulses rises to its highest level short of orgasm itself. Taking the example of cunnilingus first, as the tongue is applied to the clitoris the man feels the delicate trembling of that organ in response to the touch of his tongue. The slightly salty but not unpleasant taste also reinforces his excitement, especially if it brings back associations of the couple's last sexual experience together. Because of the special sudoriferous glands around the labia and vagina, this area has a distinctive smell which most men find sexually arousing—unless they have been talked out of it by puritanical parents or advisers who never experienced it.

What about the woman?

She can perform the same kind of stimulation for him.

At the same time?

Yes. In addition to sexual nerve impulses being additive, they are reciprocally reinforcing. If a woman takes a man's penis into her mouth while he is stimulating her genitals in the same way, their mutual excitement is likely to quadruple as the nerve transmissions double and redouble in response to increasingly acute stimulation. She feels the insistent throbbing of the organ against her lips, and experiences a slightly salty taste, as well as the characteristic but not unpleasant odour of the sudoriferous glands of the area. Because the penis is much larger in comparison to the clitoris she can also see the male genitals as she proceeds.

By simultaneous cunnilingus and fellatio every possible sense is brought to a fever pitch and a mutual orgasm occurs rapidly unless the couple switches to a penis–vagina position. The most presumably undersexed man or woman will be brought to an explosive orgasm by using this technique, providing they are willing to do it.

Why shouldn't they be willing to do it?

One reason might be that for the past twenty years they have been told that it is dirty, perverted, and abnormal, to name a few of the milder adjectives applied to cunnilingus and fellatio. In spite of this, about seventy to eighty percent of Americans engage in it. A lot of them feel guilty about it but they do it just the same because it is so much fun.

Is there anything wrong with fellatio and cunnilingus?

As a form of heterosexual activity incidental to penis–vagina intercourse, mouth–genital stimulation is not only perfectly all right to practice, but in many situations desirable.

It provides the final surge of stimulation to assure the firmest erection in a man and brings a woman to the point where her orgasm should occur rapidly and vigorously. One of the best methods of assuring orgasm in the so-called frigid woman and encouraging a strong erection in a questionably potent man is this powerful form of total sexual stimulation.

If fellatio and cunnilingus are so gratifying, why shouldn't they take the place of penis–vagina intercourse?

If that were to happen the birth rate would quickly fall to zero and there would be no one around to do it with. But the most important reason that oral intercourse will not replace penis–vagina activities is that regular copulation is even more enjoyable than fellatio–cunnilingus. The most desirable use of oral stimulation is to make the final stage of intercourse as exciting and rewarding as possible. By following an act of sexual intercourse from its origin to its conclusion we can see the role of total sexual stimulation.

Sexual intercourse really begins when the decision is made in the mind of the participants. As the man and woman form images in their respective minds about what is going to transpire, the first sensory changes begin to take place. In the man this usually takes the form of an erection. From the standpoint of nerve impulses, erections tend to be self-perpetuating. The flow of blood into the penis causes stretching of the very sensitive penile skin and intensifies the sexual excitement. The clitoris and labia minora react in somewhat the same way; the main difference is that clitoral erection and maximum sensitivity tend to lag a little behind the penis at first and surpass it later on as intercourse progresses.

As the couple undress, the sight of each other's bodies visually reinforces their degree of excitement. As they begin to kiss and caress, taste, smell, vision, touch, and hearing all begin to interact. At this early stage the various types of sensory stimulation are diffuse—later on they will become much more concentrated.

Why is that necessary?

For orgasm to occur, the full force of the bodies' entire nervous energy must be concentrated on the sexual organs. Successful orgasm requires that every microvolt of electrical energy be mobilized and directed toward the penis and clitoris–vagina. No one reaches orgasm while playing the violin, reading the sports page, or sorting the laundry.

In the early stages of copulation the sexual energy is scattered, like light rays from the sun. Erotic impulses come from the lips, the breasts, the back, the buttocks, the thighs, the tongue, and to a lesser extent, the genitals themselves. Gradually the stimulation becomes more concentrated, somewhat as the sun's rays might be focussed by a magnifying glass.

In another sense, it is like a big picture—at the beginning everything is in focus except the penis and vagina. As the sexual interaction rushes toward orgasm the entire body goes out of focus except for the genitals which come sharply and intensely into focus.

How is this accomplished?

As intercourse proceeds, the caresses and mutual interest begin to gravitate more towards the sexual organs themselves. The man begins to caress the woman's clitoris and labia, first slowly, then more intensely. The woman directs most of her attention to his penis and to a lesser extent, testicles. Here too, the additive effect of sensory impulses can be brought into play.

For most women, stroking of the clitoris is exciting. Many others also enjoy having the vagina stimulated by the finger, in imitation of the penis. If the man inserts his index finger into the vagina and uses his thumb to gently stroke the clitoris, the degree of sensation is multiplied many times.

The woman can use the same technique by caressing the penis at the same time that she gently strokes the testicles and the perineal area directly behind them.

Depending on the wishes of the couple, the next step may be mutual oral stimulation as the final step before inserting the penis into the vagina. Among other things this brings total sexual stimulation to its peak with all five senses being stretched to their maximum receptivity. Virtually every nerve cell is sending and receiving at the limit of its capacity during this stage.

Finally penis and vagina are brought together. These two most sensitive receptor organs of the entire body are ultimately used to stimulate each other. Generally, the intensity of sensation becomes so great that all the nervous energy which has been building throughout intercourse is suddenly reversed and released in a pulsating orgasmic discharge. Once more a man and a woman have enjoyed the most transcendent of all human experiences. If next time they go about it with the same freedom and directness, the experience should be as good or better.

Do the man and woman have to reach orgasm at the same time?

It depends on the books you read. Most manuals of sexual technique insist on simultaneous mutual orgasm. This is in the American tradition of doing everything well every time. But copulation is not flycasting or kicking a football; sometimes there are other factors which intervene. Although there is certainly no denying that mutual simultaneous orgasm is very enjoyable, there is also something to be said for consecutive orgasm. Since the precise moment of orgasm usually brings on a lapse of consciousness, neither man nor woman is able to enjoy the orgasm of their partner. If a man occasionally reaches his climax first, the woman is able to concentrate on feeling the pulsations of the penis within her vagina and perhaps even the sensation of the sperm as it is ejaculated against the cervix and vaginal walls. In the same way, a man, if a woman has her orgasm first, can sense the spasmodic contractions of the muscles around the vagina alternately compressing and releasing his penis. He can also manœuvre his penis in such a way as to intensify the acuteness of her sensations at that moment.

How can he do that?

It depends on her individual preference. Some women prefer the deepest possible penetration at the precise time of orgasm. If the man has not yet gone into his own orgasmic trance, he can plunge his penis as deep into the vagina as possible when it is most effective. Other women like to feel the head of the penis thrusting against the cervix as they reach a climax. If the man is not distracted by his own sensations, he can make sure that the two structures come into direct contact.

The woman of course can do similar things for her partner. As they reach an orgasm some men like to have the woman grab their buttocks as she pulls the penis deeper into her. Others like the woman to gently caress their testicles while they are ejaculating. Since the testicles are such delicate structures, a woman who is going through her own orgasmic frenzy sometimes squeezes too hard—that can bring everything to a grinding halt.

So while mutual simultaneous orgasm has its advantages, there are benefits to consecutive orgasm as well.

Is there anything a couple can do to control the timing of their orgasm if they want it to be simultaneous?

Yes. If the wife is slower than the husband he can stimulate her clitoris with his finger at the same time the penis is thrusting in the vagina. If the husband seems to be approaching a climax too quickly he can simply slow the pelvic thrusts and his excitement will quickly fall to a lower level. If he slows down rather than stopping, he will probably not change his wife's timing significantly.

Often, directing the penis to another part of the vagina can make a big difference in the rate of sexual excitement. Some women are greatly stimulated if the penis rubs against the upper wall of the vagina along the ridge just below the bladder. These women probably have some nerve fibres from the clitoris buried in this area which transmit sensations directly from the vaginal wall to the clitoris itself.

Sometimes changing positions can be helpful also.

How can that help?

There are two factors involved. Mechanically, some positions increase pressure and emphasis. In addition, each individual finds certain positions psychologically much more exciting than others. This doesn't mean that successful sexual intercourse requires a pair of double-jointed acrobats. No matter what the bodies are doing, the brain retains its same relative position. But new approaches and new ideas can sometimes increase sexual gratification.

One of the most effective of the variations is having the man lie on his back with his legs slightly apart. The woman rolls on top of him and drawing up her knees slightly, slides her vagina downward over his erect penis. This accomplishes several things. First, it shifts the pressure of the penis from the sides of the vagina to the top and produces more stimulation of the upper surface of the vagina. Second, it applies more pressure to the glans, or head, of the penis, intensifying the pleasurable feelings there. It also brings the clitoris and labia directly down on the shaft of the penis itself and allows the penis to caress the clitoris with every thrust. The woman can change the pressure herself by shifting her body backward, forward, or from side to side. It also has the advantage of leaving both partners face to face and with both hands free. They may kiss, caress each others' bodies, and do anything else that comes into their minds as copulation progresses.

A sub-variation of this allows the woman to crouch above the man in a semi-squatting position. This allows the man to see his partner in action and to caress her breasts and clitoris at the same time.

Some men are reluctant to allow the woman to assume this position since they feel that this puts the woman in a dominant position. Because of its very nature intercourse is a cooperative venture which requires the full and enthusiastic participation of both parties to be successful. The question of who is nearer the ceiling at any given moment is not really relevant.

Many of the other sexual positions have certain theoretical advantages, but for important reasons just aren't as popular as these two face-to-face techniques. Side-to-side, rear entry, woman-sitting-on-man's-lap, standing up, are all possible but have the strong psychological disadvantage of either turning the woman's back to the man or limiting the possibilities of total sexual stimulation. They are interesting as variations and may be the positions of choice for some couples, but on the whole the supine face-to-face position seems to have the most to offer.

But isn't the rear entry position the most "natural"?

It obviously is the most natural for dogs and cats, and they really wouldn't have their sex any other way. For human beings, it doesn't seem such a natural approach. Over the thousands of years of evolution, the angle of the female vagina has changed. In the female dog, the vagina is relatively straight and accepts the dog's penis well as he approaches from the rear. The human vagina is more angular as the woman stands on all fours; this can result in a bad fit unless the woman leans far forward and puts her head and shoulders down on the bed. Many women feel that this makes sex a bit of a strain as the blood rushes to the head, distracting them from what they are really trying to accomplish.

The face-to-face positions in human beings have something else going for them too. Most four-legged animals have relatively narrow chests and abdomens with most of the sensory nerves in the skin distributed along the sides and flanks. In animals that walk upright, the front part of the body is much broader and thus presents a larger surface for stimulation. In face-to-face intercourse many more nerve endings are involved than any other position.

Is there anything else that a couple can do to increase their enjoyment of intercourse?

Yes. They can gain control over the sexual muscles.

How can that be done?

First, it is important to understand the anatomy of the sexual musculature. In the female the vagina is held in place by a wall of powerful muscles. While their main function is to hold the vagina and the related structures in place during the stress of intercourse (and later of childbirth) they can also be put to another use.

With practice and training these muscles can be brought under conscious control, so that the woman can squeeze, stroke, and caress the penis while it is in the vagina. There are two major groups of muscles which can be developed most effectively.

The first and most external pair of muscles is called the "bulbocavernosus," or vaginal sphincter muscle. This muscle is split into two halves, one on each side of the vaginal opening. As it contracts, the orifice of the vagina is squeezed almost shut. (The motion is the same as that made by the lips in pronouncing the sound "wh" in the word "whip.") As the muscles relax, the vaginal opening also relaxes.

The second muscle controlling the outer vaginal area is the urethral sphincter muscle. The major purpose of this muscle is to shut off the flow of urine at the end of urination. However, it also compresses the vagina like the vaginal sphincter, except it acts just inside the vaginal outlet. Most women can gain control of both these muscles by doing a simple exercise. If she concentrates on the same motion she uses in trying to hold her urine back —a sort of drawing inward of the pelvic muscles—the muscles will respond correctly. This exercise needs to be repeated at least twenty times a day and should be done deeply while it is held for a moment or two. It also carries the added bonus of strengthening the urinary muscles and increasing bladder control.

The second group of muscles which can be harnessed for increased sexual enjoyment are the levator ani group. There are three muscles in this segment, the pubococcygeus, iliococcygeus, and puborectalis. They extend from the anal area to the pubic area and surround the deeper part of the vagina. As these muscles are constricted, the walls of the vagina are brought together firmly and gently squeeze the penis along its entire length. This muscle group is rather powerful and can make a big contribution to sexual pleasure if used correctly. The best exercise for developing the levator ani group is to make the motion designed to hold back a bowel movement. This causes powerful constriction of the three muscles involved. Proper control and development of these structures also comes with practice; about twenty contractions a day for several weeks should give good control.

How are these muscles used during intercourse?

First separately, then in combination. After the penis is in place within the vagina, contracting the external sphincter muscles will intensify the erection and increase the man's sexual excitement. At the same time it increases the stimulation of the sensitive nerve endings at the vaginal opening and adds to the woman's pleasure. These muscles also expand the clitoris as they contract, which intensifies the overall effect. The penis can be alternately squeezed and released by constricting the deeper group of levator ani muscles. This considerably augments the sensations of both participants.

By using the two muscle groups in combination, some interesting effects can be obtained. If the man remains perfectly still with his penis deep in the vagina, the woman can gently and rhythmically massage his penis from the base to the tip by contracting first the superficial muscles, then the deeper group. With practice she should be able to reverse the direction of this caress and stroke the penis from tip to base as well. This can sometimes be enough to bring the man to orgasm by itself.

Another possibility is for the man to thrust deeply into the vagina, hesitate a moment while the woman contracts the deeper muscles, withdraw slowly, then pause while the woman constricts the sphincter muscles around the tip of the penis which still remains in the vagina. Many such combinations are possible; they are best worked out by the parties involved.

Can men control their sexual muscles, too?

Not quite as expertly as women, but there is room for development there too. In the male the bulbocavernosus muscle compresses the erectile tissues of the penis during erection and causes a marked increase in diameter of the organ. Since the muscle cannot be contracted for more than a few seconds, the increase is temporary, but the change in size can be felt distinctly and pleasurably by the woman. The motion of drawing back on the urine causes the muscle to constrict, just as in women, and the exercise is the same.

The levator ani group in men, when it is contracted, thrusts the penis forward and temporarily increases its length. This motion can be very stimulating to the woman especially if the tip of the penis is against the cervix. Men can train this muscle with the same exercises recommended for women.

If both partners have good muscle control, they can synchronize and combine the contractions and do even more for each other.

What else can be done to increase the pleasure of sexual intercourse?

One good place to start is repealing the unwritten law that men must take the sexual initiative. Although every woman knows that females have been pulling the sexual strings since the beginning of the human race, women have been forced to maintain a façade of being pursued. During the past hundred years women have made great political and vocational advances—it is about time for them to approach sexual equality, too.

What can a woman do to initiate sexual intercourse?

The range of possibilities is almost unlimited. The approach can be tailored to meet the exact requirements of the situation. For some men, a dinner by candlelight is enough to get the ball rolling. Others need a more direct hint such as not-so-subtle body pressure while dancing. If the circumstances are appropriate, a back rub with either party doing the rubbing often leads directly into intercourse. This is especially good for wives with reluctant husbands. After a hard day with the boss, the relaxation and stimulation of a gentle massage may be just the right transition to a night of love.

In sex there is always room for boldness and imagination. Taking a shower together can be physically relaxing and sexually stimulating at the same time. Even in bed a wife should let her husband know what she wants and how she wants it. It helps a man to perform better if he is sure he is gratifying his partner.

Then the only thing that counts in sex is how much fun everybody has?

Not exactly. The ideal act of sexual intercourse combines reproduction, deep mutual love, and profound physical pleasure. Most people will experience this combination less than a dozen times in their life span. If they are very fortunate, they will frequently be able to combine an expression of love with a real physical enjoyment of sex. But at the very minimum intercourse should provide the maximum sexual gratification possible to both man and woman. If they can accomplish that, at least it is a first step toward achieving the rest.

5

APHRODISIACS

I've often heard the word "aphrodisiac" used. What does it mean?

The word aphrodisiac, derived from Aphrodite, the ancient Greek goddess of love, designates something that increases sexual desire or excitement. Usually it refers to drugs such as Spanish fly and others, but its meaning can also include sexually stimulating books or movies, sexual exhibitions, and even plastic surgery on the sexual organs.

Plastic surgery on the sexual organs? Is this kind of plastic surgery common?

It depends where you live. In the United States, for example, *more than fifty per cent of the people have had plastic surgery on their genitals*. In Britain fifteen to twenty per cent undergo this form of surgery. There are some areas of the world where everybody has these things done as a matter of course. One is not even considered socially acceptable until the sexual equipment has been remodelled. As a matter of fact, there are more than a dozen operations in use today directed at overhauling the sexual apparatus to make sex more fun for everyone.

What are these operations like?

They range all the way from complex procedures done at the famous Mayo Clinic in America to primitive hacking performed with a piece of broken glass in the African jungle.

One example which falls midway between is the *ampallang* of Southeast Asia. This is typical of do-it-yourself jobs.

The sportier males of that area make several slits in the loose skin on the underside of the penis near the tip. The openings average about an eighth of an inch in diameter and run at right angles to the shaft. Just before intercourse short rods are inserted into the slits perpendicular to the penis. These are usually scraps of copper wire, bits of ivory, or among the jet set, gold and silver. The purpose obviously is to enlarge the business end of the penis and increase its friction against the vagina.

What does the man get out of it?

Clearly there is no increased sensation for him. The only compensation for this sacrifice is likely to be renewed popularity with the ladies. The results must be something special for them if they manage to persuade a proud male to ventilate his precious penis this way.

For those willing to go one step further, there is a somewhat more elegant refinement. Instead of simply poking holes in the organ, a ring of small incisions is made around the head of the penis. Little pebbles are placed into the resulting pouches, and the skin is allowed to heal over them. A month or so later, the result is a penis crowned with a rocky wreath. Fully healed, the courageous gent emerges to claim his reward; presumably the girls are standing in line to get the benefit of his new equipment. A plain old normal penis must look pretty tame by comparison.

Isn't there an operation like this that gives the man more pleasure?

Only if he happens to be a music-lover. The Burmese have added an aesthetic note.

They use the same slit procedure, but instead of burying small stones under the skin, they use little bronze bells. Conceivably a talented Burmese lover can do justice to his sweetheart and play a catchy tune at the same time. There are other advantages too. If a Burmese husband comes home unexpectedly and walks in the door to the music of the bells, somebody is in big trouble.

Are there any other operations on the penis?

There is one in particular which has resisted all attempts at explanation. No one knows its origin, significance, or function. The technique of subincision has been practised for hundreds if not thousands of years among Australian aborigines. It is a vital part of their lives, performed on every male member of the tribe. At puberty, a longitudinal incision is made along the base of the penis near the scrotum. It penetrates to the urethra and allows the contents to drain through the new opening. As a result semen and urine no longer travel the entire length of the penis but are short-circuited and simply drip out of the incision.

What is behind this mass mutilation? The most obvious explanation—a primitive means of birth control—doesn't hold up. Conception occurs without difficulty; the semen merely drips into the vagina. The reason for this painful and disabling procedure remains a mystery.

Certainly nothing like this is ever done in America, is it?

Not as far as anyone knows. However, there are some cases where nature has done to men what the aborigines do to themselves. In this condition, called "hypospadias," a child is born with a gaping hole or slit along the underside of the penis. Perfectly suited for life in one culture, he is imperfect in another. As with his Australian counterpart, urine and semen will drip out through the defect.

In school he must sit down to urinate like the girls; later his sex life will be a catastrophe. The man whose version of sexual intercourse is dribbling all over his girl friend's privates will not exactly find his services in demand.

Modern surgery undoes the damage. A simple rearrangement of the layers and urine and sperm can flow freely through the appropriate orifice.

What about operations on a normal penis?

Although we don't usually think of it that way, the most commonly encountered form of sexual plastic surgery is circumcision of the penis. As everyone knows, the prepuce or foreskin, the caplike covering of skin that fits over the end of the penis like an old-fashioned candle snuffer, is cut away. This leaves the head of the penis (or glans) exposed.

Circumcision originated long before the birth of Christ, who was himself circumcised along with the twelve disciples. The operation was regularly done in ancient Egypt and was even common among the Aztecs. Today it is performed by such diverse groups as the Australian aborigines, the wild Tacuna Indians of Brazil, Abyssinian Christians, and of course modern Jews and Moslems. In the Bible, the first reference to circumcision is in Genesis, 17:11, "And ye shall circumcise the flesh of your foreskin; it shall be a token of the covenant betwixt me and you." In those times the penis was redone with a sharp stone as prescribed in Exodus, 4:25, "Then Zipporah took a sharp stone and cut off the foreskin of her son and cast it at his feet and said, Surely a bloody husband art thou to me."

The same implement, a sharp stone, is used today by most primitive tribes; those who are more advanced use a broken piece of glass. Among the Jews, a ceremonial steel knife is wielded by a ritual surgeon, called a *mohel*, who restricts his practice to circumcisions. He operates on the squirming eight-day-old infant freehand—something few modern surgeons would attempt. Modern medical circumcision is standardized and nearly automatic. The infant is strapped to a rack—usually plastic—and a bell-shaped device, also plastic, is slipped between penis and foreskin. A loop of nylon thread is knotted around a groove at the base of the bell, constricting the prepuce. The surgeon runs the scalpel blade once around the penis and it's all over. The bell is left in place a day or two, the infant meanwhile urinating through an opening in the top of the bell.

Aside from religious beliefs, the origin of this operation is unknown. There are obvious sexual advantages, but it is unlikely that they formed the original basis for this procedure.

What are the sexual advantages of circumcision?

Circumcision adds to sexual pleasure in many ways. First, a cheesy, bad-smelling substance called "smegma" accumulates between the prepuce and glans. The staggering odour of smegma is capable of cancelling the world's most powerful aphrodisiac. With the prepuce gone, there is no place for the smegma to accumulate.

Second, the nerve supply of the prepuce is insignificant compared with that of the glans itself. With the head of the organ uncovered and in direct contact with the vagina, far more exquisite sensation is possible. Although the foreskin is designed to retract over the glans during intercourse, it is sometimes adherent and prevents total contact.

Third, bacteria multiply rapidly in the smegma and infection of the head of the penis (or balanitis) can occur. A red, immensely swollen organ banishes all thoughts of sex.

Last, least common, and most terrifying, cancer of the penis occurs only among *uncircumcised* men. The treatment for penile cancer is amputation of the penis. And *that* is *that*.

Are women ever circumcised?

Yes, but not nearly as frequently as men. The clitoris being a mini-ature version of the penis also has its own mini-prepuce. At one time some doctors felt that a foreskin adherent to the clitoris was the major cause of female sexual difficulties. Thousands of women underwent circumcision—better called "mini-circumcision"—until it became obvious that little improvement resulted.

In contrast to male circumcision, which is much more common in advanced societies, female circumcision is more frequently performed in primitive cultures. As usual in this sort of thing the reasoning behind it remains obscure. The suggestion has been made that it represents a way for a husband to take some of the zing out of sex for his wife so that she won't be tempted to stray from home. Other tribes go even further. Their ritual involves removing the labia minora and even amputating the entire clitoris. This no doubt does cut down on sexual sensation. Few western ladies are willing to hold still for this one.

Then most sexual plastic surgery in this country is done on men?

Not exactly. Women account for a hefty proportion of sexual re-construction. Take for example the "husband's knot." Most girls who give birth to their children in the hospital have an incision made in the vagina called an "episiotomy." This is to prevent the baby's head, relatively large in comparison to the small vaginal opening, from overstretching and tearing the delicate vaginal tissues. After delivery the mother is left with a gigantic, gaping vaginal entrance. The doctor immediately sets to work repairing the incision by sewing the cut edges of tissue together. The whole procedure takes about five minutes. If the doctor is also sexually knowledgeable, he takes another minute and adds a little plastic surgery. He carefully gauges the size and location of his stitches so that besides closing the wound he takes up almost all the slack in the vagina—caused by years of intercourse as well as the pressure of the baby's head lunging through. In sixty seconds he restores that most vital of all spaces to its pre-copulatory dimensions. He tops it off with a special super-secure non-ravelling knot, known affectionately as the "husband's knot."

Doesn't the vagina stretch again with the next baby?

Certainly. But as long as the doctor is there with his needle and sutures, neither husband nor wife will ever know the difference. Everything will fit like a glove—or even better.

What if the doctor doesn't do this little operation?

The vagina will continue to stretch more and more with intercourse and childbirth until it no longer firmly grips the penis during intercourse. The poor penis, dwarfed by the massive vagina, flounders aimlessly within its former home. It also develops the unhappy characteristic of flopping out at the most inopportune moments.

Fortunately, years ago a sympathetic surgeon devised a suitable cure. The operation, called "anterior and posterior plastic repair," or "A-P repair" for short, is simple, effective, and solves a lot of problems at once. It is basically a version of the "husband's knot" technique, but more extensive. The vagina is reinforced, reconstructed, and reoriented in relation to neighbouring structures.

That's fine if the vagina is too big—what about something for a vagina that's too small?

A vagina that is really too small is very rare indeed. Usually the difficulty is simply an undersized entrance or "introitus." Most often the hymen is to blame. That small bit of tissue that stands guard at the gates of love sometimes does its job too well. Even the most determined midnight battering by a nervous and sweating bridegroom is occasionally insufficient—it will not yield.

The following morning the tearful bride and red-faced groom appear at the doctor's office. In this case the scalpel is mightier than the penis and in a flash of the gleaming knife the portals swing wide. Nature's defect undone by Man!

But aren't there some cases where the vagina is really too small?

Very rare. Almost invariably either the vagina is big enough (perhaps with some stretching) or it isn't there at all. Nowadays there is even help for the girl who is born without *any* vagina. These unfortunate young ladies have a rare deformity which leaves them with a short blind pouch or in the most severe cases merely a dimple. Utilizing an ingenious procedure, a man-made but sexually serviceable vagina can be fashioned. There are two drawbacks. Obviously pregnancy is out of the question. Furthermore the new vagina is recommended for married girls only since it requires frequent and energetic use to keep it open.

Breast operations seem to be getting a lot of attention lately—what sorts of operations are done on them?

Although breasts are not primarily sexual organs—they were originally designed as organs of nutrition, to feed babies—they do have strong sexual significance and deserve to be included with sexual plastic operations. The best known of the breast revisions is the silicone injection operation. This is the latest in a series of techniques devised for making mountains out of molehills. Earlier operations used materials such as plastic sponges and fluid-filled plastic bags to build up the contours of the breasts. Unfortunately they were sooner or later rejected by the body and the poor girl was left worse off than when she began. The latest attempts at breastmanship consist of pumping those organs full of silicone foam under pressure. After a time the foam hardens. "Hardens" is the key word, since the breasts are big but rock-hard—nice to look at but about as resilient as a concrete kerbstone. There is also another jarring note—some individuals who receive this type of plastic procedure later develop cancer in the area where the foam was injected.

What about girls with oversize breasts?

In the bosom department it's apparently feast or famine. There is a sizeable group of women who are dismayed because their breasts are too large. Now there is even help for these over-endowed lovelies. The details are a little unsettling but the results are generally acceptable. First the nipples are cut off and set aside in a container of saline solution. Then a large portion of the fatty tissue of each breast is excised along with a certain amount of skin. The nipples are retrieved from their jar, reattached, and everything is sewn up in its approximate place. Carefully done, the main giveaway is a thin scar underneath the breast—barely visible even in a topless waitress.

Are there any operations like that for men?

With one exception, there is no practical way to add or take away from a man's natural endowments. Since almost every penis can be made to work no matter what its size, and since there is no way to make it longer or shorter anyhow, the situation is essentially static. The exception is the testicles. Although they are not directly involved in the sexual act, they play a strong symbolic and psychological role. Even in those cases where the absence of testicles is fully compensated for by hormone substitution, with an empty scrotum flapping in the wind, a passionate night of love just doesn't seem the same.

That scrotum may be vacant for a couple of reasons. Sometimes after birth the testicles fail to descend from their resting place in the abdomen. They may even resist all surgical attempts to bring them down. Occasionally they act like yo-yos, sliding up and down, in and out of the scrotal sac. In other, more tragic, cases, they have been permanently lost, accidentally or as the result of a malignant tumour.

There is still an answer. Two egg-shaped artificial organs of plastic or tantalum can be slipped into the scrotum and anchored there so no one will be the wiser. Well, hardly anyone.

What about the "real" aphrodisiacs, for instance Spanish fly? What is it? What does it do?

Spanish fly, strangely enough, is simply a Spanish fly. Almost. Actually it is made from small, shiny, iridescent beetles found in southern France and Spain. The bodies of these insects are dried and pulverized, then treated chemically to extract a drug called "cantharidin." Then, supposedly, the real fun begins. All one has to do, according to the stories, is slip a few drops into your girl friend's drink. No matter how cold she has been to you in the past, she will be transformed instantly into an insatiable sex maniac begging you to quench her pelvic fires.

Remember the story about the fellow who slipped some Spanish fly to his date, drove out to the lover's lane, and awaited the results? The young lady became worked up, exhausted her boy friend's resources after four good times, and proceeded to have intercourse with the gear lever and most of the knobs on the dashboard? Nice story.

Here's a more likely version: Ten minutes after drinking the "love potion" the girl collapses in convulsions—she goes to the hospital and Casanova goes to the jail. If she lives (fifty-fifty chance), he gets off lightly. If she dies, it's manslaughter.

If it's so dangerous, how did the idea get started in the first place?

Spanish fly is a truly great aphrodisiac—for farm animals. This is the problem: in humans the dose that works and the dose that kills are about the same. If you are an eighteen-year-old girl, five feet two and weigh nine stone, one drop too much and you've had it.

If you're a twenty-cwt. cow, it doesn't make that much difference. The stakes are different, too. If your date for the evening won't see it your way, tomorrow night you can make it with someone else. If you have a precious breeding animal that wants to remain a virgin, some risk-taking is in order.

Well, then, how does it work in animals?

The drug cantharidin is tremendously irritating. After being swallowed it finds its way into the bladder and is excreted in the urine. It burns the lining of the bladder and urethra as it goes by and reflexly stimulates the sexual organs. It causes erection of the clitoris, engorgement of the labia, and tingling of the vagina in females. In the male it causes an immense and painful erection. Animals who get a shot of this stuff copulate mainly to try to get rid of the intense discomfort. No one watching the performance ever wants to try it that way themselves.

There *is* one important use of Spanish fly for humans. In greatly diluted form it is a fair substitute for a mustard plaster.

Isn't it true that certain foods are sexual stimulants, like oysters?

That would be too easy. In man's eternal quest for the bigger and better (and more frequent) orgasm, hundreds of foods and food combinations have been tried. Some of them depend on a physical resemblance to the sexual apparatus. For example, oysters, clams, eggs, and onions resemble the testicles. Celery, sausages, and asparagus resemble the penis. The theory, apparently, is "like breeds like." It could work, but not necessarily the way it's intended. A strict diet of celery might conceivably make the penis resemble a celery stalk—wet and soggy.

Other foods have a more obvious effect. Feeding your best girl a juicy steak at a classy restaurant may set the mental wheels in motion and land both of you in bed; the secret ingredient is in the atmosphere, not in the steak.

Isn't there anything in the food line that works?

There was one that came pretty close. During the Victorian era men who were "under par," as the polite term of the day went, were advised to "partake of prairie oysters." This was a euphemism for bull's testicles. Since they contained a fair dose of male sex hormone, eaten absolutely fresh and absolutely raw, they might have done *some* good. Apparently in those days few men were that desperate. Even then the outcome would have been problematical; most of the hormone is destroyed by the gastric juices.

How about those Oriental cures—like powdered rhinoceros horn?

That too was based on the "like makes like" principle. You can almost visualize a poor Chinese daydreaming: "If my penis only looked like the horn of the rhinoceros . . ." Obviously if he gazed at the opposite end of the rhino, he would see the beast had something else going for him. Strangely enough, among Chinese believers, the demand for rhino horn has so outstripped the meagre supply that most of the product reaching the market is powdered boar tusk or pig bone.

There is however one Chinese remedy that may have something to it. In Chinese it is known as *goo-lai-sam*—we call it ginseng. Prepared according to a strict recipe, it has many users who vouch for its effectiveness.

Does ginseng really work?

In the aphrodisiac line, that's the problem. The mind has such a dominant effect on sexual performance that often if a person thinks a remedy works, it does. Ginseng is typical. The most powerful form, according to the Chinese, is the variety in which the whole root is shaped like a little man. Again, "like makes like." The only way to be sure is to try it. With ginseng root selling at about £30 a pound, it takes a serious student to pursue the subject—or a desperate one.

What about the drug called Yohimbine?

Another example of the power of suggestion, this time made from the powdered inner bark of the African Yohimbe tree. It has been used countless times as an aphrodisiac. It has never worked.

However, there is another nineteenth-century compound which has some power as a sexual stimulant. It carries the quaint name of "nux vomica," better known as *strychnine*. Rat poison? Correct. This drug, in small amounts, kills by making the victim's nervous system sensitive to the slightest stimulation. Someone who has taken it goes into endless convulsions from the noise of a door slamming. Death usually comes from exhaustion via repeated excruciating convulsions. In *very minute* doses it may increase the response to sexual stimulation. Take a little too much and six men will walk slow with you. But then we're back to the problem of Spanish fly. It is one thing to live it up—sudden death is another story.

Isn't there anything that works?

The official story about aphrodisiacs, for obvious reasons, is that no such things exist. That is almost true, but not quite. Apparently the Guardians of Public Morals, mostly self-appointed, feel that if ordinary people get their hands on a good aphrodisiac, they will turn our genteel society into one big orgy. Or perhaps they're afraid of the seduction of the innocents, whoever they might be these days.

There are three effective aphrodisiacs available in our society today. They are all illegal. There is a fourth which is a poor substitute. Predictably, it is legal, cheap, and widely used. It is alcohol. In spite of all the pious talk about alcohol being a "dangerous depressant," it is simply a tranquillizer. That's the way it works in the sexual department, too. Fear is the enemy of sexual stimulation. Ask anyone who's tried to make mad love with a jealous husband knocking at the door. Alcohol calms *all* fears including the dozens of anxieties surrounding sex. After three martinis when he says, "There's nothing to worry about," she believes him. Alcohol is a sexual lubricant in another way. It surrounds everything with a nice glow. So you don't do so well— who cares? Who remembers? Its real defect is that it actually interferes with full sensation, co-ordination, and enjoyment of sex. That's probably why it's legal.

A true aphrodisiac is the male sex hormone, testosterone. By acting on the entire body it causes powerful, almost irresistible sexual desire. It works equally in men or women. The onset is slow, but the effect is profound and long-lasting.

Of course there is a catch. In men it results in atrophy of the testicles, not a small thing. In women it can cause masculinization. The clitoris enlarges, hair appears on the face, the voice deepens and other somewhat unattractive changes transpire. In both sexes it can cause serious liver damage if used indiscriminately. Its use, except by a licensed physician, is illegal and should remain that way. Not as immediately dangerous as Spanish fly or strychnine, it can make plenty of trouble of the worst kind.

What about the other two?

The other two are fascinating drugs. The first is marijuana. One of its most powerful effects, and the one which is played down publicly, is sexual arousal. Intense sexual fantasies, heightened sexual desire, and increased sexual sensation are reported by many who use the drug.

Isn't marijuana a narcotic?

Yes and no. According to federal law in America it is classed as a narcotic. Scientifically that is incorrect. It is not considered by drug experts to be addicting. It falls into the category of "habituating drugs." These are substances which do not cause physical dependence but are "habit-forming." That can be a giant-sized problem in itself, as anyone knows who has tried to quit smoking. This is why tobacco is classed as "habituating" by most pharmacologists.

In spite of controversy, two things about marijuana are clear: first, it is a sexual stimulant, and an effective one. Second, it is an illegal drug. Setting new records in the bedroom is not worth doing time in jail.

What about the last one?

The last one is the toughest—LSD. LSD has a multitude of effects on the mind, most of them poorly understood. One thing clearly understood by anyone who takes it is that it packs sexual dynamite. Those stories in the Sunday newspapers moralizing about bad people who take LSD leave out one thing: the real reason they take it. Sometimes it leaks through the antiseptic accounts. The subject says, "I felt as if I possessed all the women in the world." What do you think he means by "possessed"? Regular users are always talking about "love." When they say "Make love, not war," they don't mean the hearts and flowers kind.

If it will help them to get more pleasure out of sex, why shouldn't people be allowed to use LSD and marijuana?

It is presently against the law to buy, sell, use, or even possess either drug. Furthermore they may be harmful, particularly if used indiscriminately. Most of the supply available today on the illegal market, because of its unsupervised production, is potentially dangerous.

Because of moralistic restrictions, bona fide scientific research with LSD and marijuana is virtually impossible. If these drugs were carefully studied and understood it is certainly possible that everyone might benefit.

It is one of the ironies of life that the drug which we are allowed, even encouraged to use, alcohol, is a powerful destructive force in our society.

6

IMPOTENCE

What is impotence?

Impotence is a penis that won't do what it's told. In spite of an unbelievably complex copulatory control system maintained by the body, the penis may fail to respond to its commands at appropriate times. This upsets the precise progression of events necessary for successful intercourse and the entire undertaking fails. For real disappointment, nothing matches the sputtering out of a reluctant penis.

Exactly what happens in impotence?

There are several distinct types of impotence but they all have one thing in common—sexual intercourse becomes impossible.

The most frustrating potency defect of all is absolute impotence. In this condition, the penis acts as if it is dead—it just hangs there forlornly. No amount of stimulation can encourage it to become erect. The harder a man tries, the less he accomplishes. Of course there is no possibility of sexual intercourse—it would be like trying to unlock a door with a wet noodle. An accurate description can only come from a man afflicted with this form of impotence. Jerry is such a man. He is forty-one, has been married three times, and is desperate:

"I have been through a lot, Doc. Married three times, going through two divorces, they take a lot out of a guy, but it's never been as bad as this. It doesn't even work! I mean, take last night. Arlene, that's my wife, got herself all dressed up at bedtime—the works. A black transparent negligee, perfume, she even had a couple of drinks to loosen up. And she's really built! Any other guy would give his right arm for a chance to swing with her."

Jerry shook his head in despair.

"Damn it, so would I! If I were still a man. I let her play with it, I rubbed it against her, I did everything with it but paint it green. All it did was get smaller. I thought it was going to disappear!"

Can a penis actually disappear?

Not really, but some men who are made frantic by relentless impotence begin to think so. Among the Chinese it takes the form of a disease called "kuru." A Chinese suffering from impotence may become obsessed with the fear that his penis is receding into his body. He is terrified that it will then be lost to him forever. Impelled by fear he resorts to desperate measures to restrain the wandering organ. He establishes a twenty-four-hour watch manned by members of the family to keep the penis in sight at all times. Frequently he pierces the phallus with a small nail or series of pins which he attaches to the bedpost with a stout cord. Alternatively the free end of the cord may be entrusted to the most dependable member of the family with instructions to jerk vigorously if the penis begins to wriggle upward into the body.

Is "kuru" an actual disease?

It is as real as impotence to the man who suffers from it. There is actually no chance that the penis will disappear into the vast emptiness of the abdominal cavity to be seen no more. But try to tell a hysterical Chinese that. Ninety-five per cent of the time absolute impotence is simply a cruel practical joke played on a luckless man by his own emotions. But the victim doesn't understand. Let Jerry finish his story:

"We've been doing the same thing for the two weeks in a row. Every night we go to the starting gate, every night I get scratched before I even get started. If my wife doesn't get some action, this is going to be divorce number three for me."

Even if Arlene does get "some action," it may still mean divorce. Many wives caught in this position look elsewhere for sexual intercourse. When the husband finds out, he often rings down the curtain on the marriage—more as a way to avoid facing his own problem than anything else. If he doesn't break the stalemate, his wife probably will. When the divorce complaint says "mental cruelty," it may refer to a mind that won't let the penis work. That form of sexual torture can be as cruel to the frustrated donor as it is to the disappointed recipient.

Is absolute impotence very common?

In a sense, yes. At one time or another, every man suffers from it. Because of the design of the male sexual equipment, immediately after ejaculation, the erection usually disappears. (It may linger for three to five minutes on certain occasions, but this is unusual.) For a variable period of time, no erection is possible and no further intercourse can take place. This is temporary absolute impotence. Even that transient experience is somewhat unsettling and can cause feelings of insecurity if erectile capability does not return in fifteen to twenty minutes. Actually this form of enforced relaxation protects the sexual mechanism from being overworked; it operates like a fuse or circuit-breaker. When the nerve pathways controlling copulation are overheated by orgasm, a fuse temporarily blows, shutting down the powerline to the penis. After things cool off, power is restored, and another reproductive rocket is ready for launching. The average "down time" is about thirty minutes; the normal range is twenty minutes to one hour.

Can't some men have subsequent orgasms much closer together than that?

Everyone has heard of cases of super-potency where men have five to six orgasms per hour. This can occur in three types of situations.

After a long period of sexual deprivation, say two to three months, the quiescent period of the sexual reflexes is shortened. After ejaculation, erection can occur again in as little as five minutes. This is a relatively rare situation and is soon replaced (regrettably) by a more conservative waiting period.

Under circumstances of unusually strong sexual stimulation it is also possible for re-erection and ejaculation to take place several times in an hour. At the outset of a new sexual encounter or in a relationship with an especially exciting woman, a significant number of men have expanded ejaculatory capabilities. This, too, tends to fade with time as the level of sexual excitement and the novelty of the situation diminish.

The other explanation for sensational male orgasmic performance is the one that applies more often.

What's that?

A lot of men expect more from their genitals than they were designed to deliver. These fragile structures are controlled by delicately tuned mechanisms oriented to quality, not quantity. Copulation is not a competitive sport. Yet men who compete intensely in every other area of their lives find it hard to take sex as it is. Super-potency is dangled before them on television (implicitly), in the films (explicitly), and in novels (very explicitly). After enough exposure to this sort of thing, they begin to believe that anyone who can't make it every eleven minutes is in difficulty. Their own track record, which actually may be more than adequate, seems pale by comparison. So they do what every human being does when he begins to feel insecure—they tell lies. But the lie makes their problem worse instead of better.

How's that?

Say Charlie has intercourse twice a week with one ejaculation each time. Unfortunately, all the books he's read describe the exploits of supermen with super-penises; compared to them his performance is sadly lacking. He doesn't realize that his sex life is about average for his time of life. When the subject comes up in the locker room at the country club (every week), he says it this way: "There's never been a night in my life when I didn't go back for a second round!"

Mike, his golf partner, who is lucky to have one orgasm a week, counters with: "Half the time, I can go all night!"

Charlie knows he lied and he thinks Mike is lying, but he's not sure. He loses even more confidence in his sexual powers and tells better lies the next time. The problem compounds when his lack of confidence really begins to affect his capabilities. Then when the boys start bragging, he just shuts up.

Does confidence have that much effect on potency?

More than any other human endeavour, male sexuality is a confidence game. The rule is, "If you think you can do it, you probably can." An erection is so perishable that a sudden noise, a critical word, even a rejecting look can demolish it. One of the real problems of absolute impotence is the "vicious cycle."

How does that work?

Assume that the man fails to obtain an erection on a particular occasion for some insignificant reason—he is tired, preoccupied with work, sick. If his wife or girl friend ridicules him or compares him unfavourably to other men, the stage is set. The next time he is in trouble. He failed once—what if he fails again? Just worrying about how his penis will act may keep it from giving any performance at all, confirming his worst fears. He now has two strikes against him and will likely fail for sure tomorrow night. A new conditioned reflex has been established—as soon as he approaches a naked woman his phallus goes to half-mast. It can be a terrible experience. It happened to Simon:

"I still remember the first time as if it happened yesterday though it was almost a year ago."

As he sat before the doctor, Simon gulped a pill without any water. "Damn it, I've been so nervous since I lost my manhood I have to take pills before I can do anything. I only wish I could find a damn pill to put me back together again, if you know what I mean." Around the armpits his shirt was soaked with sweat.

"It's my own fault. I was out with this dame one night and I took her over to my place. She was one of those 'high-class' call girls. After we got to bed—we were both kind of high; she took my, you know, organ in her hand and said, 'Is this all you've got?' It was like someone stuck it with a pin—it just collapsed." Now the sweat had spread to Simon's forehead. He mopped his brow.

"Then she must've been afraid she'd lose a client because she did everything to it and put it everywhere she could think of—she thought of a lot of places. But no matter what she did, all I had to show for it was a wet noodle. She killed my penis!" His face was bright red and Simon gulped another pill.

"Every time since then I've been afraid. As soon as I bring it out, I'm afraid it's too small. Sometimes the girls don't say anything but I'm sure that's what they're thinking. The more often I try, the worse it gets."

"Do you ever have erections?" asked the doctor.

Simon grinned pathetically. "Oh, sure. I have them every night —as long as I'm all alone. I can make it every night by myself— but I tried to give that stuff up when I was fourteen!"

This is one of the most frustrating and humiliating aspects of absolute impotence. Ninety-five per cent of the time the penis works fine—when there's no work to do. It's almost as if the organ has been frightened by a vagina; in a sense it has. Fear and potency are mutually exclusive.

Is there any other kind of impotence?

There is another kind that masquerades as super-potency. It works like this: Erection is no problem at all. Swift, hard, and urgent, the penis strains toward the vagina. The moment penis and vagina make contact, ejaculation occurs! For the man, it's ten seconds from approach to orgasm. For the woman, nothing. The apologies of her partner are no substitute for a sexual climax.

Does this condition have a name?

The scientific name for this condition is "premature ejaculation." It comes in many forms, all equally frustrating. The male orgasm and ejaculation may come on even before the clothes come off—hard on the underwear and on the feelings.

Sometimes everything goes smoothly until pelvic thrusts begin—with the first forward motion, everything spills out. The variations are almost endless but they all have one thing in common: ejaculation occurs long before there is any possibility of satisfying the female.

Is premature ejaculation really abnormal?

Most women think so. After being stimulated to a high pitch of sexual excitement, their reward is a warm shower of sticky semen deposited on the vulva. Some men try to alibi their problem by insisting that speed of ejaculation is synonymous with potency. "I'm just too sexy!" they say. If their race is against the clock, they are probably right. But in heterosexual intercourse the penis is trying to keep time with the vagina. If the two sexual systems run neck-and-neck and arrive at the finish line more or less at the same time, the race has two winners. If the man always has to cross the finish line before his girl gets to the first turn, both of them are apt to lose.

But don't male animals all ejaculate quickly? If it's normal for them, why shouldn't it be normal for men?

This is the logic applied by Kinsey (a biologist) in his survey of human sexuality. He noted that a large proportion of the men interviewed by his staff reported premature ejaculation. He compared the performance of men with that of animals and concluded that since animals ejaculated fast, it was fine for men to do the same. He even suggested equating speed of orgasm with masculinity. Kinsey overlooked a few things. The dog, for example, has extremely rapid orgasms. He also chases cars, drinks from puddles, and dies at the age of fourteen. If it is normal to be like a dog in one way, why not follow his example in all the others?

Another point Kinsey forgot to mention is that during intercourse the dog's penis becomes trapped in the female's vagina. No matter how fast he may ejaculate, the dog stays where he is until his mate is satisfied—unless he wants to leave his penis behind. One more man–beast distinction: in animals resembling man, the anatomical location of the clitoris in the female brings it into direct and forceful contact with the penis. A minimum of stimulation by the male animal almost guarantees orgasm for his partner.

There is one group of women who adore men with premature ejaculation: prostitutes. On the evening that a girl is lucky to find a dozen gentlemen who are quick on the trigger, she can be home in bed (her own) by nine-thirty.

How does this condition affect men who suffer from it?

Men who are honest enough to look behind their smoke screen of alibis aren't very happy with their speed. Rick is twenty-seven; he is an actor playing bit parts in films. He also plays bit parts in the bedroom.

"I thought I was the best stud in Hollywood. I was ready to swing with any chick any time. I was really great—while I lasted. Only problem was I didn't last too long. I'd leap into bed with a dame, make a great entrance, and I was offstage in half a minute." Rick shook his curly head.

"I even thought it was their fault! Most of the time I'd pick a fight and tell myself I never wanted to see them again. The truth was I didn't want to run the risk of letting them know what a flop I really was. I went out with a different girl every week for almost six months! But it didn't last—the word got around that Ricky-boy couldn't go the route.

"The thing that really made me face the music happened about a month ago. I met this new babe on location for a picture I was working in. This was the first girl I actually cared about. And she was really a knock-out! After a week or so, I took her over to my motel. We had a few drinks, I undressed her, slipped off my own clothes and we got into bed. She was ready—I've never seen a girl so worked up! She wanted me even more than I wanted her! She took hold of my penis to guide it into her—as soon as she touched it, I went off! God, what a lousy feeling! She didn't say a word. She just got up, put on her clothes real fast, and walked out. I never saw her again; I picked up my bill the next day. I went to a head-shrinker that afternoon and started to get myself straightened out."

Is there any other form of impotence besides premature ejaculation?

Yes. There is another type midway between absolute impotence and premature ejaculation. It is called "copulatory impotence." This is a particularly unpleasant condition because everything seems to be all right, until all of a sudden it isn't. Erection proceeds normally, insertion goes without a hitch. Even pelvic thrusting gets under way nicely. All of a sudden, the penis goes limp. The poor victim has two choices: he can retreat in humiliation by taking his penis out or wait a few seconds and let it come flopping out itself. Neither choice is appealing. Continuation of intercourse with a soggy organ is impossible. Like all other forms of impotence, the disease is not contagious. The woman remains sexually eager and excited, much to her partner's (and her own) dismay. Once the penis conks out like this it stays down for the count. With luck, another erection can be expected in about an hour.

Fortunately, copulatory impotence is the second rarest potency disturbance. It is difficult to deal with since few men even recognize it for what it is. They blame it on "being tired" or "run down" and hope for better luck next time. Sometimes they're lucky and sometimes they aren't.

What is the rarest form of impotence?

This is another case of impotence sailing under the flag of superpotency. A wife of the victim, a victim herself, can describe it best:

"For the first two years of our marriage. I thought there was something wrong with *me*. I just couldn't satisfy Chuck. He would get such hard erections and beg me for sex so often I just couldn't understand it. And he would go on for hours. I'd have a climax and then another one and maybe two more but he'd still be hard at work. By then it was three in the morning and I was exhausted. When he finally took his penis out, it was just as hard as when it went in. In the morning he'd want to try again and it would be the same. I was just happy he had to go to work. Weekends were hell. It was sex, sex, sex, for hours and hours. Finally I got him to go to a psychiatrist and in a few weeks, everything was fine. To tell you the truth, I couldn't have taken it much longer. He was about to wear me out."

This dramatic condition has the equally dramatic name of "psychogenic aspermia" (P-A). It is very much as the haggard wife described it. Everything about the man's sexual performance is flawless except he never ejaculates. Not only does he fail to ejaculate, he never reaches orgasm. It is the male equivalent of female frigidity. The erection stays rigid, sensation is more or less intact (except for soreness after the first hour), but for the man there is no end. Ironically, a man with P-A is in the same sexual boat as one with absolute impotence—neither of them can complete the sexual act.

The one advantage for the P-A sufferer is that with expert psychiatric help, normal sexual functioning can be restored *rapidly*. Curing other forms of impotence may take longer.

What is normal sexual functioning for a man?

As in every other area relating to human behaviour, there is no absolute standard. There is however a range of "normal" male sexual capacity. The first test is the ability to obtain an orgasm under reasonable circumstances. This presumes the presence of a sympathetic, sexually attractive woman and a reasonable amount of sexual stimulation. The next step is the capacity to deliver the penis to and into the vagina without losing either the erection or the seminal fluid. The third criterion is the capacity to prolong intercourse sufficiently so that a relatively normal woman can reach orgasm as a result.

This is one of the most variable and difficult to measure aspects of potency. A woman who has had extensive genital stimulation by her partner just before insertion may reach orgasm rapidly. If intercourse begins with little or no clitoral and labial petting, orgasm for the female can take considerably longer. A reasonable yardstick for male potency is the ability to continue intercourse for five to ten minutes. During that time a normally potent male will deliver from fifty to one hundred pelvic thrusts.

Frequency of intercourse is affected by so many outside factors that it is difficult to define a normal pattern. A man who has intercourse more than once a week and less than twice a day is probably in the range of normal.

After orgasm, how long should it take before a man is ready to have intercourse again?

Recovery time after orgasm depends on the strength of sexual stimulation, frequency of intercourse, and age. A man who is strongly stimulated by his wife or girl friend, who has not had intercourse for six weeks, and who is under the age of forty may be able to have a second erection five minutes after ejaculation. On the other hand, a man having intercourse every night may have an erectile recovery time of thirty minutes or more. This relates to another area of masculine insecurity. The average man is capable of about one ejaculation per session without straining himself. The woman can (and some prostitutes do) service a regiment in the same interval. Every man knows that but somehow feels compelled to serve second and third helpings. Food and sex have much in common. In eating, the first bite is the tastiest, the first helping the most appetizing. The third serving of strawberry shortcake just doesn't taste as good as the first time around. The third copulation of the evening is more for the record books than the enjoyment of the participants.

How common is impotence?

Every man in this world has had a potency disturbance at one time or another. The exact incidence of chronic impotence is hard to calculate since this is not the sort of event that men take ads in the newspaper to announce. If premature ejaculation is included (as it must be), probably fifty per cent or more of all men are chronically impotent.

What is the treatment for premature ejaculation?

Like remedies for all forms of impotence, you pay your money and you take your choice. Because premature ejaculation is such a blight on sexual enjoyment, for women as well as men, virtually every possible cure has been tried—along with some that are obviously impossible. The most primitive approach is simply to repeat intercourse until the sexual reflexes become sufficiently fatigued to delay ejaculation. This is a tedious business at best and requires sending the lady to the corner to buy the paper or something while the man is waiting thirty minutes until the next erection arrives. Some men even masturbate in advance so that what appears to be their first orgasm of the evening is really number two. With this approach masturbation can become the main event and intercourse is an anticlimax. As one sufferer said, "After I blast-off myself, what do I need a girl friend for?"

Other men try to delay orgasm by "thinking of other things" during intercourse. This is the technique recommended by some "experts" in the field of marriage counselling who should know better.

A fellow who tried this remedy tells about it:

"I'm only twenty-four but I felt like seventy-four. No matter what I did, I came too fast. I couldn't find a girl who'd go out with me twice and so I went to this counsellor. He told me all I had to do was 'control myself'—I didn't have to pay to hear that. Then he suggested as soon as I got into the vagina, I should think about my job instead of sex. I sell cars. So I started thinking about my customers, especially the chicks. There's this one who's really built. As soon as I thought about her, I went off—even faster than before. So I went back to him and he told me to do arithmetic problems in my head. So I tried that. I'm not too good at multiplying so I was saying it kind of out loud like, 'Thirteen times eleven is . . .' and the girl I was making it with heard me. She got real mad and pushed me off and went home."

Another variation is to think of something "disgusting" to delay orgasm. If the patient can think of something "disgusting" enough, he may solve his problem by losing his erection completely. The whole concept is self-defeating anyhow. Imagine sitting down to a sizzling steak dinner and trying to conjure up the image of a trash can full of discarded food.

Two other wild-eyed methods involve the wife or girl friend. In one, the woman is asked to masturbate the man almost to the point of ejaculation, then stop. She does this repeatedly until he's had enough. This is supposed to teach him how to last longer. This approach actually has two hidden advantages. It allows her to get even for the times he has disappointed her, and also shows him what it feels like to be left high and dry. As far as curing his disease, it doesn't do much.

The other method calls for the couple to merely lie next to each other in bed naked and think of other things. They are to avoid any sexual stimulation at all. This "calms down over-excitable men who tend toward prematurity." For the man who ejaculates prematurely and the woman who has to contend with him, lying around thinking of other things instead of having intercourse is not much of a thrill. That's what they've had to do most of the time anyhow.

Are there any methods that work?

There are some that almost work. These depend on decreasing the sensitivity of the penis to the friction of the vagina. Unfortunately this is the physical equivalent of thinking of other things in the sense that it takes away much of the physical pleasure of copulation. It can be accomplished in several ways. The easiest (and cheapest) method is for the man to wear two (or more) condoms. These layers of rubber may dull his sensation enough to retard orgasm. They also give him the unmistakable feeling he is making mad love to a rubber glove. If sensation still comes through, a special "prolonger" is available via mail order. This "prolonger" is a super-thick condom with extra layers of rubber at the head of the penis. At £3 each, they put a premium on orgasm, but many men are willing to pay this for a complete experience.

Isn't there something like an ointment that slows down orgasm?

Yes. The most common preparation is dibucaine ointment. It is a local anaesthetic related to the medication the dentist injects before pulling a tooth. It numbs the sensory corpuscles of the penis and sometimes delays orgasm. It may also prevent orgasm completely and convert premature ejaculation to psychogenic aspermia—at least for the night. The other disadvantage is that some men are allergic to this chemical. If they are, the entire penis breaks out in red, oozing, itching blisters. It can do the same thing to an innocent bystander, the vagina.

The real problem with anaesthetic ointments is that in the long run they make premature ejaculation worse. The penis becomes negatively conditioned and gradually less and less stimulation is required to trigger orgasm. After a few months of using the ointment, the touch of a woman's hand on the erect penis may be enough to jettison a full load of semen then and there.

What about treatment for other kinds of impotence?

The problems of men afflicted with absolute and copulatory impotence are a veritable gold mine for peddlers of nostrums and quack remedies. A hundred years ago it was snake oil, today it is Activated Enzyme Capsules. The list of alleged cures is endless. They all have one thing in common: they don't work. In the electronic age there should be electronic remedies—and there are. As mentioned previously, a transistorized erection machine is available which will also produce ejaculation. Unfortunately this is not a cure. Copulation with electrical impulses will never replace a warm and friendly female. There is another mechanical gadget which comes closer to normal intercourse however.

What's that like?

It is simply a hard rubber doughnut. To benefit from it, the man must first obtain an erection (which makes it unfeasible for absolute impotence). Then he passes his penis through the hole in the doughnut and slides the ring down to the base of the organ where it fits *tightly*. The effect is purely mechanical—the blood which has rushed into the penis at the time of erection stays there because it can't get past the area of compression. No matter what happens, as long as the doughnut is on, the erection is in. This gadget is also used in premature ejaculation; even if orgasm occurs instantly, the penis remains more or less rigid until released from the grip of the rubber ring.

Does that device work?

An honest answer is, Yes, and No. It does keep the penis somewhat rigid no matter what else happens. But it doesn't prevent premature ejaculation and it doesn't make an impotent man potent. Besides it is artificial, unnatural, and cumbersome. Making love with a rubber chaperone bumping up against the pubic bones leaves something to be desired.

That is also the drawback of the other remaining potency appliances. Basically they are splints for sagging penises. Some of them allow the glans or head of the penis to be exposed and come in contact with the vagina. Others enclose the organ in a solid rubber cylinder reinforced with spring steel. The more imaginative ones are rubber replicas of erect penises designed to fit phalluses that have lost their enthusiasm.

Their basic defect is that they eliminate sexual intercourse and substitute for it mutual masturbation. The man is copulating with an imitation vagina made of plastic or rubber tubing and the woman is being masturbated by a plastic or rubber penis. Husband and wife can use these same gadgets and get the same results even if they live a thousand miles apart. Why bother?

Possibly. As a first step he has to realize that impotence is actually not a defect of the penis. Men with this condition often become obsessed with this organ to the point of ignoring the underlying problems. Take Mel, for example. He has absolute impotence and has tried everything—except understanding his problem:

"All I can think about these days is my penis. I look it over whenever I go to the toilet. I try to massage it a little bit every day to 'build it up.' Sometimes I think I'm going to get an erection and I get all excited but by the time I get a chance to look at it, it's usually wilted again."

Mel is looking at the wrong end. The penis is simply an extension of the sexual areas of the brain. As the brain (and spinal cord) ordain, so the penis performs. The conscious part of the mind plays a very small role in sexual endeavours. Erection and ejaculation are possible when the man is asleep, unconscious, and even when the spinal cord is severed. The conscious mind only adds a little garnish to the sexual banquet at best and at worst brings everything crashing down.

Flawed potency originates in a man's emotional makeup. There are some men who are potent only under certain, very special circumstances. For example, they can only obtain and maintain an erection if they are in danger—like making it with the wife of a policeman when the officer may return at any moment. Others require their partner to act out a special scene—for example, the woman must resist until the last moment as if she were being raped. These are examples of partial impotence. If the emotional conflict is great enough, the brain prevents the penis from functioning at all.

What about a man who is potent with some women and impotent with others?

In this relatively common situation, total impotence is waiting in the wings. A man may be impotent with his wife and dramatically potent with a prostitute or girl friend. With these occasional encounters there is no emotional relationship and no need for the brain to cast its veto. Let him leave his wife for his new lady love and that emotional weather vane, the penis, will signal stormy weather again.

Then the wife or girl friend has something to do with a man's impotence?

In many cases she does. There are actually two possibilities. The reluctance of the brain to allow normal intercourse may be a reflection of its owner's feelings about all women or simply one woman in particular. In either case, an impotent man uses his penis like a weapon—a blunt, flabby weapon, but a weapon nevertheless. He refuses to supply sexual gratification to the woman or women he wants to hurt. The fact that he injures himself in the process is unimportant to him. The element of revenge is particularly prominent in premature ejaculation. A girl-victim can describe it best. Natalie is thirty-one and very pretty. She has been married to Jack ten years—he has been impotent in one way or another most of that time. For the past four years his problem has been premature ejaculation:

"I just don't know what to say! He tells me it's my fault but I'm willing to do anything! I just don't know what to do!" She bit her lip to hold back the tears. "I'm tired of crying! It doesn't do any good any more!

"It's the same every time. We go to bed, Jack says he'll be great this time. He plays with me long enough to get me all excited. And then he goes to put it in. As soon as his organ touches me, he comes right away. It's driving me crazy! The worst thing is his smile! At least he can look disappointed. It's almost as if he's doing it on purpose!"

Natalie put her finger on it that time. Jack is doing it on purpose. Only he doesn't realize it. He expresses his resentment of Natalie eloquently with his phallus. The results are hard on her but easy on him. He has regular and frequent intercourse, with an orgasm every time. Natalie hasn't had an orgasm (except when she masturbates) for almost ten years. The smile is characteristic of men with premature ejaculations—they are all profusely apologetic but their regrets have a hollow ring.

What about the other kinds of impotence?

Absolute impotence, copulatory impotence, and premature ejaculation are all manifestations of the same basic problem. They all effectively deny pleasure to the woman.

Impotent men are willing to starve themselves just to get revenge. They, in effect, will gladly cut off their penises to spite their wives. The worse thing about it is most of them aren't even aware of what's going on behind the scenes. Harvey's reaction is typical of men with potency problems:

"I want to! I want to! If only I could! Doctor, I'd give anything just to be able to do it once! I've spent a fortune on pills and massages and chiropractors and phoney plastic penis gadgets. I'd give still more if I could only have my manhood back!" What Harvey doesn't want to know is that his brain has decided, without consulting him directly, that erections and ejaculations are not for him.

Is there any proof that impotence is an emotional problem?

There is convincing evidence that the source of male potency is the brain. Without going into the complicated theories involved, some psychiatrists have excellent results in curing men of impotence. Simply by talking, that is, helping them understand the emotional conflict underlying their sexual handicap, normal potency is restored. If the defect were physical, all the words in the world wouldn't have the slightest effect on a crumpled penis. Further proof comes from research using hypnosis. In response to suggestions implanted during a hypnotic session, erection and ejaculation can be restored and precisely controlled. These events can even be placed under the conscious control of the patient. A man who has experienced it tells what it's like:

"Looking back on it, it all seems so easy. I suffered the agonies of hell for about seven years until I found a psychiatrist who was able to help get me back in the groove. After a few visits he hypnotized me and told me that whenever I wanted to have intercourse with my wife all I had to do was wait until we got into bed and fluff up my pillow. We agreed on that as the trigger for the hypnotic suggestion—it seemed a good idea. I wasn't really convinced but that first night my wife was turning out the light, kind of disappointed as usual. I said, 'I'll just fluff up this pillow a little before we go to sleep.' As soon as I did, I got the hardest erection you can imagine—it almost scared me. I didn't know my penis could get that big—it was throbbing. My wife couldn't believe it but we didn't waste any time. That was one of the best nights in my life! I didn't get too much sleep though; I spent most of the time fluffing up the pillows and, well, you know how it is."

Men with premature ejaculation who have been treated in this fashion can delay orgasm as long as they wish. When ejaculation is desired they merely give the post-hypnotic signal (such as blinking three times) and orgasm starts immediately. Obviously the signal must be chosen wisely to prevent a chance gesture from bringing on orgasm. A vigorous sexual climax while riding the bus to work can be embarrassing. When the man's confidence is restored, hypnosis can be discontinued. Generally hypnotic therapy is not a specific treatment—it only buys time and holds the marriage together while more basic problems are being solved. The most important contribution of hypnosis to impotence is that it proves, once and for all, that the overwhelming majority of potency problems are emotional.

If impotence is an emotional problem, what's the solution?

The only known cure for emotional problems is psychiatric treatment. Fortunately, in many cases the symptom, impotence, can be treated without launching into a full-scale psychoanalysis. Sometimes the wife needs to understand her contribution to the problem—if she is willing to help, the job is much easier.

What can be done for men whose impotence is purely physical?

About five per cent of impotence is on a physical basis. Even this small group has some emotional problems, but they are generally an effect of the potency disturbance rather than a cause of it.

Many diabetic men are impotent. No one really knows the reason, therefore no treatment exists other than bringing the diabetes under control and hoping for the best. (It is however equally possible for a man with diabetes to have an emotional cause for his potency defect.)

Surgery on the prostate gland in older men results in impotence about one third of the time. These unlucky fellows must look for a substitute for sexual intercourse, if such a substitute exists. Another physical basis for defective potency is the male menopause—restoration of the missing hormones often sets everything straight. Any serious physical illness can also upset sexual effectiveness. Treating the disease itself usually gives the best results.

Is there any hope for the many with physical impotence?

Most men with physically determined potency disturbances have absolute or copulatory impotence. Those with copulatory impotence are sometimes helped by using positions for intercourse which trap the penis in the vagina and keep it semi-erect no matter what happens. If he can manage to get his penis into the vagina, the woman can close her legs tightly while the man opens his legs wide. The vaginal muscles clamp down tightly on the penis and often orgasm is possible for both. This position is effective with the man on top or the woman uppermost—it doesn't really matter. There is another position named by the patient who used it, "the better-than-nothing-technique." That about describes it. The woman lies in the usual position, on her back with legs spread. The man lies on top with his penis still limp. However, by placing the penis against the vulva and moving back and forth, he can sometimes provide her with an orgasm. As the patient said, this method is better than nothing—but not much better.

If the woman is willing, cunnilingus can also provide her with regular orgasms. These adaptations are all desperate ones with obvious defects. They only have one thing to recommend them— in an otherwise happy marriage where a man loses his potency because of a physical defect, they keep the wife from suffering unnecessarily. They are not a solution for the ninety-five per cent of men whose impotence is emotional and can be treated.

Sex is one of the few renewable pleasures in this life. It is tragic for a man to allow his emotions to deprive him of what is justly his—at least without putting up a good fight.

7

FRIGIDITY

What is frigidity?

Frigidity is the word used to describe impaired sexual feeling in women. It covers the entire range of substandard sexual response from total avoidance of sexual contact to an occasional missed orgasm. The word frigidity is a misleading one and was probably coined by a man.

Why is that?

It shows a certain lack of understanding of women's sexual makeup by confusing a symptom with a disease. Inability to respond sexually is not a way of life that any woman chooses for herself; it is imposed on her by conditions beyond her control. Besides, the word already has its mind made up—frigid means cold and implies that the lady is deliberately sexually rejecting. That may not be true at all. Perhaps a better term would be orgasmic impairment. This, after all, is what all frigid women have in common. More important, it does not prejudge the situation and assign blame.

What are the different forms of frigidity?

Like impotence, orgasmic impairment ranges all the way from undeniable and obvious sexual failure to the more subtle manifestations which may even masquerade as being presumably oversexed. The basic problem in orgasmic impairment (O-I for short) is that the brain and vagina are not reliably connected to each other. It is like a telephone with loose wires. Sometimes the line goes dead in the middle of a conversation. Sometimes the message gets through but is garbled in the process. Sometimes the parties get the wrong number. Sometimes the phone doesn't even ring.

What happens if the phone doesn't ring?

Then the O-I is total and absolute. For all practical purposes the sexual organs don't even exist. A woman afflicted with this condition has renounced all interest in sex and things sexual. She is misunderstood by her family and friends and relegated to the social shadows as a "frustrated old maid," a title she certainly doesn't deserve. Total orgasmic impairment is a serious emotional problem and deserves to be treated as such.

How does it come about?

Like every other emotional problem, it has its roots in the victim's past. No psychiatrist has ever seen a woman with this condition who was raised by loving parents in a warm, secure family environment. Most women with total O-I suffered serious emotional deprivation during childhood and after. Their adult behaviour often appears to be an unconscious means of perpetuating the coldness and isolation they experienced as children. A lot of bad things had to happen to turn a happy five-year-old moppet into a cynical, withdrawn, forty-year-old spinster. Unfortunately the emotional problem penetrates to every facet of the woman's personality.

Sexual intercourse is simply a specialized type of social relationship; before a woman can have sexual intercourse with a man she must have social intercourse with him. The emotional blunting which is so obvious and dramatic in the sexual sphere permeates most other aspects of the woman's personality as well. Emily is a good example; her sister Hilda can describe her best:

"Emily is only thirty-four but you wouldn't think so if you saw her, doctor. She teaches history at the junior college and most of her students think she's at least forty. It's a shame, too, because she's such a nice girl. I mean she took care of father for ten years until he died last May, and he wasn't the easiest man in the world to get along with. But she doesn't have the slightest interest in men and because of the way she acts, there aren't many men who are interested in her. And the clothes she wears—she doesn't have to wear mini-skirts, but no one else in the whole college wears skirts below the knee. And I can't even get her to wear lipstick. The worst part about it is that Emily is basically such a nice girl."

"What are her other activities besides school?"

"None, really. Since father passed away she spends even more time by herself. Occasionally a fellow will still ask her out, but she's just not interested. The thing I can't understand is how she changed so much. When she was younger she was cute as a button and I was sure she'd be married before she got out of high school."

Emily finally came for a psychiatric interview, primarily, as she said, "to please my sister," the only person with whom she still maintained emotional contact.

"I don't know what Hilda told you, doctor, but I just don't care about sex. I don't even want to talk about it. If you want to discuss something else, I'm willing to listen. But sex, no."

Hilda was right. Although Emily was attractive, her dowdy hair style and dress made her look much older.

"We don't have to say a word about sex if you don't want to. Why are you so unhappy?"

Emily gave a gasp. "I didn't know it was that obvious!" She tried to talk, but started crying. After a dozen pieces of Kleenex and a cup of tea she started to talk again.

"I can't explain it. For the past fifteen years I've just been drying up. At first I tried to fight it off—you know, I'd try and go out on dates and find new interests but nothing worked out. Everyman seemed to be after one thing—sex, and that just scared me."

"I thought you didn't want to talk about sex."

"Oh, I don't care. I'm so miserable now it won't make any difference."

Emily entered psychiatric treatment for her basic problem: depression and anxiety, with a big burden of guilt. Gradually she recognized how she had been unconsciously trying to reproduce in her present life the dreariness and disappointment of her youth. Her interest in clothes and her own appearance increased and she began to go out on dates. She stopped picking men who were experts at disappointing her and began to look and act her age—or younger. After six months of treatment, Emily eloped with the assistant dean of the college. After her honeymoon, she stopped in to see her psychiatrist.

"I'm happy to say, doctor, this is just a social call. I wanted to tell you how happy I am. I don't know what it's done for other people but psychiatry did what Mother Nature couldn't do—it made a woman out of me!"

The only effective treatment for total orgasmic impairment is psychotherapy, because the condition is a psychiatric one. The sexual difficulty is simply a manifestation of a deeper emotional dysfunction.

When is a woman too old to do something about that sort of thing?

From a practical point of view, never. As long as she has the desire to come to grips with the condition and try to overcome it, treatment is worthwhile. Of course, as the patient gets older there is less and less time to enjoy whatever results are obtained, but on occasion women in their fifties or sixties improve so much with psychiatric treatment that they marry for the first time. Orgasmic impairment can also affect those who are just stepping over the sexual threshold.

How does that happen?

Every thirty years or so our society goes through a so-called sexual revolution. Young people finally tire of the sexual restraints imposed on them by their "old-fashioned" parents and teachers. Instead of being held captive by the obsolete morality of the establishment, as avowed sexual freedom fighters, they shake off their bonds and surge toward sexual liberty. Unfortunately they overlook two things.

First, their stodgy parents did exactly the same thing years before—they called it "The Roaring Twenties." Their grand-parents also slipped their sexual bonds—those days were known as "The Gay Nineties." Characteristically each new generation is in revolt against the expressed morality of the generation that preceded them. This is basically a sociological problem and tends to work itself out. If every securely married forty-year-old mother succeeded in imposing her own code of conduct on her twenty-year-old daughter, this would be a much less interesting world. Fortunately mother doesn't succeed. Moreover, twenty years from now, the daughter, by then a mother herself, will be trying to do the same thing with her daughter.

If the daughter doesn't understand this clearly, it can lead to trouble. Many young people, say between the ages of eighteen and twenty-five, are enthusiastically dedicated to the principle of sexual freedom but the brain sometimes short-circuits the message before it gets to the sexual organs. In effect there are two messages on the line—one says, "Anything goes! Do whatever turns you on!" Sometimes the other voice talks a little louder. It says uptight things like, "What if you get pregnant? Does he really love you?" Sex plus fear means no orgasm. Sex plus guilt means no orgasm.

Why does fear prevent orgasm?

In human beings, sex is optional. Copulation is not vital for survival; we only seek it when more urgent needs have been met. Food, shelter, and a minimum feeling of security come first. When danger threatens in any form, Nature clears the decks for action. One of the first functions to go overboard is orgasm. (Next goes erection in the male, followed by complete loss of sexual desire in both sexes.) A nineteen-year-old girl who deep inside wonders if it really is all right may have just enough fear to keep her from reaching a sexual climax.

A twenty-five-year-old secretary, divorced with two small children, may worry just enough about getting pregnant ("Did I remember to take my pill today?") to wipe out any chance of orgasm.

Another factor is best described as the vaginal compromise. In many sexually active unmarried girls there are two diametrically opposing forces: "I want sex! I need sex!" and from an earlier edition of their personalities (still intact just below the surface), "Sex before marriage is wrong! Save it for your husband!" Since the brain cannot reconcile such opposing viewpoints, it bows out and leaves the job to a more versatile organ, the vagina. The net result is intercourse without guilt (almost) and incidentally without orgasm. The "crime," sexual intercourse, is immediately followed by the "punishment," orgasmic impairment. The vagina is both judge and executioner—the perfect compromise. Perfect, that is, if you don't object to cruel and unusual punishment.

Why is it so cruel?

For two reasons. First it is like Tantalus, the king of Phrygia who, according to Greek mythology, was condemned to stand forever in water up to his chin. Racked by thirst, each time he bent to drink, the water receded out of his reach. Some women with O-I know how King Tantalus must have felt. There are few tortures more agonizing than being brought to the brink of sexual fulfilment and having orgasm snatched away at the last moment.

The second and most unfortunate aspect of this punishment is that it never need happen. There is no reason whatsoever that requires a normal adult to relentlessly punish herself for not adhering to a moral code neatly tailored to the needs of a ten-year-old girl. It is hard to justify sexual intercourse three times a week for a young lady of 13 or 14 years (although some of them are doing it). It is hard not to encourage the same frequency in a vigorous twenty-two-year-old girl who is bursting with sexual vitality and sexual hormones. Every form of sexual behaviour has its best time and place. If a girl isn't going to copulate when she is twenty-two, when is she going to do it? At sixty-five?

But isn't it better for her to wait until she's married?

Yes, probably. But in the meantime taking a cold shower every night isn't going to improve her mental health either. The most important principle to keep in mind is that sex is right. Human destiny is constant relentless copulation, in spite of all the barriers and the obstacles. The instinctive compulsion to breed is irresistible. It is most desirable to enclose sexual activities within a framework that provides the greatest security and broadest gratification for both partners—for a lot of people that framework is marriage. But if marriage is not possible (for any number of reasons), then sex without marriage is the only alternative. (No sex is so stupid it is not even worth considering as a possibility.)

But what will society think?

Ninety-eight per cent of society doesn't really care about the sexual behaviour of its members. The other two per cent who are so obsessed with what others are doing probably doesn't have the courage to go out and find the same thing for itself. If our society were as diligent about observing sexual proprieties as some moral guardians would have us believe, there wouldn't be nearly as many new members born into it every day for the moralists to guide and purify.

A great deterrent to sexual happiness and orgasm is fear of doing wrong. Sex, for grown-ups, is not wrong. Unless that message penetrates, a lot of unhappiness can ensue. A girl who has suffered can give a better idea.

Joni is an airline stewardess. Originally from a farm in Iowa, she has come a long way. She has a veneer of sophistication and a beautiful twenty-three-year-old body that she knows how to use— almost.

"I guess there's no need to lie to you, doctor." She crossed her legs and tugged at her mini-skirt—a futile gesture.

"I have everything a girl could ask for—an exciting job, complete freedom, as many men as I want to choose from every day. But I can't seem to—I mean—the one thing I really want to have . . ." Tears and makeup flowed into each other.

"Have you ever been able to reach an orgasm?"

"No. The more I try, the worse it gets! I seem to be getting further away instead of closer. I'm afraid if it keeps up this way, pretty soon I won't even feel like doing it!" Tears triumph over makeup.

Whether she realizes it or not, when she swings with the jet set at the ultimate moment, unconsciously Joni enforces the moral code of rural Iowa—the one she learned from her mother long before she ever saw an airplane.

By using the understanding and intelligence that helped her progress in her career, Joni began to recognize that the things her mother told her fifteen years ago on the farm did not necessarily apply to her present life. Back in those days she wore dresses made from flour-sacks. But just as her body had outgrown the flour-sack fashions, her personality and way of life had outgrown the flour-sack morality. As she came to understand this, reaching a sexual climax became easier for her and she ultimately married happily. At Christmas time she wrote to her doctor, "I may have been a stewardess, but I really 'won my wings' in the psychiatrist's office!"

Is there ever a physical reason for frigidity?

From a mechanical point of view, the female genitalia is probably the most perfect example of fail-safe design in the world today. Every mechanism has an alternative process to fall back on just in case something goes wrong. In spite of that, something physical does go wrong occasionally. Until it is adjusted, orgasm becomes impossible. The greatest stumbling block, physically, is the hymen. This little membrane can stop the works if it is so inclined.

If the hymen is tough and thick it can successfully repel all assaults of a determined penis. Each time the penis bounces off the drumhead of the hymen, it leaves more soreness and swelling behind. The pain can become so great that the most passionate virgin is willing to call it an evening. The reluctant hymen is merely another burden of modern "civilization." In simpler cultures, the old women of the tribe obliterated the hymen with a sharp stick on the first day of the first menstrual period. That took care of that.

What can a modern girl do?

She must settle for a scrubbed-up version of the old lady with a stick. In the doctor's office, draped in sheets and suitably tranquillized, the patient reclines while the doctor performs a "hymenotomy." With a stainless steel scalpel he makes an incision in the hymen in the form of a cross. That is the first half of the operation.

The second half of the procedure is the most important. Just as when ears are pierced, the incision must be kept open. A week or so after the operation, when the soreness has disappeared, the husband or boy friend dilates the opening with whatever instrument seems appropriate. Regular and frequent intercourse for the first six weeks is essential to obliterate the remnants of the hymen and allow the vagina to heal satisfactorily.

Is that the only trouble the hymen can cause?

No. In addition to male consternation about its alleged presence or absence, the hymen makes other mischief. In women over the age of forty the place where the hymen used to be (assuming it has long since served whatever purpose the hymen serves) may become inflamed. Instead of a few tiny tattered remnants of hymen around the vaginal orifice, a hard tender knot forms. This is called a "hymeneal caruncle." It sits, like a sentinel, atop the lower rim of the vaginal opening. Every time the under surface of the penis glides over it, it causes exquisite pain. The usual treatment is relieving the oestrogenic hormone deficiency that brought it on in the first place.

Is there any other form of frigidity that involves younger women?

Yes. Probably the most common form of O-I (and one that is usually temporary) is the so-called "honeymoon frigidity." Adjusting to a delicate and intimate association like sexual intercourse can take a little time. To expect instant orgasm on the honeymoon is courting disappointment. Even if the wedding night is not the couple's first time in bed together, the anxiety and nervousness of the occasion may be enough to eclipse any chance of orgasm. Sometimes it can be even worse. Sue tells what happened to her:

"I can almost laugh at it now but that night I thought it was the end of the world. By the time the wedding and the reception and the dinner were over it was almost midnight before Tony and I got to our hotel. After we talked for a couple of minutes, I undressed and got into bed. That was the first time we ever really did it together. I mean before we got married we fooled around with each other a lot but we never went all the way. Well, he came into bed and we were both pretty excited. He was kissing me all over and I started to pull him on top of me but then all of a sudden he stiffened up.

"I couldn't imagine what was wrong—I got a little scared. Then he said, 'Did you bring them?' I said, 'Bring what?' He said, 'The protection. You don't want to get pregnant tonight, do you?' Well, he forgot the, the protectors and goodness knows, I didn't have them. Well, we decided to go ahead anyhow because nothing could stop us by then—or at least that's what we thought. Then he couldn't get it in. The harder he pushed, the more it hurt me. I tried to help, but after a while it was so painful I had to ask him to stop.

"Well, it was about three a.m. by then so we rested for a few minutes and he found some Vaseline in the bathroom. He used some of that and I gritted my teeth and he finally got it in and we thought we were going to be able to do it. Then I suddenly felt peculiar and I thought maybe he tore something. But I remembered it was about time for my period and so I told him. It wouldn't have mattered anyhow. As he was taking his penis out he started coming and that was that. We were just about to go to sleep when the sun started to come up. That was the worst night of my life!

"But I really can't complain. My period only lasted three days and by then we had both recovered from the turmoil of that wild experience. The rest of our honeymoon was perfect—Tony and I more than made up for that silly beginning!"

Sue's experience was extreme. Rarely do all these things happen at the same time though it can turn out that way. Only occasionally is ecstasy on the agenda for the wedding night, but that really shouldn't bother anyone. Like any other complex operation, sexual intercourse has a breaking-in period. The couple need to get used to one another's responses, they must learn to coordinate their sexual reflexes, and sometimes they need to discard unrealistic expectations.

What kind of unrealistic expectations?

Copulation, in its commercialized portrayals in films, books, and on television, is depicted as two flawless bodies, perfectly matched, ascending to the heights of human sensual delights. Theoretically this may occur, but it does not describe the average sexual experience. The woman who expects pleasure beyond her wildest dreams each time a penis approaches her vagina is begging to be disappointed. Sex can be wonderfully gratifying, but it is after all a psycho-physiological interaction between two human beings and has all the limitations and defects of any human endeavour. Expecting too much guarantees disappointment. If everything isn't perfect the first time or the second time or even the twentieth time, during the course of their marriage the average couple will have another 7,000 opportunities to improve their performance.

Then frigidity problems always clear up by themselves?

Unfortunately not. Sometimes in spite of "good intentions" on both sides, they get worse. It may simply be a matter of ignorance. Wendy has been married six months, she is twenty-four. She went to her doctor originally because she "couldn't get pregnant." There was more to it than that:

"You see, Ted and I are very anxious to have children. I was an 'only child' and so was he. We want a large family as soon as we can."

"Well, six months is a little early to get discouraged. Have you ever used contraceptives?"

"What are contraceptives, doctor?"

That was enough for the doctor to guess at the problem.

"You don't really feel anything during intercourse, do you, Wendy?"

Wendy shook her pretty head vigorously as the tears gushed down her cheeks. "I don't even know what I'm doing! There must be more to sex than this. It's like—like—doing nothing! But at least it doesn't hurt the way it did before!

After the nurse prepared her for examination, the doctor found exactly what he suspected. Wendy's hymen was perfectly intact—for all practical purposes she was still a virgin. However, the urethra was widely dilated—it would admit an index finger with no resistance. As far as sex was concerned, Ted and Wendy were in the dark—literally.

Right from the beginning Ted had found his way to the wrong orifice and since Wendy expected intercourse to be painful, she tried not to complain. The urethra finally yielded to the constant assault, but it was not exactly the route to pregnancy. The doctor performed a hymenotomy and provided Wendy and Ted with an anatomical road map; pregnancy followed three months later. An intact hymen and knocking at the wrong door—that about completes the list of physical causes for frigidity.

But aren't some women "built" differently—in a way that makes it hard for them to reach a climax?

The configuration of the sexual organs is probably the least important condition for orgasm. Orgasm is possible in women without a clitoris, in women without a vagina, and even in those with artificial vaginas.

Are there women without these structures?

Yes. The vagina and clitoris may just never develop in a small percentage of girls. In other women, malignancies require that these organs be surgically removed. In spite of their loss or absence, these women can and do have orgasms.

Plastic surgeons have developed a technique for improvising an artificial vagina by forming skin from the inner aspect of the thigh into a cylinder and suturing it into place where the vagina should be. The adaptability of the body is so great that with frequent intercourse the skin stops being "skin" and takes on most of the characteristics of normal vaginal lining. Even more dramatic, within six months, about seventy per cent of women experience regular orgasms. The nerve supply to the vulvar area is so rich that stimulation of whatever is there can bring on a sexual climax. There is no reason why every woman should not have regular and frequent orgasms, if she wants to.

Then why do so many women have trouble reaching an orgasm?

Because they are victims of an internal rebellion. A woman who has an unsatisfactory relationship with a man—husband or boy friend, it doesn't really matter—often is unable to express her feelings openly. Her husband may be a good provider but indifferent to her sexual needs. Consciously she is willing to settle for what he gives her, in spite of the emotional emptiness. Unconsciously, her emotions fight back.

One external manifestation of this revolt may be suppression of orgasm. It happened to Angela and this is how she described it:

"Alex and I have been married for ten years now and I just don't know what to do. I've tried everything I can think of and I'm ready to give up.

"The worst part of it is I don't really have anything to complain about. Alex works hard, makes a good living, and most women would be glad to have him for a husband. But sex with him—and I know I shouldn't be saying this—is fine until the end; then it just falls apart. I haven't really had an orgasm in seven years."

"You said 'most women' would be glad to have Alex for a husband. How about you?"

"I'm beginning to wonder. Every weekend, we go to visit his mother. When he's there, he acts just like a little boy. He forgets all about me and all he thinks about is his 'little mother.' I—I almost hate her!" Angela's face turned red and her knuckles turned white as she ground out her cigarette with a vengeance. As later sessions revealed, Angela didn't "almost hate" Alex's mother; she hated her with a passion. In a real sense the passion she directed at her mother-in-law was almost mathematically subtracted from the passion she could have used in intercourse with her husband. The sacred figure of Alex's "little mother" had never been discussed between them—Alex wouldn't allow it. So Angela fought back the only way available to her—unconsciously, in bed, with her sexual organs. She withheld from Alex approximately the same degree of emotional feeling he diverted from her. As retribution it was almost perfect—except it ruined her enjoyment of sex.

Resolving the inner conflict required the cooperation of Alex. At first he resisted: "No psychiatrist is going to come between me and my mother!" After a few sessions he began to realize that "mother" was coming between him and his wife. He had the courage to make the break—almost. He visits mother once a month and *tries* to see her through grown-up eyes. Things are getting better—the only time Angela misses a climax is when she has intercourse with Alex on the night they get back from mother's.

Does orgasmic impairment always involve the husband, too?

Almost always, though sometimes the connection may not be so obvious. Take the case of Ellen:

"I don't know what it is, doctor. I try to do everything right just the way Jim tells me to. I've read all the books he brings home on sexual techniques. I let him do everything to me we can think of but I still don't feel a thing."

"How does Jim feel about it?"

"Well, he's read all the books too and he feels just terrible. He really thinks there's something wrong with him if he can't satisfy me. If he has a climax before I do—that's ninety-nine per cent of the time—he gets all depressed. Sometimes he can't even go to sleep afterward." Ellen managed a wan smile. "I tell him it's not important—just to go right ahead without me. I've given up long ago."

Intercourse with Ellen is as exciting as doing your laundry— and Jim arranged it that way. After they had spent several sessions together with the psychiatrist, the story unfolded. Both Jim and Ellen had little sexual experience before marriage. Ellen "put herself in Jim's hands," as she described it, because "the man should know everything about that sort of thing." Jim *didn't* know everything, and he panicked. Their sexual life was a succession of chapters from the latest sex manuals—a sort of sex-by-the-book. Everything was scientifically accurate except the human part. Poor Ellen didn't know any better *consciously*. Unconsciously she resented her husband's Popular Mechanics approach to copulation—and with good reason. In sexual intercourse, real human emotions can make up for any lapses from perfect form. Even if the technique lacks perfection, love and tenderness can fill in the gaps. Once they realized that, Jim threw away his books, Ellen felt more like a wife than a lesson, and orgasms replaced disappointments. As Jim said some time later, "To tell you the truth, Ellen and I learned more from a few wild nights with each other than from all the books put together!"

What happens if the woman doesn't recognize that her orgasmic impairment is an emotional problem?

Then she may be in for a lot of disappointment. Sometimes the result is a "Jack Spratt' marriage. A woman with O-I unconsciously selects an impotent husband. He can't last long enough to stimulate her—even if he could her orgasm probably wouldn't materialize. By selecting a man with a complementary emotional problem, a woman can insulate herself from ever arriving at what she unconsciously wants most to avoid—sexual gratification. Sometimes the result can be tragic.

How is that?

If the woman begins to feel that achieving orgasm is only a matter of finding the "right" penis, she may decide to do something about it. The common name for such a quest is nymphomania. The woman, unaware of the real nature of her problem, goes from man to man, from cocktail party to cocktail party, looking for "real satisfaction." The men who try to satisfy her think they are "getting something." Nothing could be further from the truth. They are simply taking advantage of an unhappy victim of a neurotic conflict. When all the glamour is scraped away, any nymphomaniac would trade her "exciting" life for three orgasms a week with a man she loves. Her search for the "magic penis" is doomed to failure because the obstacle to orgasm is not in the penis nor even in the vagina—it is in her own mind.

Do nymphomaniacs ever have orgasms?

Yes. Nymphomania is an ironical disease. Like an impotent man who can have an erection as long as there is no chance of using it, "nymphos" can have an orgasm as long as there is little chance of repeating it. It can be disappointing.

Sometimes a woman with this variety of orgasmic impairment thinks her search is ended. At a party, in a cocktail lounge, at a ski lodge, she meets the man who can turn her on. After a night (sometimes two or three nights or more) of relatively normal sexual functioning, she is elated. Her "search" has paid off, and she can finally settle down to enjoy it. Then something happens. Something *always* happens to these unfortunate women. As soon as the relationship becomes more than casual, the brain resigns and orgasm goes out the window.

Why does that happen?

Often sex is acceptable to them as long as it's a game. When it becomes apparent that a fully-fledged relationship at an adult level is about to develop, they want out. Nancy, a photographer's model, is a good example:

"Doctor, I'm worried—I'm twenty-eight now and I'm still frigid. Oh, I keep up a good front. I don't act as depressed as I feel about it. I try to be bright and gay and all that but I never really get anything out of sex."

"You mean you never have an orgasm?"

"No, that's just it. Maybe it would be easier that way. Most of the time, I can't reach a climax—that's true. But about every six months I find a man who's different. With him, everything comes easy—at least for a while. Whenever we sleep together, it's magnificent and I think, 'Well, Nancy, you've finally found him!' Then I move into his apartment and within a week—*nothing*. As long as it doesn't matter—as long as there's no chance it will last, sex is perfect. What's wrong with me? Why can't I be like other women?"

As long as sex was just a sophisticated hobby, Nancy did fine. When it came time to take on the role of a mature woman, she really wasn't up to it, and the genitals, under the influence of the brain, promptly resigned. As she came to understand her problem, and many other things about her personality, Nancy made some changes. Her choice of men shifted to those who were more mature and could bring out the best in her. Missing an orgasm became an exception instead of a rule. As Nancy finally said, "Growing up may take a lot of work but I can tell you—grown-ups have more fun!"

But aren't some nymphomaniacs that way because they are "oversexed"?

That's what they would like to think. No woman wants to admit that the sole reason for playing "musical beds"—changing partners as soon as the music stops—is her lack of sexual satisfaction. The role of a glamorous, insatiable siren is much easier to play, if not to live with. Some of the best acting in this country is not done on the stage but in motel bedrooms. Shrieking, gasping, clutching, moaning, are sometimes the way of saying, "This is what I want—not what I'm really feeling." Orgasm among nymphomanics is as rare as orgasm among prostitutes, but both groups know how to project an image. The nymphomaniac needs a reputation for being "good in bed" to assure her a steady supply of men in her search for the penis that pleases.

Are there different kinds of frigidity?

Yes. Depending on what the woman is trying to say, she (unconsciously) chooses various forms of expressing herself. For example, if in spite of her conscious desire for intercourse, she wants nothing to do with the penis, vaginissmus may be the result. In this symptom, the lips of the mouth may say "yes," but the lips of the vagina are shouting "NO!"

Just like the mouth, the vagina is surrounded by circular rows of powerful muscles. In forming the sound "Aw," the muscles around the mouth relax. This is the way the vaginal opening should be at the start of intercourse. As the lips form the first sound of the word "What," the muscles are constricted; if the vagina takes the same position, no penis can enter. If in spite of this warning, boy and girl attempt to proceed with intercourse, the results can be disastrous. It happened one night with Gene —he will never forget it.

"I once read about it in a book but I thought it was a lot of baloney. I can tell you from my own experience, it's something awful. I was out one night with this girl, her name was Audrey— I'll never forget that. We had a good time and a few drinks and then went over to her place. She had this apartment with a couple of girl friends. She was a little nervous like she didn't do it all the time, but we got along all right. After we were in bed, I started to put it in her but she said, 'It hurts.' Well, a lot of them are like that —you know, they want you to think it's the first time and all that. It *was* kind of tight, but she said to go ahead and try it anyhow. I wish I'd just got up and gone home." Gene took a nervous drag on his cigarette.

"I pushed it on in but right away I knew there was something wrong—it just didn't feel right. Then it happened. She screamed, and her whole business clamped right down on me. I felt like I was caught in a bear trap! I tried to pull out but that was my next mistake. Her, her, you know, grabbed me even tighter and it hurt like hell. All the time she was screaming—it must've hurt her too. Then the people in the next apartment started knocking on the door and I yelled at her to keep quiet. That was a bad move. When they heard me yelling they thought something funny was going on and they called the cops. Man, I wanted to get away but I couldn't move the way she was hanging on to me. Well, to make it short, the cops broke down the door and found us on the bed like that. They must've seen this deal before because they started laughing. *Then* her two girl friends came in. Wow! By then I would've left my organ behind if I could've got away! But the cops just covered us up, kicked everyone else out, and left us alone. In about ten minutes, she quieted down and I got loose. We never saw each other again and now if a girl just doesn't seem right, I tell her, 'Why don't you save it for marriage, honey? We'll both feel better that way.' "

Most cases of vaginissmus are not as dramatic as the one Gene experienced. When he finds the vagina locked, the average man doesn't try to force his way in. But if it's locked every night and he can't find a key, it means trouble for everyone. This spastic contraction of the vaginal orifice usually stems from fear—fear of pain, fear of intercourse itself, fear of pregnancy. When the fear disappears, so does the spasm. If the couple can understand the source of the vaginissmus themselves, the condition clears up promptly. Usually, they are not so fortunate, and it may go on to dyspareunia.

What's dyspareunia?

"Dyspareunia" is derived from a Greek word that means "unhappily mated as bedfellows." It couldn't be more explicit. In this condition, attempted entry of the penis into the vagina is painful. Pelvic thrusts are painful. In the rare cases where orgasm occurs, orgasm is painful. Instead of fun, copulation becomes an ordeal. The woman promptly puts an end to her pain by putting an end to sex.

What causes dyspareunia?

In a minority of cases, the underlying cause is physical. Any infection of the pelvis or genitals naturally makes intercourse uncomfortable. These conditions are generally obvious and yield rapidly to treatment. Minor damage to the sexual organs caused by an aggressive penis working against a tough hymen, a spastic vagina, or a nervous girl who zigs when she should zag may cause pain which vanishes when the basic mechanical problem is solved. A further source of painful copulation later in life may be the lack of oestrogenic hormones during the menopause. Once the deficiency is corrected, there should be no more pain.

Physical reasons for dyspareunia make up about ten per cent of the total. The other ninety per cent of women who find sexual intercourse painful are merely saying with the vagina what they are unwilling or unable to say in words: "Sex hurts me." It is their way out of a tough spot. Instead of declaring to her husband, "I hate you and the thought of intercourse with you makes me sick!," the unhappy wife makes it come out, "Of course I want to have sex with you—I can't help it if it causes me excruciating pain, can I?" The second message is much easier for her to live with but the net effect on her (and her husband) is the same in both cases. Unbearably painful intercourse may be the solution for some women; others do it just the other way.

What do they do?

By unconsciously making the appropriate adjustments, they manage to have intercourse *without any feeling at all*. *All* the wires are down—they have emotionally isolated the brain from the vagina. The reproach to their husband (or boy friend) is clear: "Use me any way you want—if that's the way you have your fun. But don't try to get me involved in this sex business." Strangely enough, a large proportion of the women with this form of orgasmic impairment are mini-skirted, bikini-wearing, hip-wiggling swingers. There is even a certain correlation between super-sexy clothes, conversation, and mannerisms, and loss of sexual feeling.

How is that?

One has to go back to the early years of the nineteenth century to find a time when sexual exhibitionism was more "in" than it is now. During the Empire period, coinciding with the reign of Napoleon I, it was fashionable for women to affect floor-length dresses, with high waists and one or both breasts completely exposed. Modern fashions seem to be heading the same way and from both directions. This is particularly pleasing to a certain category of girls with sexual anaesthesia. Often they are compelled to show as much of their equipment as the law allows to demonstrate to all comers that they are *really* sexy. Once the mini-skirt and the low-cut blouses are neatly folded at the foot of the bed, the show is over. The best part of their performance has been swinging their hips, seductively crossing their legs so their skirts slide up provocatively, and bending over to fix their stockings so that their low-cut bras are well displayed. When it comes to the main event, they sit on the sidelines. The most dramatic example of the disparity between showing the merchandise and delivering the goods is the strip teaser and her swinging sister, the go-go girl. Impaired orgasm is common with these girls. Virtually all their sexual energy goes into displaying their charms;

none is left over for more productive purposes. In a sense unveiling their sexual appendages en masse is the emotional equivalent of an orgasm—there is no impetus remaining to do it the regular way.

Then girls with sexual anaesthesia don't feel anything at all?

Not necessarily. The condition exists in many gradations. The extreme form is total and permanent lack of feeling during intercourse. This variety is rare though it does exist. More commonly the absence of sensation is relative and selective. Usually it affects a woman as it affects Jenny:

"I wish I knew what was going on. When I think everything is going to be perfect, I don't feel anything. If I resign myself to just going through with it, suddenly everything becomes alive. It's getting a little hard to take."

"Can you give me an example?"

"Yes—last night. Jeff, my husband, finally got fed up with me. He's been going through this business—he calls me 'Sleeping Beauty'—for almost five years now. He said, 'This time how about just letting me have a little for myself? We won't try to awaken Sleeping Beauty or anything like that. Okay?'" Jenny sighed deeply. She sounded as if she'd had a lot of practice sighing.

"I agreed. I know how he must feel. Well, he went to work not paying any attention to me. All of a sudden I got more aroused than I had been in years. Like I really wanted it!"

"What happened then?"

"Like he came about ten seconds later and I was back playing Sleeping Beauty."

Jeff was playing a little game of his own. His sexual martyrdom was his way of avoiding any real involvement with sex. Jenny had to pay a big price for it—and it wasn't really necessary. The approach she finally hit on worked. Let her describe it:

"So the next time I said, 'Look Jeff, just do whatever you want—I'll manage.' You should have seen the look on his face! Well,

I finally got him to do it that way. I didn't feel much for the first couple of weeks but then all of a sudden everything began falling right into place. I started having orgasms about every third time, then every other time, and now I'm almost batting a thousand. You know, for a while there I was beginning to think of myself as some kind of a handicapped person or something. Sleeping Beauty? Not me!"

Can't some women just enjoy sex without reaching a climax?

Some women tell it that way, but "enjoying" sex without orgasm is about as satisfying as "enjoying" a nice dinner without being able to swallow it. Instead of finding excuses for tolerating orgasmic impairment, instead of suffering in silence, it makes more sense for a woman to devote her energies to solving the problem. As a human being she at least has the right to fully enjoy the pleasures that are available to the family cat and dog. If she doesn't like her sexual existence the way it is, she can do something about it.

What can she do?

In some cases a woman can do a lot to help herself. Orgasmic impairment is almost like self-induced sexual amnesia. At one time in her life virtually every woman had strong sexual impulses with almost certain orgasmic capability. Then something happened. Either mother came down hard on the entire idea of sex or a rejecting man squashed the budding orgasmic potential. This, piled upon whatever other emotional problems were fermenting below the surface, sharply curtailed her chances of orgasm. But with the help of an understanding and sympathetic man and a real desire to overcome the difficulty, this latent orgasmic capacity can often be revived.

How is it done?

The first step is for a woman to become familiar with her own sexual endowments. She can make the best of her sexual capacities if she understands the design and interactions of her sexual structures. A few minutes spent in private before a mirror sometimes makes a big difference. The next helpful step can be masturbation with a vibrator.

What's the purpose of that?

The goal is twofold: a woman who never reaches orgasm any other way can almost always achieve a climax with a vibrator. A woman whose orgasms are erratic and unpredictable can make them automatic and reliable. The reflex pathways that determine the sexual climax are reinforced over and over again until orgasm is no longer a "sometimes" thing, but occurs regularly like clockwork. It is essential for a woman to realize that orgasm is not magic—it is an easily attainable neuro-vascular reflex. This in itself goes far to restore a woman's confidence in herself. In addition, the more intense the orgasm, the better the reflexes are reinforced. Once a woman is capable of reaching orgasms with regularity by this method, she is ready for the next stage.

What's that?

Transferring the reflex mechanism to sexual intercourse. Masturbation re-establishes the association between pleasurable sensations and stimulation of the genitals. The obvious sequel is to extend that association to copulation itself. In the beginning it is important to set the stage carefully. All possible distraction should be banished from the environment. Children, in-laws, dogs, and cats, need to be sent on an outing. If necessary, the doorbell is disconnected and the telephone is put off the hook.

Sometimes it is easier if the husband starts by using the vibrator on his wife. When she is sufficiently aroused, a few pelvic thrusts with the penis may be enough to trigger a strong orgasm. Success is only the cue to repeat the process again. As the wife begins to respond, more and more reinforcement of the orgasmic reflexes is the key to victory. Sometimes an effective transition from the vibrator is the husband's lips and tongue applied to the clitoris. A woman may be reluctant to mention this at that stage—her husband should suggest it. If it helps her overcome her problem, it is worthwhile. If this technique of orgasmic re-awakening is going to be successful, the results will soon be apparent.

What if this method doesn't work?

That simply means the solution to the problem lies deeper. Psychiatric treatment is indicated and there is still an excellent chance of restoring full orgasmic capability. However, the psychiatrist must be selected carefully. Successful treatment requires a doctor with just the right combination of compassion and scientific perspective. He must be perceptive and relentless and willing to consider the problems of the husband and/or boy friend as they affect his patient.

Is there any way to prevent frigidity?

Yes. The first and most important defence against orgasmic impairment is knowledge. It starts at home at the age of three or four. Honest, straightforward sexual education is the first step. A vital part of this programme is continuing education to keep pace with the maturing sexual requirements of the child. The five-year-old girl doesn't need to know that the clitoris is the centre of orgasm. If she gets the story of where babies come from, she is well equipped for any problems that she might face in the next few years. On the other hand if someone neglects to tell her sixteen-year-old sister that fellatio and cunnilingus are common means of sexual expression, they are letting her in for trouble.

Sex is a normal function—it always has been. But in the last 200 years or so, it has got a bad name. Self-appointed religious leaders and "moral guardians" have sold us on the idea that "sex is bad"—our guilt is their bread and butter. If the pressure keeps up, pretty soon they will have us feeling guilty about eating (apparently some people do already). Sex, like eating, can cause tremendous suffering if misused—but then so can going to church. Guilt is not the answer—knowledge is a better solution.

The second line of defence against orgasmic impairment is emotional education. If the final goal of sex were simply orgasm, the ideal form of sexual activity would be masturbation. It is cheaper, cleaner, and saves a lot of time. It lacks one important ingredient—emotional involvement with another human being. Sex without emotional feeling soon becomes sex without physical feeling. Selecting a partner whom she can love and respect is one basic thing a woman can do to minimize orgasmic problems.

If a woman is having regular orgasms, can she ever have trouble with them later on?

Yes. But most of the difficulties will be temporary. Anything that affects her emotionally may temporarily interfere with orgasm. When the problem passes, orgasm should return promptly. Occasionally, during regular intercourse, for some unknown reasons she may just not reach a climax. This is probably just one of those short-circuits in the sexual wiring that occurs now and then. Unless it is frequent and persistent, it isn't worth worrying about. The best way to assure frequent orgasms is to have frequent intercourse. The sexual apparatus, like any complex machine, works better with regular use.

Sigmund Freud, in one of his more pessimistic moments, said, in effect, "Among human beings, sex is a dying function." It doesn't have to be that way if we don't want it to be.

8

MALE HOMOSEXUALITY

What is male homosexuality?

Male homosexuality is a condition in which men have a driving emotional and sexual interest in other men. Because of the anatomical and physiological limitations involved, there are some formidable obstacles to overcome. Many homosexuals look upon this as a challenge and approach it with ingenuity and boundless energy. In the process they often transform themselves into part-time women. They don women's clothes, wear make-up, adopt feminine mannerisms, and occasionally even try to rearrange their bodies along feminine lines.

Do all homosexuals act this way?

Not all of them. There is a wide range of variation in homosexual behaviour; however, most homosexuals at one time or another in their lives act out some aspect of the female role.

Aren't some people just naturally that way?

Being naturally that way is one of the many explanations homosexuals grope for in an attempt to understand their problem. Back in the nineteenth century some homosexuals described themselves as "urnings." An urning was supposed to be a man who had a woman living inside him, presumably trying to get out. Apparently not even the self-styled urnings were happy with this concept and the whole idea simply faded away.

Couldn't homosexuality just be a hormone problem?

Hormone imbalance is another explanation homosexuals reach for. Unfortunately it doesn't hold water.

The basic idea stems from the fact that men and women have the sex hormones of both sexes circulating in their bloodstreams simultaneously. According to the hormone theory, if the female hormone dominates in the male, effeminate characteristics and homosexuality emerge. When tested experimentally the idea falls apart.

First, it doesn't explain masculine homosexuals. A certain number of men who appear muscular, athletic, and manly in every respect are actually enthusiastic homosexuals. Some of those over-muscled young men whose pictures adorn the physical culture magazines are only interested in the endowments of other young men. Obviously they have enough male sex hormones.

Second, injection of massive amounts of male sex hormones should counteract homosexual impulses. It doesn't. As a matter of fact, quite the opposite. Active homosexuals who are given large doses of male sex hormones become even more active as homosexuals.

Why should that happen?

Further research demonstrated that the male sex hormone, testosterone, is responsible for sexual drive in both sexes. Testosterone given to women causes a surge of sexual desire. The ladies also sprout whiskers, become baritones, and undergo other changes which interfere with the enjoyment of their new interest in sex. The same effect appears in men. Predictably with this hormone homosexuals develop more interest in sex, but only their kind of sex.

: *Is that all they discovered?*

No. Medical researchers are a thorough group and rarely let go of a problem until they squeeze the last scrap of information from it. They turned the picture around and injected high doses of female sex hormone, oestrogen, into men; first, heterosexual men, then, homosexuals.

What happened to the heterosexual men sexually?

Nothing. Actually less than nothing. All of them promptly became incapable of any sexual activity whatever. No erection, no ejaculation, no orgasm, no desire. Not one of these men was ever known to solicit in bars trying to pick up male partners. The only observable effect of the female hormones was seen in a few members of the test group. They developed gynaecomastia —enlargement of the breasts—and they lost their body hair. They were upset.

What about the homosexual men?

Exactly the same. They lost all interest in sex too. Their sexual organs refused to function. They even stopped looking for male partners. A few of them developed enlarged breasts and loss of body hair—they were delighted.

Couldn't homosexuals just be born that way?

A lot of homosexuals would like to think so. They prefer to consider their problem the equivalent of a club foot or birthmark; just something to struggle through life with.

This explanation is a little tragic. It implies that all homosexuals are condemned without appeal to a life some of them say they enjoy so much. Actually for those who want to change there is a chance.

How?

If a homosexual who wants to renounce homosexuality finds a psychiatrist who knows how to cure homosexuality, he has every chance of becoming a happy, well-adjusted, heterosexual.

What do homosexuals really do with each other?

An almost unbelievable variety of ingenious things. Since their equipment is a bit limited, they need a lot more imagination in sex than the average heterosexual couple.

The usual homosexual experience is mutual masturbation. It is fast, easy, and requires a minimum amount of equipment. The chaps simply undress, get into bed, and manipulate each other's penises to the point of orgasm. Three to five minutes should be enough for the entire operation.

Don't homosexuals do others things too?

Certainly. The next most common variety of homosexual behaviour is oral intercourse. This is also known as fellatio, which means the same thing except in another language. In this variation, one man sucks the penis of the other. Sometimes they then reverse roles, sometimes not.

Generally the circumstances are far from romantic. According to one homosexual, it goes something like this:

"Whenever I feel like sex, I walk into the men's room, find an empty cubicle, go in, take down my pants, and sit on the toilet. Then I wait. It never takes very long.

"Pretty soon another guy sits down in the next cubicle. I watch his feet. If he's a gay guy, he'll slide his foot over and kind of nudge mine. That means he's 'cruising.' If I'm interested, I nudge back. Then we get started.

"I always use a piece of toilet paper to write some kind of note—usually I just say 'Do you suck?' Sometimes if I have plenty of time I add something else like, 'How big are you?' I throw the paper on the floor, he picks it up, comes over into my cubicle, and sucks my penis. That's how it ends—sometimes I suck his penis but usually I just go home." No feeling, no sentiment, no nothing.

Are all homosexual contacts as impersonal as that?

No. Most are much more impersonal. The majority of gay guys, when they cruise, dispense with the courtship. They don't even have time for footsie or love notes on toilet paper. Homosexuality seems to have a compelling urgency about it. A homosexual walks into the men's washroom and spots another homosexual. One drops to his knees, the other unzips his pants, and a few moments later, it's all over. No names, no faces, no emotions. A masturbation machine might do it better.

Surely there must be more to homosexuality?

There are dozens of variations but they all have this in common: the primary interest is the penis, not the person. A homosexual may have as many as five sexual experiences in one evening—all with different partners. He rarely knows their names—he is unlikely to see any of them again. Besides, few homosexuals use their real names. They generally go by aliases, choosing first names with a sexual connotation. Harry, Dick, Peter, are the most favoured.

Some gay guys write their telephone numbers on walls—in telephone booths, men's toilets, railway stations, anywhere other homosexuals pass. Occasionally they note their specialty. These fellows call themselves telephone hustlers (by identification with heterosexual prostitutes).

They go home and wait for the phone to ring. It never takes very long. Another gay guy calls, they quickly exchange qualifications, and make a date. A few minutes later there is a knock on the door, penises are produced, and another homosexual affair is concluded. Elapsed time from portal to portal, about six minutes.

Isn't that kind of dangerous?

Homosexuals thrive on danger. It almost seems part of their sexual ritual. For reasons he doesn't understand himself, the average homosexual thinks nothing of inviting a stranger to his apartment at two a.m. for a little run. Sometimes things go wrong and he gets more than he bargained for. In every large city the morning newspaper occasionally carries an item like this: "Police found the nude body of Zack Ulmer, a busboy, in his apartment early this morning. According to the medical examiner he had been beaten to death with a heavy candlestick. Neighbours reported seeing him admit an unknown man shortly before midnight. No motive was immediately apparent."

Murder is exceptional—assault, robbery, and blackmail are commonplace. Identifying with their female counterparts, homosexual prostitutes, or hustlers, think nothing of absconding with their customers' wallets in the wee hours of the morning. Disagreements over sexual procedures and prerogatives sometimes lead to savage beatings. There is even a subcategory of homosexual known as the "S and M." This is the one type of gay guy the others fear. Rarely will any homosexual knowingly pick up an "S and M."

"S and M"? What does that mean?

Technically, sadist and masochist. Literally, trouble. Those who combine homosexuality with sadistic and masochistic aberrations are among the cruellest people who walk this earth. In ancient times they found employment as professional torturers and executioners. More recently they filled the ranks of Hitler's Gestapo and SS.

How does an "S and M" work?

They specialize in luring other homosexuals to their apartments, trapping them, and torturing them. Fortunately the tortures are usually low-key and childish. Fear of arrest and punishment keeps them in line. Let one of the victims describe it:

Gary is twenty-six and has been a homosexual for about nine years. He is a college instructor.

"I should've known there was something funny about that character when he came up to me in the bar. He wasn't really my type—too crude, if you know what I mean. But I was curious and—you know how it is, I had a couple of drinks." He giggled nervously.

"If I'd only known. Anyway, we went up to his place and it started like always. We undressed, got into bed, and I started sucking him. Before I knew what happened, he grabbed my head between his knees and started choking me. Man, was I scared!" He giggled again.

"He put these kind of leather handcuffs on me—they always like leather, you know. Then he tied me to the bed with a gigantic strap. He put out all the lights except for a candle over the bed, went over to the closet, and took out this whip. It was terrible!" More nervous giggles.

"By this time he had a real hard erection so I said, 'Why don't you put that thing away and let me take care of you?' Boy, that was the wrong thing to say! He pulled out this straight razor and yelled, 'Now I'm going to make a woman out of you for good!'"

Gary smiled wryly and went on. "I like a good time as much as the next guy, but how can I have a good time if he takes all my good times away? Then the phone rang. He answered it, talked a while, and by the time he hung up, he wasn't so excited. He just masturbated a few times, sucked me once, and then let me go home. I don't go to that bar any more."

Gary's experience was typical. Terror, intimidation, gratification with the victim's pleading, usually satisfy the "S and M." Unfortunately the outcome is unpredictable. Occasionally the torturer gets carried away, the evening escalates and ends in mutilation, castration, and death. Sadly, that's all part of the homosexual game.

What else do homosexuals do?

Virtually every possible interaction of the sexual organs has been pressed into service by homosexuals diligently trying to get along without women. They masturbate by placing their penises between each other's legs. One lies on top of the other and they rub penises together. The penis is slid rapidly back and forth against the abdomen or thighs of another homosexual until ejaculation occurs. The only limitation is the imagination of the participants.

In every group we find those with special tastes, homosexuals are no exception. Sometimes it takes the form of oral-anal stimulation. (Or as one homosexual put it, oral-anal simulation.) One fellow licks the anus of another. Rarely is this enough to bring on a climax; it is usually a prelude to masturbation.

But isn't that unusual?

It all depends on how you look at it. From a homosexual's point of view, he is doing the best he can. Mother Nature didn't see fit to provide him with a vagina so he gets his fun where he finds it. Since one penis can't fit inside another he must search for a place to insert his organ. Every orifice and skin-fold is a potential candidate. For many homosexuals, there is only one solution.

What's that?

The anus. Of all the structures of the body that is the one which most resembles the vagina. Of course, there are certain differences. The anus was designed as the terminal end of the gastrointestinal tract—it is not really prepared to receive the erect penis. This in itself provides certain formidable mechanical obstacles which must be overcome before this brand of homosexuality becomes possible. In contrast to the vagina which is tremendously elastic (as it must be to accommodate the infant's head at birth), the anus hardly stretches at all. However, determined assault by the homosexual penis, generous amounts of lubrication, and intense pain on the part of the "recipient" ultimately result in "success." As the homosexual progresses from partner to partner, the orifice loses most of its muscle-tone; fine for "fun" but it doesn't do much for bowel function.

In anal intercourse doesn't the one on the bottom always play the part of the woman?

That brings up an interesting point. Superficially, the majority of homosexuals are indistinguishable from their heterosexual brothers. The rest have divided themselves, by choice, into "male" and "female." In the sardonically poetic language of the gay world, the effeminate male homosexual is known as a queen. Some of them do justice to their name.

Long blonde hair (usually a wig), a full complement of make-up, removal of all body hair, and lots of perfume are the first steps. Then come the clothes. Most queens reign in drag, that is, women's clothes. (Those who are diffident about appearing in public in female attire are cattily referred to as closet queens.) Few real women have such alluring clothes as the queens. Among homosexuals, expense is no object and there is never a husband in the background complaining about the cost of a new dress. No self-respecting queen would ever be caught dead in last year's outfit.

What they wear underneath is also very important to the queens. Generally they favour the same underwear as female prostitutes: lots of transparent black nylon with black lace trim. Upstairs, understandably, they prefer padded bras. The peek-a-boo look around the bosom will never catch on in homosexual circles except for a tiny group of the most daring queens. (More about that later.)

What about down below?

They even have something going there. Carefully moulded female genitalia of pliable rubber are very popular with those who strive for authenticity. They are complete in every detail. If function is desired, an artificial vagina is available.

An artificial vagina?

This is a mail order item. It runs up to £8 postpaid and arrives (obviously) in a plain brown wrapper. The catalogue describes it this way:

"No. 237. Artificial vagina. Flesh coloured, soft pliable plastic. Designed to reproduce the female sex organs in every detail. Feels identical to the real thing. Can be inflated to depict the labia majora and labia minora as enlarged by sexual desire. Sanitary, re-usable." The artificial vagina is built into a pair of flesh-coloured nylon stretch panties—one size fits everyone.

Actually the market for this deceiver is rather limited—most homosexuals prefer other ways.

What about masculine homosexuals?

Homosexuals have a tendency to overdo this sort of thing. There never was a man more manly than a butch, as the queen's alter-ego is known. Butches lean heavily toward masculine trappings such as leather motorcycle jackets, tight pants of coarse material, super-masculine shirts, heavy boots, and other exaggerations of men's wear. In most large cities there are shops catering to the sartorial requirements of butches. For rural homosexuals, several mail order operations supply their needs.

Don't a lot of heterosexual men dress the same way today?

Yes and no. Since butch costumes are simply normal dress carried to extremes, there are bound to be some similarities. But it is the exaggeration that gives them away. Two men may wear what superficially appears to be the same shirt; the homosexual's is just a little tighter, a little brighter, just a little more.

Recently, the gay guys have been leaning toward costumes. A good example is engineers' pants. White denim trousers with vertical blue stripes have long been worn by locomotive engineers and firemen and hardly anyone else. Homosexuals decided that this line of work was very butch and appropriated the uniform —tight striped pants with a bright red bandanna around the neck. This trend has been picked up by homosexual designers and others and now has a place in men's fashions.

Various looks like the Nehru look, the Cossack look, and the Leather look, all had their start among the gay crowd. Many heterosexual men, to their dismay, find little else offered at their haberdashers these days.

Unfortunately for butches, clothes do not make the man. This is especially true of underclothes. Peel off the top layer of a butch and there is a queen underneath. Their underwear is truly amazing. Some take pleasure in men's shorts so tight they can barely meet the needs of nature. Others choose briefs so brief they barely exist. Most butch underthings are little better than skimpy athletic supporters. The ultimate *is* an athletic supporter —two straps and a sack attached to the tails of a super-tight shirt. It works fine—the shirt is always tucked-in, the genitalia held tightly. The only problem is that the poor fellow can't bend over.

Why do homosexuals do that?

One of the main reasons for such concern with underwear is the homosexual's desire to display his genitals. They are his stock in trade and he wishes to show them to best advantage. What a good uplift bra is to a prostitute, a good pair of undershorts is to a homosexual. Held high, thrust forward, *clearly outlined* by almost unbearably tight clothes, his sexual organs are there for all the (gay) world to see. This is part of the homosexual courtship and in the areas where homosexuals gather, it is really something to see.

Some lean against buildings—they are available—others stroll leisurely along the pavement—they are cruising. Each group casually but shrewdly sizes up the other. Mentally they measure penis length, try to guess each others' specialities, sneer at the types they dislike. There are always a few "S and Ms" on the prowl looking for "chickens," and, just to make things interesting, one or two detectives ready to make an arrest.

What about the new trends in men's fashions and hair styles?
Are all the men who follow them transvestites?

No. Social customs and cultural patterns in themselves do not determine emotional problems. If long hair and sideburns are socially acceptable as masculine, as they are currently, transvestites must look elsewhere for their gratification. If all men in our society can wear bright silky shirts and sexy clothes without criticism, the transvestite isn't interested.

Why is that?

Transvestites have a strong emotional interest in *women's* garments. Men's clothing with a feminine cut doesn't interest them. Nor does women's apparel with masculine overtones—transvestites rarely enjoy wearing capris or ladies' stretch pants. Symbols of femininity are what they seek.

In Scotland, a modified skirt, the kilt, is acceptable for wear by men. Scottish transvestites are not tempted. They want to dress like girls, and the more authentic their wardrobe, the better.

The other important element is the lure of the forbidden. A big part of transvestites' fun comes from the "secret pleasure," as one of them put it, of knowing they are flouting the rules of society.

Now that the new styles are "in," what effect does this have on transvestites?

It forces them to be more daring in their dress. They may sport ensembles at the extreme outer edge of social acceptability. A ruffled shirt that is *almost* a blouse may appeal to them. Men's cologne with a distinctly feminine aroma is their scent. Paradoxically the new freedom in dress may drive some transvestites farther underground. What was once "thrilling" has now become commonplace. Some take to wearing garter belts under their clothing—obese transvestites prefer girdles. Instead of jockey shorts, lacy panties do for underwear. Some go so far as to wear an entire female costume (including mini-skirt) under a business suit. If these transvestites are injured in a car accident they create a sensation at the hospital emergency room as they are undressed for treatment. One nurse had that experience:

"It was about midnight on Saturday and they brought this man in from a collision. At least I thought he was a man. I'm still not sure. He was dressed very nicely. I told an orderly to undress him while I called the doctor. It was really quite a surprise. Under his suit he had on a white knit mini-skirt and a blue silk print blouse. It was lovely! He even had a cute red silk scarf and a tiny pearl scarf pin. But I couldn't imagine why he was wearing them. When we got those off, he was wearing a bra underneath, a panty girdle, and nylons. I've seen a lot of things working nights in the emergency room, but this was something! The doctor explained to me what the problem was, and I guess it won't be such a surprise the next time, but now whenever we get a late Saturday night accident in, I wonder what he has on underneath."

Aren't homosexuals afraid *of being arrested?*

Maybe they should be, but they aren't. Lack of fear of the consequences is one of the puzzling characteristics of homosexual behaviour. *In reality no homosexual need ever be arrested for his sexual deeds.*

From a rational point of view, men who wish to masturbate each other can do so discreetly, secretly, and leisurely. (It is far easier to rent a hotel room for a homosexual act than for a heterosexual one.) They could entertain themselves at length with whatever variations of sexuality might appeal to them. No one would discover them, no one would arrest them, no one would disturb them.

Most homosexuals do it another way. They have a compulsion to flaunt their sex in public. A public washroom is frequently their stage. Bus stations and parks, are haunted by gay guys. Random and reckless selection of partners is the trademark. The fact that the stranger is likely to be a policeman, an "S and M," or a syphillitic never seems to occur to them. This is the core of homosexuality.

But all *homosexuals aren't like that, are they?*

Unfortunately, they are just like that. One of the main features of homosexuality is promiscuity. It stands to reason. Homosexuals are trying the impossible: solving the problem with only half the pieces. They say they want sexual gratification and love but they eliminate, right from the start, the most obvious source of love and gratification—woman. The only other possible form of sexual activity must centre around their own penis (or the penis of another man). Penis or vagina, that's it right there. No other options are available.

Then the game gets rough. The homosexual must constantly search for the one man, the one penis, the one experience, that will satisfy him. Tragically there is no possibility of satisfaction because the formula is wrong. One penis plus one penis equals nothing. There is no substitute for heterosex—penis and vagina. Disappointed, stubborn, discouraged, defiant, the homosexual keeps trying. He is the sexual Diogenes, always looking for the penis that pleases.

That is the reason he must change partners endlessly. He tries each phallus in succession, then turns away remorsefully. "No, that's not the one!" He is in a difficult position—condemned eternally to search after what does not exist—after what never existed.

What about all the homosexuals who live together happily for years?

What about them? They are mighty rare birds among the homosexual flock. Moreover, the "happy" part remains to be seen. The bitterest argument between husband and wife is a passionate love sonnet by comparison with a dialogue between a butch and his queen. Live together? Yes. Happily? Hardly.

The other part of these "marriages" that doesn't fit in with happiness is that the principals never stop cruising. They may set up housekeeping together, but the parade of penises usually continues unabated. Only this time, jealousy, threats, tantrums, and mutual betrayal are thrown in for good measure. Mercifully for both of them, the life expectancy of their relationship together is brief.

How do male homosexuals get along with female homosexuals?

About the only thing they have in common is their contempt for straight arrows, the term they use for heterosexuals. Any relationship that exists between them is based on grudging mutual tolerance. Rarely does a female homosexual turn up in a male gay bar. Usually the tensions run too high.

Most male homosexuals have rather mixed emotions about women and female homosexuals are not exactly delirious about men. In the final analysis a male homosexual is still a man, no matter what kind of haircut he may have at the moment. And a female homosexual is still a woman.

All homosexuals don't find their partners on the street, do they?

For the average homosexual there are not too many other alternatives. The usual heterosexual social situations just don't exist for them. Church meetings, singles groups, blind dates, family introductions, are exclusively heterosexual territory. Not even the ultimate in commercialized sex, computerized dating, has found a way to cash in on homosexuals.

The one refuge for every homosexual is the gay bar. These establishments cater exclusively to a homosexual clientèle and are often operated by homosexuals. They are profitable because they corner the market—no gay guy can really relax in a straight joint.

The first visit to a gay bar is quite an experience. Superficially, it seems like any other cocktail lounge. Men and women sit at the bar and mingle freely at booths and tables. There is the usual background of conversation with male and female voices balancing each other. Then it slowly begins to sink in—the entire room is filled with men!

The feminine whispers, the high-pitched laughter, the soft signs, are men's voices. The cocktail dresses, the tight black outfits, are worn by men. Even the trim, middle-aged matron entering the ladies room (one sign says "Queens") is a man.

The sexy babe in the tight mini-skirt owes her womanhood to two pounds of foam padding, a pound of make-up, and a lot of wishful thinking. In the daytime "she" parks cars.

In the corner booth, a senior citizen in a Nehru outfit is sitting with three young men. They have a hard glossy look; they mean business. Old homosexuals who have lost their charm but not their money attract a swarm of male prostitutes who will put up with anything if the price is right. Sometimes an ageing queen needs, and is willing to pay for, two or three of them to do what one could do twenty years ago.

At another table a woman—no, a man, sits glumly. He is a closet queen. This is his first time out in drag and he is nervous. He has spent hours putting on his make-up; every hair on his blond wig is sprayed carefully in place. His padded breasts strain against his tight silk blouse. A sinister-looking butch in tight suede pants and a studded belt swaggers over and drops into the chair opposite him.

"How about a drink, baby?"

The queen nods her acquiescence. Homosexual romance begins to blossom. A pastry-chef has just picked up a used-car salesman.

Homosexuals live in their own world, with their own substitute for women, and even their own language.

Homosexuals have their own language?

Not precisely a language, but a private argot that has its own cynical humour. Curiously the majority of expressions relate to food. The list reads like a menu. Here are a few:

FISH: woman (contemptuously)
FISHWIFE: a male homosexual's real wife
SEAFOOD: a homosexual sailor
CHICKEN: young homosexual
MEAT: penis
BUNS: buttocks

Other homosexual expressions come right from the vocabulary of the heterosexual prostitute with whom gay guys have a lot in common. The following are international:

DO: suck a penis
HUSTLER: male prostitute
TROUBLE: a butch who is likely to cause trouble
STRAIGHT: a heterosexual
TRICK: partner for a transient homosexual encounter

These terms are purely homosexual:

NELLY: effeminate homosexual
QUEEN: another word for the same
GIRL: more of the same
AUNTIE: an ageing homosexual
FAG HAG: a woman who is attracted to male homosexuals
R.G.: a real girl (since homosexuals usually refer to themselves as "girls" they need a specific expression to designate a real woman)
S AND M: sadist-masochist or slave-master
DRAG: female attire worn by homosexuals and transvestites
DRAG QUEEN: a homosexual who comes on in drag
DRAG SHOW: a performance by female impersonators
CLOSET QUEEN: a homosexual who denies or suppresses his homosexual feelings, usually intended as an insult; also can refer to a homosexual who is not currently active
TRADE: homosexual looking for "action"
DO FOR TRADE: giving him some "action"
BUTCH: a masculine, usually super-masculine, homosexual
ROUGH TRADE: vicious or dangerous homosexual
CAMP: be obviously and obnoxiously homosexual
WRINKLE-ROOM: gay bar frequented by ageing homosexuals

This is just a sample—the list goes on and on.

Why do so many homosexual expressions refer to food?

Food seems to have a mysterious fascination for homosexuals. Many of the world's greatest chefs have been homosexuals. Some of the country's best restaurants are run by homosexuals. Some of the fattest people are homosexuals.

The exact reason is complex but clearly food overshadows

much of homosexual behaviour. Aside from using their mouths as a principal sexual organ, food plays another role in their sexual lives.

Since Nature apparently did not anticipate homosexuality, the male has not been equipped with glands to secrete a sexual lubricant. Thus the first problem that two gay guys have to solve before making love is lubrication. Many homosexuals favour cooking grease. Salad oil and margarine are commonly used. Among gourmets, butter and olive oil are preferred. But it doesn't stop there.

Most homosexuals find their man-to-man sex unfulfilling so they masturbate a lot. Much of their masturbation centres around the anus. The question, of course, is what to use for a penis. The answer is often found in the pantry. Carrots and cucumbers are pressed into service. Forced into the anus, lubricated with vegetable oil, they give some homosexuals what they seek.

Egg white is also considered a good lubricant. Sometimes the whole egg in the shell finds itself where it doesn't belong. Sausages, especially the milder varieties, are popular.

The homosexual who prefers to use his penis must find an anus. Many look in the refrigerator. The most common masturbatory object for this purpose is a melon. Canteloupes are usual, but where it is available, papaya is popular.

Is that unusual?

Actually "kitchen masturbation" is harmless compared to some other forms of rectal recreation. When homosexuals drink, things really begin to happen. Nearly every intern in the emergency room of a large city hospital has seen this:

It is two a.m. Sunday. A young man stands forlornly at the emergency room door. He is about twenty-six years old, short, thin, with long bleached-blonde hair. He is drunk but sobering up fast. Sweat clings to his powder-blue silk shirt. He wants to see a doctor *urgently*. The intern motions him over to the examining table. The patient walks with a strange, bent-over, crab-like gait. As he walks he talks, fast. "Ya see, doc, it was an accident. I had this bet and I . . ."

"Just get up on the table please." Obviously the intern had seen this problem before.

The patient does as he is told. Pants off, on his hands and knees, chest on the table, anus in the air. He is still talking, " . . . to see who had the nerve to put this . . ."

The intern cuts him off—he knows it didn't happen that way and anyhow he doesn't care. He is more worried about what he is going to find. He inserts the anuscope, flicks on the light, and there it is: a whisky glass. He breathes a sigh of relief. Whisky glasses are easy, relatively speaking. He snaps on a special rubber-cushioned clamp, squirts in some lubricant, the gay guy gives a little gasp, and it's out.

Then things slow down a little and the doctor doesn't mind talking: "I always worry when I see these guys come in. They all have this funny walk and I know they didn't sit on a tack. It usually happens like this: Two fags are having a big time on Saturday night, you know, drinking and whooping it up. The queen rolls over and waits for his boy friend to give him the works; only he slides in the first thing he has in his hand instead, usually the whisky glass. They're both so loaded by then they don't know what they're doing.

"I don't mind those things—they go in small end first and when you turn them, they come out small end first. It's the off-beat stuff that gets me. Like the time this old fairy hobbled in. I flipped him over, slipped in the scope, started to snap on the light, and almost flipped—his whole damn rectum was as bright as day! Someone had slipped the poor moron a flashlight—he was the most turned-on faggot in town. I had a hell of a time getting it out!"

Flashlights aren't the worst—light bulbs are. Occasionally a homosexual manages to pass one of these into the rectum. No clamp can get a grip on them. Major surgery is urgently indicated and there is real danger. If the bulb bursts, the result may be intestinal perforation, peritonitis, and death.

Some of the more routine items that find their way into the gastrointestinal systems of homosexuals via the exit are pens, pencils, lipsticks, combs, pop bottles, ladies' electric shavers, and enough other items to stock a small department store.

Do all homosexuals do these things?

No. Sometimes they work the other way. The penis-in-a-bottle trick is an example. Occasionally a homosexual masturbates by lubricating the mouth of a suitable bottle. He forces his penis in (they all like a tight fit) finally ejaculates and tries to take his penis out. Not so easy. As the penis is stimulated by friction against the bottle, the erection gets harder. This squeezes the base of the organ tightly, cutting off the circulation. After ejaculation the penis stays hard, the bottle stays on, the penitent patient shows up at the hospital with a phallus under glass. The doctor does what the victim was afraid to do—breaks the bottle. He usually throws in a stern lecture and sends the unfortunate on his way. Sometimes it isn't that easy. Recently a middle-aged homosexual appeared at the emergency room at midnight in agony. This is how he told it:

"Doctor—well, you understand these things. I can tell you, can't I?" After a deep sigh, he went on. "Well, I'm not like your other men, you know I like my own kind of people. Anyhow, I got married tonight. Not to a real girl of course, I would never do anything like that. But to the most beautiful person you can imagine. Why he's just . . ." Then he remembered why he was there. "Anyhow we were starting to celebrate our wedding night when you know what he did? He was so silly; he took this beautiful gold wedding band I gave him, he took it right off his finger and he put it on my heh-heh—you know what I mean, don't you doctor?"

Examination confirmed the poor fellow's story. Around the

base of an immensely swollen purple penis was a gold wedding band, almost buried in the puffed-up tissue.

This fellow was lucky. His wedding night only cost him a few minutes of excruciating pain while the ring was immobilized and cut away, followed by a week on the sexual sidelines. Some who are victims of similar experiences wait too long, gangrene occurs, and they end up more womanly than they intended.

Are there any other parts of the body that appeal to the homosexual?

One more and probably the most intriguing of all—the *male vagina*. To possess this organ, the essence of femininity, is the consuming wish of some homosexuals. To overcome the obstacles of genetics, anatomy, physiology, to finally become a woman, is worth anything. Precious few succeed.

How can a man have a vagina? Is it possible?

With the miracles of modern medical science, virtually anything is possible. Skilful albeit bizarre surgery, audacious hormone therapy, and above all a willingness on the part of the patient to sacrifice anything makes the impossible a reality.

It goes something like this. First the patient has to find a doctor willing to do the job. Certain European surgeons are known to be willing. Not surprisingly at least one of them is a well-known homosexual himself. The operation is fairly simple:

Under general anaesthetic, the penis is amputated at the base. The testicles are also removed, *completely*. Then it gets interesting. By skilful plastic surgery an artificial vagina is constructed below the root of the penis. This part of the operation is well known, since artificial vaginas are routinely constructed in young women born with absent or abnormal vaginal canals.

Simultaneously, plastic surgery is being performed on the breasts. The usual method is injection of silicone foam, a process also used on under-endowed females. Goodbye penis and testicles, hello vagina and breasts and a man becomes a woman. Almost but not quite. Actually he is simply a man who has lost his external genitalia. He has gained a pound of chemical foam plastered onto his chest and an open wound where most of his reproductive system used to be. He still has plenty of problems.

First he must dilate his new vagina daily. Otherwise it closes up. Nature resents meddling and tries to correct man's mistakes. For the first couple of months, the new "woman" does the dilating himself. After that he looks for someone else to do it.

There is also the matter of hormones. The adrenal gland stubbornly continues to produce testosterone. It hasn't got the news. To counteract this, the "lady" must take female sex hormones to keep down her beard and keep up appearances. She also must rub hormone cream into her breasts to keep them looking feminine.

Are these the men who are changed into women?

These are the men who claim to have been changed into women. They are actually castrated and mutilated female impersonators.

Isn't this business expensive?

More expensive than most people imagine. The homosexuals pay exorbitant amounts of money, pay with tremendous pain and disability, and some ultimately pay with their lives.

Pay with their lives?

Recently, in England, two homosexuals who had undergone these operations five years previously died of cancer. Ironically they succumbed to cancer of the breast—their new female breasts. Ironically these men who wanted to be women died of a woman's disease. That's as close as they came.

9

MASTURBATION

What is masturbation?

Masturbation is sexual stimulation designed to produce an orgasm through any means except sexual intercourse. The term comes from the Latin word *masturbari* which means to pollute one's self. It is also known by such imposing terms as manustrupation, onanism, and self-pollution.

A lot of people have always felt guilty about masturbation and these ominous words haven't made them feel any better. Especially onanism.

Where does that word come from?

The Bible. In Genesis 38:8, Judah tells his son, Onan, to marry and have sexual intercourse with his brother's wife. Onan is reluctant.

"And Judah said unto Onan, Go unto thy brother's wife, and marry her, and raise up seed to thy brother. And Onan knew that the seed should not be his; and it came to pass, when he went in unto his brother's wife, that he spilled it on the ground, lest that he should give seed to his brother. And the thing which he did displeased the LORD: wherefore he slew him also."

For hundreds of years this passage was used by clergymen and parents to scare the daylights out of little children who masturbated. Their translation was, "If you masturbate, God will come and kill you." Careful reading of the passage makes it appear more likely that Onan was engaging in a rather primitive form of birth control. His execution seems to have resulted from his refusal to fertilize his sister-in-law rather than "spilling his seed."

Should children be kept from masturbation?
Is masturbation harmful?

The only thing harmful about masturbation is the guilt that is drummed into children who admit masturbating, by parents who may themselves masturbate but don't admit it. Every human being, at one time or another, in one way or another, has masturbated. Most of them have felt overwhelmingly guilty because of it. Most of them have continued masturbating.

Some of the terrible things masturbation is supposed to cause are pimples on the face, loss of manhood, pollution, and weakness. Of these afflictions only pimples are a recognized disease. All children at the time of puberty develop pimples. Virtually all children are actively masturbating at that time. It would then be more accurate to conclude that pimples cause masturbation. No minister, moralist, teacher, or scientific researcher has ever shown any evidence that masturbation is harmful in any way.

Why do people masturbate?

The primary reason is: masturbation is fun. Certainly not as much fun as fully-fledged sexual intercourse, but the next thing to it. That is exactly what masturbation is, a substitute form of gratification when sexual intercourse is impossible.

Masturbation is most common in early puberty when sexual objects are unattainable and social prohibitions against intercourse are enforceable and enforced. As social and sexual maturity proceeds, masturbation gradually recedes and is replaced by copulation. At times when sexual opportunities dwindle, it may reappear and later in life it sometimes predominates again. Childhood and old age have been called the golden years of masturbation, since sexual feelings are present but the means to satisfy them are sometimes lacking.

When does masturbation usually begin?

Deliberate masturbation may occur in children as early as six months of age. Usually, by two or three the pattern of masturbation is well established. From that point on, things don't change much until puberty.

Young boys usually masturbate by grasping the erect penis gently with the hand and stroking it repeatedly from tip to base. Others simply pull at the glans or head of the organ. Less often, childhood masturbation takes the form of lying prone on a bed and rubbing the erect penis against the mattress.

Masturbation in little girls centres around the clitoris; most small children are unaware of the existence of the vagina. Rubbing is the most popular form of activity, and any object can be pressed into use. Pillows, dolls, teddy bears, balled-up sheets or blankets, all serve the purpose for the time being.

Why do children begin to masturbate so early?

Because their mothers teach them to. Frequently it develops like this:

Marie is in the pediatrician's office. She is worried. Her four-year-old boy, Jimmie, plays with himself. This is how she tells it:

"But doctor, it's the most embarrassing thing in the world. I just can't stand it any longer!"

"What seems to be the trouble with Jimmie?"

"The trouble? Why he does this horrid thing to himself all the time! He takes his . . . his . . . his male, you know, and plays with it, right in front of me!"

"How long has he been doing this?"

"For about a year now but it's getting worse! Last week he did it in front of my mother!"

"Perhaps he has some irritation of his penis—that's common in young children."

"Why, I can't imagine how that could happen. I scrub his . . . his organ very carefully at least twice a day."

"How long have you been doing that?"

"Oh, about a year."

Just in case Jimmie didn't figure it out for himself, his mother showed him that gentle rubbing of his penis feels good. He got the message and started to produce these good feelings himself. But he finds it hard to understand the rest. If he plays with his own penis, his mother gets furious; if she does it, it's okay. Besides there must be something really great about the whole business if mother won't let him do it. The other things she forbids, like sweets and staying up late, are a lot of fun, too.

This is the characteristic pattern of masturbation—discovery (or revelation by mother) of pleasant sexual feelings and the start of masturbation—prohibition (usually by mother)—guilt—continued masturbation with added guilt. The same thing happens, of course, with little girls.

Do children really have sexual feelings?

Certainly, although not in the adult sense. The combination of pleasant sensations that come with genital stimulation and curiosity about sexual mysteries is plenty to keep them occupied for most of the childhood years. At puberty, things begin to change.

What happens then?

The sudden surge of hormones causes dramatic alterations in the sexual organs as well as the sexual feelings. This is the period of preoccupation with sex. For the first time, in an important way, orgasm enters the picture. Up until now, masturbation was primarily self-fondling with pleasant sensations. Now something new has been added—the big pay-off.

In boys the first orgasms are dry—no seminal fluid, no sperm. Later on fluid appears, followed by sperm in increasing numbers. Girls begin to feel real genital tension for the first time. Erection of the clitoris and engorgement of the labia minora force her attention to her sexual organs. Menstruation also makes her gradually more conscious of sexual matters.

Do girls have orgasms at this time, too?

Not nearly as frequently as boys. Their masturbation is usually not as direct either. They tend to continue to rub against things like playground equipment, especially swings and slides. Climbing trees and sliding down poles are effective mechanical means of stimulating their genitals.

Boys are much more active sexually at this stage and are beginning to branch out into other forms of masturbation.

Other forms of masturbation?

Yes. Group masturbation and mutual masturbation. A certain percentage of boys around the age of twelve to fourteen besides masturbating alone also masturbate in groups. It works like this:

Three to six boys get together at a clubhouse, in a field, or any other private place. They usually bring cigarettes and often girlie magazines. This adds to the forbidden atmosphere.

Gradually they bring out their penises and begin to masturbate.

There is generally a competition; the one who reaches orgasm first is the winner. (An interesting contrast to later life, where the man who climaxes soonest is usually the loser.) Sometimes two boys will go off by themselves and masturbate together. Occasionally they work up to masturbating each other.

Isn't group and mutual masturbation like that homosexual?

Not really. The sexual pressure that builds up in adolescent boys is tremendous. It has to find some outlet, and, at least in our society, approved sexual outlets for thirteen-year-old boys are few and far between. Somehow football games and cricket matches just don't do the trick. The hormones are pouring into the bloodstream, penile erections occur relentlessly, and something has to give. These types of masturbation are a reflection of this period. If they are replaced by heterosexual activity promptly, there is no problem.

Do girls do the same thing?

In a slightly different way. Adolescent "crushes" and close physical contact with other girls such as hand-holding, arms-around-the-waist, and occasionally kissing, are common at this stage. Group and mutual masturbation are rare but do occur. These activities actually pave the way for bigger things to come. In the middle teens, adult-type masturbation begins.

What is that like?

In boys, it is masturbation with sexual fantasies. During the process of rubbing the penis, the boy thinks of sexual scenes. It may be an imaginary episode or a reliving of a particularly exciting sexual experience. One boy, Frank, describes it this way:

"I started 'doing it' about three years ago when I was twelve. Some other boys told me about it but I didn't believe them so I tried it myself. I don't think it's right, but I just can't help it—I get the urge and then before I know it I'm doing it again. I feel lousy afterwards.

"Most of the time I just think about different girls I like, you know, their bodies and everything. Then I think about the party when this girl let me feel her all over. Every time I think about that I want to do it some more."

In this case masturbation acts as a bridge helping to make the transition to heterosexuality.

Adult-type masturbation in girls performs a similar function. This is one way the sexual equipment is, so to speak, broken-in. The nervous pathways are established, and the idea of sexual stimulation proceeding to orgasm is established. At that stage most girls masturbate this way:

Gentle stroking of the pubic area just above the vulva initiates erection of the clitoris and swelling of the labia minora. As sexual excitement increases, firmer pressure downward toward the clitoris, without actually touching it, begins. As orgasm approaches, the shaft of the clitoris is sometimes gently kneaded with the index or third finger. Rarely is the head of the clitoris manipulated because of its extreme sensitivity. At this point, and especially in virgins, masturbation by insertion of objects into the vagina is very rare.

Some girls masturbate by merely rubbing the vulva. Enough pressure is transmitted to the clitoris to begin the cycle and carry it through to orgasm.

Isn't it bad for a girl to masturbate like that? Doesn't all that attention to the clitoris interfere with her later on?

Often girls who masturbate are threatened that they will have trouble getting adjusted after marriage because their sexual interest is fixed on the clitoris instead of the vagina. As usual this threat is off the beam, too. Since the focal point of sexual gratification in the female is the clitoris, before, during, and after marriage, masturbation of the clitoris can only help her to get adjusted. There just isn't anything bad about masturbation.

Is it true that some girls can achieve an orgasm just by stimulating their breasts?

It is true that a number of women masturbate by fondling their breasts, especially the nipples. But there's something else going on. Because of their anatomy women can masturbate anywhere at any time. All they have to do is cross their legs and rub their thighs together. This moves the labia and clitoris against each other and soon culminates in orgasm. If carefully observed, as they have been during laboratory studies of sex, every woman who has an orgasm during breast self-stimulation is also doing a little thigh-rubbing.

After the heterosexual preliminaries have begun, the pattern of masturbation changes to imitate more closely the mechanics of petting. Girls then begin to devote more attention to the labia. They frequently pull on the labia and stroke them to simulate the action of the penis as it moves in and out. This excites the clitoris directly. At this point exploration of the vagina begins.

What are "the mechanics of petting"?

Petting is the nice word for mutual masturbation. Masturbation, in the broadest sense, is any sexual stimulation leading to orgasm except by penis–vagina contact. Whether a girl strokes her own clitoris or her boy friend caresses it for her, if that is how she is going to reach orgasm, it is masturbation. That doesn't make it bad, it just describes it.

In the back seat of a car at the drive-in movie, teen-age girls are introduced to all kinds of new experiences. They become aware of the sensitivity of the inner part of the thighs, the mons veneris, the prepuce of the clitoris, and if their dates are bold enough, the vagina itself. These are the necessary preliminaries leading to normal, mature sexual activity.

Later, when she masturbates, the girl tries to reproduce these feelings. She may begin to explore the vagina herself and determine the most sensitive areas.

Isn't it better if she finds this out after she's married?

That's fine, if she can get married at the age of fourteen. Otherwise it's asking a lot to expect a healthy, sexy young girl to wait seven long years to find out what it's all about. In certain other cultures, she would be initiated into the intricacies of her own sexuality by the older women of her tribe. They would teach her to masturbate and ceremonially help her to destroy the hymen at the onset of menstruation. In some tribes gigantically elongated labia from masturbation are considered desirable and extremely attractive sexually.

In our culture the older women of the tribe simply tell a young girl, "Save it until after you're married." It doesn't seem to be the kind of help she needs.

What kinds of things do girls insert into the vagina?

The most common object is the most available one—a finger. Many women learn by experience that stroking the roof of the vagina also stimulates the clitoris and intensifies orgasm. Deliberate insertion of other objects into the vagina is not common in women although it does occur. Candles, cucumbers, carrots, darning eggs, and many other household items are used. There is no problem of lubrication, unlike the male, since adequate supplies of natural lubricant are available. Women who are serious about masturbating this way usually improve on these makeshift devices. They frequently acquire a dildoe.

What's a dildoe?

A dildoe is an artificial penis. The earliest known dildoes have been found in ancient Egyptian tombs; they were made of clay. Since the Egyptian nobility only had buried with them things of great value that they planned to use in the next world, the dildoe must have been very important to Egyptian ladies.

Apparently these devices were popular in biblical times too. They are mentioned in Ezekiel 16:17,

"Thou hast also taken thy fair jewels of my gold and of my silver, which I have given thee, and madest to thyself images of men, and didst commit whoredom with them."

Obviously the reference to "images of men" does not refer to the entire man but merely to a specific part of the male anatomy. While few dildoes have been made of gold or silver, for economic reasons, nearly every other material has been pressed into service at some time. In the Middle Ages sealing wax was cheap and plentiful. It quickly took on the warmth of the body and softened just enough to provide a "natural" feel. Primitive tribes have used clay, unglazed for the common people, glazed for the wives of chiefs. Clay has the disadvantage of shattering under vigorous usage; cleaning up can be painful.

With the discovery of vulcanization of rubber, the French, who have always displayed ingenuity and verve in sexual matters, developed what they cheerfully called the *consolateur*, or consoler. Made of virgin gum rubber in the shape of a long, firm, but pliable penis, the device was fitted with a reservoir made in the form of a scrotum. This was filled with hot water (some ladies preferred milk) which circulated through the entire apparatus to give the effect of body heat. One model was rigged to spray a jet of warm fluid into the vagina at the psychologically appropriate time.

American technical know-how was not to be outdone. Like many other household objects, the American dildoe is made of plastic. Inexpensive (as dildoes go), sanitary (very important to Americans), and lifelike. It is available by mail. This is the way it is advertised:

NEW SUPER ARTIFICIAL PENIS—Designed to create more intense stimulation inside the vagina. It will perform all the functions of a real penis to excite the sensitive female areas. Special prominent corona [the rounded ridge behind the head of the penis] causes maximum excitement.

It is offered in lengths from five to nine inches and diameters from one and three-eighths to two inches. The price ranges from seven to twenty-five pounds which takes it out of the class of an impulse item.

The Japanese have about a thousand years head start in the dildoe line and have a good product. Traditionally their market prefers carved ivory, but, ivory prices being what they are, artificial ivory or hard white plastic is well accepted. While Westerners strive for realism, the Orientals hold out for feeling. Japanese dildoes are available in a wide variety of models from smooth, small calibre versions, for virgins just breaking into this form of sexual activity, ranging upward in size and texture. The advanced models have progressively more prominent carving along with large dimensions to provide stimulation for mature vaginas. Some of these are as thick as a man's arm and over a foot long. They probably exist as conversation pieces; they are more suitable for consoling a lady elephant.

Actually the Japanese long ago came up with a development which made all but the most advanced dildoes obsolete. They call it the *ben-wa*.

What's a ben-wa?

Japanese automated masturbation. Hundreds of years ago, clever Japanese women, possibly driven by desperation, developed a technique for masturbating that to this day remains unexcelled. When a Japanese lady wants to relieve her sexual tensions she reaches into a little plush-lined case and takes out two small, shiny metal balls. Though they may vary in size according to the effect desired, in the average *ben-wa* set, each ball is about the size of an apricot. Expensive sets are made of silver or even gold—the everyday variety is polished steel and these days, of course, plastic.

One ball is hollow, the other is partially filled with mercury. The empty ball is inserted well into the vagina, the globe with mercury follows.

The woman then lies down, or better yet, rocks in a chair. As she gently rolls her hips, the mercury slides back and forth in the outer ball, constantly nudging the inner ball against the cervix. The vibrations are transmitted outward to the entire vagina, clitoris, labia, and inward to the uterus itself. Sometimes Japanese women continue these languid movements for hours, drifting from one orgasm to another.

Do Western women masturbate that way?

Apparently the *ben-wa* has not yet found its way out of the Orient, but Occidental ladies have their own techniques. They may be cruder in some ways, but they are just as ingenious.

In the early days of the Industrial Revolution in this country, many young girls worked in garment factories. The hours were long, the pay poor, and the working conditions dismal. They operated treadle-type sewing machines which required constant pushing of the treadle with one or both feet. Gradually the girls discovered that by pushing the treadle a certain way with their thighs pressed together, they could rub the labia minora and massage the clitoris. What had been drudgery became almost a pleasure. The long hours at the sewing machines melted away as this new diversion took hold. Fortunately (or unfortunately) electric machines were soon introduced and the pleasure went out of the garment industry. The introduction of electricity was not all bad news, however. It opened up new horizons in the area of masturbation.

How was that?

The electric vibrator came on the scene. This handy little device was first introduced many years ago by physical culture enthusiasts.

Its purpose was to mechanize massage and muscle-conditioning. It did a lot more than that.

Basically the device is a small electric motor which attaches to the back of the hand with an elastic strap. As the motor operates it sets up strong vibrations in the hand which are then transmitted to the muscle or whatever else the hand is touching. If the hand happens to be holding an erect penis—motor, hand, and phallus all shake together. The sensation is not the same as sexual intercourse, but it is considerably more exciting than plain old masturbation, according to enthusiasts. More frequent orgasms are also said to be possible using this electrically augmented method of masturbation. The big plus, of course, is that applying the vibrator to a tired penis often swiftly brings on a respectable erection. It is not a question of muscle tone in this case, but only rapidly repeated stimulation of nerve endings.

It works the same way with girls. If the vibrator is strapped on and the clitoris is held gently between the thumb and index finger, things start to happen fast. The gentle surging motion rapidly causes erection and orgasm. Here, too, one orgasm follows another in swift succession. As many as sixty orgasms an hour are possible with this electronic assistant.

It also allows many variations in the technique of masturbation. Some women place one or two fingers in the vagina before throwing the switch. They claim this is the closest thing to actual intercourse possible. Others slide only the index finger into the vagina and place the thumb on the clitoris. No matter what approach is used, those who prefer this method are extravagant in their praise.

But these machines aren't sold for that purpose, are they?

Probably not, but the manufacturer can't keep the consumer from using the vibrator to vibrate anything he wants to vibrate. Some times the advertising extolling the virtues of the product can be read more than one way. For example:

Heavy-duty vibrator-massager—vibrating motor sends pulsations surging through your hands to relieve stiff areas of the body. Pat, rub, stimulate—makes you glow all over.

Are there any other products like that?

There is another type of vibrator which consists of a small motor in a plastic case. The motor causes a steel shaft to oscillate; assorted rubber tips fit on the end of the shaft. The plastic case also serves as a handle to get into tight places. While these vibrators are sold for "tight muscles" generally there is only one type of muscle they can loosen up.

The most useful of the various tips is the small suction cup that fits nicely over the clitoris. The gentle motion is perfect for multiple orgasms. Some women get more pleasure from one of the other tips: two dozen or so tiny rubber fingers attached to a small disc. This is placed carefully against the clitoris and the juice is turned on. Twenty-four tiny fingers gently prod the organ a thousand times a minute. Orgasm is only moments away.

Can't that vibrator be used for other things too?

Of course. There are probably thousands of people with a nice little vibrator tucked away in a dresser drawer who never use it for anything more exciting than massaging their scalp. But it is questionable if they need all those wonderful qualities built into the average drugstore vibrator:

"Four speeds, infra-red heat, 'spring action,' natural feel, deep massage." And it is doubtful if they buy the thirty-dollar, de luxe models which are "instantly ready to penetrate . . ."

There is another vibrator product that leaves even less to the imagination. It is called a "personal vibrator."

What is that like?

It is offered as the first massager invented to fit *every contour* of the body. . . . It is made of white plastic and not surprisingly, is shaped almost exactly like a penis. It contains a small electric motor powered by two flashlight batteries.

The advertising also indicates that the device is not affected by bodily secretions, is easily washable, won't break in use, and gives the ultimate sensation due to deep penetration and strong vibration. The claim that it will not break in use is apparently to reassure the timid.

While this vibrator is primarily designed as an electronic dildoe, it also sees service among homosexuals who use it for anal masturbation. It is certainly much more hygienic than using household objects such as hairbrush handles and broomsticks; the effect is also said to be more satisfying.

Do homosexuals have orgasms from anal masturbation?

Sometimes they do. More often they use anal masturbation in conjunction with masturbation of the penis. Some homosexuals insert an anal vibrator and then proceed to masturbate, either alone or with other homosexuals.

Are there any other types of masturbation beside genital and anal?

Yes. Most people don't talk much about urethral masturbation but it is relatively common. In this form of sexual stimulation, the passage from the bladder to the outside is stimulated by inserting objects and moving them back and forth gently. So far no one has come up with a mechanized way to do this, but, with transistors and miniaturization, it can happen any day.

This type of sexual play is most common in a woman, probably because her urethra is more sensitive sexually. Located between the clitoris and vagina it is well supplied with nerve connections to these structures. The most common object used for urethral stimulation is the handiest one—a hair pin. Inserted gently and slid back and forth it rarely brings on orgasm itself but facilitates and intensifies clitoral and vaginal masturbation. Safety pins (closed), pencils, rubber bands, and even lipstick cases will do the trick. As the urethra is used more and more this way, it stretches until it will admit the tip of the finger. Women who enjoy this technique then masturbate with one finger on the clitoris, one in the urethra, and one in the vagina. They say that each area multiplies the sensations from the others.

Men also use urethral masturbation but to a much lesser extent. The greater length of the male passage requires longer objects, but these are easily found. Small pieces of wire, lengths of plastic tubing, large calibre pencil leads, all find their way to the urethra.

Don't these things ever get lost?

Occasionally they do. Then it requires a trip to the hospital. The doctor who extracts a safety pin from the bladder usually doesn't have to ask how it got there. If he does ask, he should be prepared for an original answer:

"Why, doctor, I must have sat on it! I'll have to be more careful in the future, won't I?"

This excuse isn't available to men, of course. When their urethral stimulator gets into the wrong chamber all they can do is mutter something about an accident and let the doctor get on with the retrieval.

Some women insist they never masturbate. Aren't they telling the truth?

In a way. If they mean they have never deliberately masturbated they are probably being honest. But there are a lot of other ways to accomplish the same thing.

One common form of clandestine masturbation is the vaginal douche. For many women douching (the word *douche* means shower in French, and in that country both men and women take *une douche* to keep clean) is simply a form of personal hygiene, especially after sexual intercourse. For others this vaginal shower bath takes on other meanings.

It is probably not accidental that many douche nozzles are almost perfect replicas of the penis—they could double as dildoes any time. Dildoes are contraband; douche outfits are available everywhere. With a daily douche (or even twice a day for fastidious ladies) some sexual stimulation is unavoidable.

Is there anything wrong with that?

Not at all. It is a simple answer to a real physical and emotional need. Sexual intercourse with the right man is more desirable, but masturbation in this form is certainly better than suffering. Moreover, it appeals to those who have a deep feeling of guilt and would never consider "touching themselves."

Are there some women like that?

Yes, and many suffer intensely as a result. There is a condition which plagues middle-aged women, especially those who live alone. It is called pruritus vulvae, a medical way of saying itching of the vulva, and a ferocious itch it is. These women have a constant compulsion to scratch their sexual appendages to relieve the itching, burning, tingling sensations they feel there. It goes something like this:

Violet is typical. She is forty-seven; she has never married, and has spent most of her life caring for her mother. Mother passed on last year and Violet began to itch. Why did the itching start then? Well, mother was an invalid and required so much attention that her daughter never had time to think about herself. Now that mother is gone, time hangs heavy on Violet's hands. She has never admitted any sexual feeling. "I felt I was above all that." She never admitted masturbating either, but was careful to "keep clean." This means two vaginal douches a day and cleansing vaginal suppositories, "whenever I felt the need." She suffers terribly with her new symptom:

"It's horrid. All I can think of is my 'private parts.' I want to scratch them constantly, but I know I shouldn't. Sometimes I just can't help it and I douche myself as hard as I can—then it goes away for awhile.

"When I go out visiting, it's awful. I was with my club at the minister's house last week, and it started then. What could I do? I couldn't be still but I couldn't scratch in front of all those people! I rubbed against the chair as much as I dared but finally I had to go home. Then I could scratch as much as I wanted. It makes me feel terrible, but what can I do?"

Some doctors would prescribe powerful chemicals to deaden the nerves of the vulva. Others might suggest strong tranquillizers to keep her from reacting to the itch. There are even some who would cut the nerve supply to the sexual structures to take away all feeling whatsoever. Fortunately Violet's doctor was more understanding. He prescribed a routine that keeps her busy. She douches three times a day, rubs cream into the vulva after each meal and at bedtimes (especially at bedtime), and inserts vaginal suppositories four times a day. Her itch has cleared up. Regular sexual intercourse would do the same thing, but Violet can't face that. Masturbating once a day would also bring relief from the itching. Violet can't face that either. But she doesn't have to feel guilty about following doctor's orders.

Then is masturbation just a substitute for sexual relations?

That's usually the purpose it serves. Sometimes people masturbate as part of sexual intercourse. It often happens with homosexuals. In anal relations among homosexuals the sensation of the penis in the anus is rarely enough to bring about orgasm. Usually the one on the bottom will masturbate by rubbing his erect penis against the bed or just masturbating in the regular way. Many of the sexual relationships between homosexuals are based on mutual masturbation; they massage each other's penises to the point of ejaculation.

What about oral sex? Isn't that masturbation too?

If we define masturbation as stimulation of the sexual organs, except heterosexual intercourse, directed at an orgasm, fellatio and cunnilingus can be considered to be masturbation.

But isn't that abnormal?

Hardly. Fellatio, in the heterosexual sense, is when a woman kisses, licks, or sucks her partner's penis. It is probably the most common form of heterosexual activity next to copulation. It is harmless in itself. The only possible bad effect, as mentioned before, is from the guilt some women feel over it. They can stop worrying. They are not perverted.

The same thing holds true for cunnilingus. *Cunnus* is the Latin word for vulva. In translation it has lost a couple of letters, but the meaning hasn't changed. *Lingus* is Latin for tongue. Put the two together and you have the word and the action itself. Many women, as noted before, enjoy the feeling of a man's tongue and lips stimulating the clitoris, labia, and outer parts of the vagina. Many men enjoy pleasing their sexual partners this way. Wrong? No one has even been able to explain why. Guilt? It just doesn't make sense.

Isn't that the kind of thing homosexuals do?

Yes. But heterosexuals needn't feel perverted when they do these things. If oral sex is a prelude to intercourse, it's hard to find anything harmful or wrong about it. If the man and woman both enjoy it and can resist the temptation to feel guilty, it can be a source of pleasure to both of them.

What if it isn't a prelude to intercourse?

Then it depends why they're doing it. Some people can't do anything else. Men with spinal injuries are frequently incapable of penis–vagina sex in any form. For them cunnilingus may satisfy their wives, keep their marriages intact, and make them feel worthwhile sexually. To condemn them is unfair. A woman who, because of cancer (which sometimes requires the removal of the entire vulva) or some other disease, just can't have normal sexual relations, may find fellatio satisfying to her and to her husband.

On the other hand if a man or woman who is sexually intact chooses oral sex instead of genital sex, there may be an emotional problem involved.

Is there any situation when masturbation is more desirable than sexual intercourse?

There are several. For example, when the individuals are not emotionally equipped for intercourse. A thirteen-year-old boy and an eleven-year-old girl may be all set genitally but regular copulation will cause them more problems than it solves. Masturbation may be more desirable there.

Another possibility is the woman who has difficulty achieving an orgasm. Sometimes sexual training in the form of masturbation can help her to overcome this problem.

Masturbating is a cure for frigidity?

Not necessarily a cure, but it can be helpful on occasion. The principle is that the nerve pathways from the brain and spinal cord to the sexual organs operate more smoothly and the sexual apparatus itself responds better with practice. For years it has been known that many women develop greater sexual capacity with more frequent intercourse.

Following this plan, a woman masturbates to orgasm using a vibrator. She practises at least once a day and has an average of five to twenty sexual climaxes each session. In addition to exercising the sexual equipment, this practice also develops a taste for sexual gratification which acts as an incentive later on in regular intercourse.

Are there any other situations where masturbation is desirable?

In those who cannot obtain sexual satisfaction in any other way. Men and women in prison, very old people, and often the blind are restricted in their sexual outlets.

The blind?

Until recently, blind people were shut off from the rest of the world, socially as well as visually. One of their few sources of sexual gratification was masturbation. In blind schools masturbation was made more difficult because those who masturbated could not tell if they were being observed. Blind girls particularly became adept at secret masturbation.

A favourite technique was to sit in a chair with one foot tucked under them. The heel of the foot was pressed against the vulva and the girl slowly rocked back and forth. Other than a momentary change in expression from time to time there was no sign of anything happening.

Well, then, is there anything at all wrong with masturbation?

Masturbation is simply a sexual expedient which serves an important purpose. It was the primary sexual activity for most people shortly after they came into this world. It may be their main source of sexual pleasure shortly before they leave this world. In between, if they can arrange it, sexual intercourse is a lot more fun.

10

SEXUAL PERVERSION

What are sex perverts?

Anyone who isn't interested in the penis–vagina version of sex is often considered a pervert and shunned by normal people.

This includes such types as exhibitionists, Peeping Toms, sadists, fetishists, masochists, and those with similar tastes. They are thought of as wild-eyed drooling maniacs, lusting for an innocent victim. It just isn't that way.

Why not?

First of all, pervert is an unkind and loaded word. It is derogatory rather than purely descriptive. A better word is sexual variant.

Sexual variants start out the same as everyone else—they just never grow up sexually. An average person advances from one stage of sexual development to another—the variant gets stuck at one point and never moves from there. The Peeping Tom is a good example. Everyone starts out sexually as a Peeping Tom.

How is that?

The only sexual activity available to small children, except for masturbation, is peeping, or looking at other people sexually. At about the age of three or four years little boys and girls become interested in each others' bodies. The boys want to know, "How come girls don't have one?" And girls want to know the same thing. Even at this first tentative moment, sex is mysterious and alluring. From that point on children seize every opportunity to observe the sexual makeup of their companions. Mutual inspection of genitalia is the primary basis for those childish games, Playing House and Playing Doctor.

While mother is busy in the kitchen studying a new recipe, the children are busy in the playroom studying each other. This is a normal and essential part of the process of sexual maturity. There is really nothing naughty about it. The childish pastime of "you show me yours and I'll show you mine" is a phase most children pass through rapidly. It soon gives way to more advanced peeping. At school the boys watch the girls and the girls watch the boys. As puberty begins, sexual interest becomes more refined and centres around breasts, later buttocks. In high school, girlie magazines are passed around among the boys and mutual sexual exploration begins on dates. Ultimately, observing the body of the opposite sex becomes part of the enjoyment of sexual intercourse. Looking at the body of the sexual partner becomes one of the pleasant events leading up to copulation.

Then isn't everybody a Peeping Tom?

No. The peeper gets short-circuited along the way. His peeping does not lead up to sexual intercourse—it stops right there. All he wants to do is look—almost.

What else does he want to do?

Masturbate. His sexual outlook is infantile and limited. He looks, is sexually aroused, and masturbates. He makes no effort to go any farther.

Some peepers devote tremendous energies to their hobby. They keep track of the best places to go and the best times to be there to get an eyeful. Listen to an expert:

Ralphie is a fry cook. He is thirty-two and never married. He doesn't go out with girls any more. He went on a few dates when he was younger, but they made him nervous. He is thin, well dressed, and nervous. As he talks his eyes dart about the room.

"Well, I don't know. I don't think there's any harm in it. I don't touch nobody, I just look. It ain't against the law. I mean everybody's got a right to look, don't they? I just sit there and look. Like on the subway for example. I know the right stops. I get on where all the girls from the offices get on and I just sit there. The train stops, they come in, they sit down and cross their legs. That's when you see it! When they cross their legs. Last summer I even saw one without any panties on!"

Ralphie gets a little excited at this point as he remembers what he has seen. If Ralphie were in the second grade and was going through that two-week period where he wanted to look at little girls' panties, it wouldn't be a big deal. Well, that's exactly where he is, only he's twenty-five years too late.

"Then after I ride around for about an hour I get pretty excited. So I go home and play with myself."

That is the extent of Ralphie's sex life—looking at women's underwear and then masturbating.

Some peepers are more dedicated. Take Arnold, for example. Arnold is a stockbroker. He is in his early forties and was married for a year or so when he was twenty-two.

"It just didn't work out—she was too immature."

Arnold describes his favourite technique.

"On the days the market is closed, I go to the Public Library.

I go back in the stacks and pretend I'm looking for a book. I always poke around on the bottom shelf which means I have to be on my hands and knees. Begin to get the idea?

"I wait until some girl comes along—she has to be a good-looker—and then I swing into action. I kind of work my way over to her, real slow so she doesn't suspect anything. Then I get out my equipment. I have this little magnifying mirror and I hold it by her feet so I can look up her skirt and get a perfect view of the entire situation."

For some reason, peepers love to refer to the object of their peeping in vague, general terms—"entire situation" is a good example.

"To get a really good look, I carry this pocket flashlight. I shine it on the mirror, it reflects up her skirt and I get to see everything. Pretty scientific, huh?

"One of these days I'm going to get me a little camera and then I can take some pictures—that really ought to be fun."

Arnold will probably never get that camera. Most peepers like to get a look at live objects—they find the risk of being caught extra exciting. To them, a photograph just isn't the same.

For awhile after the divorce he used to go to dances with a mirror fastened to his shoe but he complained he couldn't get a decent image. Actually, having to dance with real girls made him too anxious. Like Ralphie, after he's seen enough, he goes home and masturbates.

What about the ones who look in windows?

These are the elite of the peeping fraternity. As far as they are concerned, fellows like Ralphie and Arnold are just amateurs. Window peepers take big risks and get big thrills.

What kind of risks do they take?

Crawling around someone's back yard at midnight is a risky thing to do. If the housekeeper doesn't make a grab at them, the policeman might when he arrives. If they get caught, they go to jail. For most peepers this just adds to the thrills.

What are the thrills?

Looking at other human beings after they have taken their clothes off. Window peepers hope to catch glimpses of naked women. The age or physical attributes of the subject are not important. The other vital requirement is that she be a victim in the sense that her privacy and her feminine modesty are violated. Window peepers are visual rapists—this is a vital part of their sexual gratification. Otherwise they would be content to sit in strip clubs or topless joints day after day.

If they hit the jackpot, they may be able to observe a man and woman having intercourse. This is especially exciting to most of them and provides enough material for months of masturbatory fantasies.

Irwin's case is typical. He is a vice-president of a small bank. Irwin is married unhappily. He has intercourse with his wife every month or so. He would rather just peep.

"I don't know—there's something about sex that just isn't fulfilling. As far as I'm concerned nothing can match getting a real eyeful. Why last week I saw something you could go a lifetime without seeing. It was over on 24th Street—I get over there about once a month."

Like most serious peepers, Irwin works on a schedule. He covers the entire town every six weeks. He varies his route to minimize trouble from the police.

"There was this perfect set-up—a girl with this guy in the living room. They were in front of a picture window so I could see everything. First he undresses her—real slow. Then she undresses him, only fast because she's getting hot—you can tell."

After peeping for twenty years, Irwin considers himself something of an expert on human sexual responses.

"Then he had a hard erection—just like I get when I get a real eyeful. He put her down on the couch and he was just starting to really get going when she reached over and turned off the light."

That is one of the occupational hazards of window peepers. Their victims sometimes choose darkness at the last moment. There are other drawbacks, too.

Like what?

Irwin has been arrested eleven times and convicted twice. One arrest was just too much good luck, as he puts it.

"I really hit it big one night. This babe was undressing in front of a mirror one night—I could see everything, front and back. I got so excited I couldn't wait until I got home so I, uh, relieved myself in the car."

A passing police patrol caught Irwin masturbating in the front seat of his car. He was convicted as a sexual psychopath.

"Why you'd think I was some kind of criminal—I never hurt anyone. I just keep an eye on things."

Do window peepers look for anything else?

Occasionally a homosexual peeper goes in search of views of naked men. However, those in search of homosexual sights usually operate more directly. In many public washrooms holes have been drilled in the partitions separating the toilets. A homosexual will sit on the toilet for hours watching other men urinating and defecating.

For a more frankly homosexual experience, they prefer homosexual hang-outs, like Turkish baths. Often ten or fifteen peepers will crowd around to watch one man performing fellatio on another.

Are there any other types of peepers?

Certainly, only their peeping is socially acceptable. Men who like stripping shows, topless waitresses, and beauty contests are not usually thought of as peepers, but they are. The difference, of course, is that their type of peeping is accepted by society and is often a preliminary to sexual intercourse.

A direct example of peeping leading up to copulation is the use of mirrors in certain high-class houses of prostitution. The good rooms have mirrors on the ceiling, and the best rooms have mirrors on the walls as well. Some customers would probably like to have their sex lying on a mirror too, but there are technical difficulties involved.

Are there any women peepers?

For some reason this game doesn't appeal to ladies. Women do a lot of looking, but peeping in the real sense doesn't seem to be their style. What would be a dream come true to the average male peeper merely offends them.

What's that?

An exhibitionist. Exhibitionism is almost an exclusively male field too (with some exceptions). Exhibitionists specialize in forcefully displaying their penises to women in public places. Occasionally they try to catch a woman's eye while masturbating. They are timid and usually harmless, but are somewhat of a nuisance.

They hang around parking lots, bus stops, and ladies' washrooms. Of all the sexual variants they are the most passive and childish. Much of the time they are under the influence of alcohol when they exhibit. They rarely try to avoid arrest. A detective on the Vice Squad tells it this way:

"I never have any trouble with them. In fact most exhibitionists are such nice guys I hate to lock them up. But we must keep them off the streets—that's orders. I know most of them by now and I can pretty well tell by the description who it is. I just call them up and tell them to come down to the station the next day. They come, I book 'em, and that's that."

Exhibitionists need psychiatric treatment badly, but they are a puzzle to most psychiatrists. The psychiatrists do their best, but the exhibiting usually goes on.

What about female exhibitionists?

Most of them are professionals. Strippers and topless dancers are good examples. No matter what they say, most strippers enjoy their work. They derive sexual satisfaction from displaying their breasts to large groups of men. They don't need much encouragement to display everything else. More than one stripper has obliged an enthusiastic audience by taking it *all* off, G-string and all, and parading around nude. She gets what she wants and they get what they want. Everybody is happy, no harm is done, except to Public Morals, whatever that means.

Predictably, strippers don't get much other sexual satisfaction. They usually have trouble attaining orgasm and never find much real pleasure in genital sex.

The same holds true in general for beauty queens. Their activities have more social approval, but the game is the same. They show off their breasts, hips, buttocks and a discreet outline of the vulva (through a bathing suit) to admiring men. Miss Artichoke of 1966 has a lot in common with Bubbles LaTour and her Magic Balloons.

Are there any men who are professional exhibitionists?

Very few. Basically it's an economic problem. There just aren't enough people around who will pay to watch a hairy man strip down to his jockey shorts to music. The single exception is the female impersonator.

Female impersonators are homosexual men—actually queens who capitalize on their condition. As one of them said, "I do what I want to do anyway, sweetie, and get paid for it."

Some of them do a very good job. Every hair is painfully

removed from their bodies. Carefully powdered and made up, dressed in expensive gowns, dancing gracefully (more or less) under coloured lights, in a dimly lighted club they look almost like women. Of course they are limited in the amount of clothes they can discard if the illusion is to be preserved. Their sexual lives are the same as most homosexuals—perhaps with a bit more glory because of their careers.

Do peepers and exhibitionists ever get together?

More often than one would imagine. Of course the strippers, beauty queens, and female impersonators must have an audience of peepers to turn on. No audience, no performance. But sometimes peepers encounter willing amateur female exhibitionists. It happens quite by accident. It happened to Irwin:

"I watched this girl take off her stuff about eleven o'clock one night and the next month when I came by she was doing it again. Just for fun I broke a rule and came again the next night—there she was! Now I go past her place every Tuesday. She has a new outfit every week and puts on a good show. But, you know how it is, I have the whole town to pick from and I get tired of seeing the same thing over and over again."

Mental rape is no fun if the victim is willing.

Those who like to look and those who like to be looked at have another way of finding each other. Some of the newspaper advertisements offering photographers' models are just girls willing to pose in any position. While they work for money, they also enjoy what they are doing.

Is there anything wrong with that?

Aside from being naughty in the moralistic sense of the word it is hard to see how any harm is done. Certainly no one's virtue is compromised; a seventeen-year-old virgin is not likely to advertise:

"Female photographer's model; experienced all poses. Attractive. 123-1879, eves."

Peeper and exhibitor both know what they are after.

Is it fair to prohibit male exhibitionism and let women exhibitionists go unpunished?

Probably not. But the laws that attempt to regulate sexual behaviour were not passed in an atmosphere of fairness.

What are transvestites?

Transvestites are individuals who wear the clothes of the other sex. There is no prohibition against women wearing trousers, neckties, men's shirts, men's shoes, or any other item of masculine apparel. Let a man appear on the street in a skirt and blouse with high heels and he is asking for trouble. The women are just following fashion, the men are "sex perverts."

Are there any men who would want to wear women's clothes?

Quite a few. Their activities are not as well known, since unlike homosexual queens, they rarely appear publicly in drag. Most transvestities qualify as wardrobe queens.

The typical transvestite usually starts out trying on mother's clothes about the age of six or seven. This phase passes and is then revived at puberty. Only this time when he dons the dresses, somehow he feels sexually stimulated.

Martin can explain it better. He is a chemist at a large plant, married, with two children. He is forty-seven and has been a transvestite for about thirty years.

"I will never forget the day I first put on my special clothes. I was seventeen and mother was out for the afternoon. It was a grey plaid skirt and a pale blue angora sweater. I stripped myself naked and dressed slowly in front of the mirror. By the time I got those clothes on I had a hard erection and I was trembling. I looked at myself from every angle but I felt something was missing. I finally slipped on a pair of panties and ejaculated almost immediately. Ordinary sex can never approach a wonderful feeling like that."

Martin married at the age of thirty-six, after his mother died. His wife knows about his hobby and approves, as do most wives of transvestites. She was a little surprised at first but she soon recognized how important this little peculiarity was to her husband.

"My wife is so understanding. She helps me shop for my new outfits—she has wonderful taste. Especially in underwear. I used to have the most horrid underthings; you know, bloomers and ugly girdles like mother. How was I to know? I never saw what other girls wore."

Characteristically, transvestites have a close attachment to their mothers and little contact with other women.

"Now I have the right things. I have stunning peek-a-boo midnight blue bikini panties with a matching garter belt and a transparent bra to go with it. I wear it with my little blue chiffon hostess gown—I never wear a slip—and silver lame slippers."

Are transvestites homosexuals?

Not necessarily. Some are heterosexual men who enjoy wearing women's clothes. Their heterosexual potency is not strong, but many of them never consciously consider homosexuality. Of course there are homosexual transvestites, too. Probably the best way to put it is: Not every transvestite is a homosexual but many homosexuals are transvestites.

Many little boys go through a stage where they put on their mother's lipstick and carry her handbag. Usually they quickly desert this period to emulate daddy. If they get stuck with mummy, they may become transvestites. Martin frequently uses his female clothing sexually. He has intercourse about every six weeks. He is completely impotent unless he wears some article of woman's clothing. Sometimes a pair of nylon stockings is enough.

Most transvestites become more attached to ladies' clothes as they grow older. In the last year or so Martin has begun to wear "something" to work everyday. At first he wore an anklet under his socks. Then he got a little bolder and tucked a frilly hankie into his pocket so the end just barely poked out.

"It was thrilling. There I was, doing it in front of everyone and they didn't even suspect!"

Because of their preoccupation with things like underwear and women's shoes, some transvestites' behaviour borders on a fetish.

What is a fetish?

A fetish is a strong sexual attachment to an inanimate object or an isolated part of a person's body. People who engage in fetishes may be strongly aroused by articles of clothing, for example. Some men are sexually stimulated by black lacy panties and insist on making them part of their sexual experience. Without these panties, sex isn't any fun for them.

That doesn't seem unusual. Aren't many normal men like that?

No. A fetishist is aroused even if the panties are empty—he usually prefers it that way. His sexual interest centres on the object, not the wearer.

Fetishist favourites are feminine underthings—panties, bras, garter belts, girdles, bikinis. (Some modest fetishists are stimulated by slips.) They collect these items eagerly and are intimately acquainted with the qualities and advantages of various brands. Most fetishists are specialists—a panty-man has no interest in garter belts.

There is specialization within categories; the brassiere collector may specialize in strapless models or D cups and waistpinchers only. Social distinctions also exist; a G-string collector may look down on a girdle-fancier as crude. Collections, which may run to hundreds of items, are not for sale, though exorbitant prices (for anyone who is not a fetishist) may be paid for rare or exotic items.

When do they wear these things?

Usually they don't. That is where the transvestites and fetishists part company. It is a rare fetishist who ever dons his garments. Wally, who has an outstanding collection of panty girdles, tells how it's done.

"What I need most of all is peace and quiet. I go into my den, usually when the kids are asleep and my wife is out at a meeting, and lock the door. Then I take out my girdles—I keep them locked in a big filing cabinet. I spread out all my dainties—I call them my dainties because that's the way I feel about them—and then I look at them. Usually that's enough to get me aroused. I handle them a little, thinking about where the different parts of a girl would go. By then I have a good erection and I masturbate, usually into the blue one with the roses on it."

Like Wally, most fetishists masturbate with, in, or onto the objects they collect.

Do women ever engage in fetishes?

It is very rare for a woman to be sexually stimulated by an article of clothing or similar object in itself. Wearing a filmy negligee or a plunging neckline may be exciting to them, but primarily from an exhibitionistic point of view. In this sense they are more practical than men—why settle for a pair of undershorts when you can have the entire contents?

Do fetishists get married?

A lot of fetishists do marry, but women really don't gratify them nearly as much as their collections. Sometimes their married life starts off routinely, except for an unusual twist or two. They may ask their wives to wear long black net stockings (and nothing else) during intercourse. Gradually they add other items and just as gradually their interest shifts from the woman to the object. Finally they avoid intercourse completely. The object has displaced the person.

Don't women object to this kind of thing?

Some of them do. Others obtain sexual stimulation themselves by wearing exotic garments. While most fetishists are men, they have no trouble finding women to cooperate with them in their sexual embellishments. There are even ways to combine business and pleasure.

How is that?

Some men choose a line of work where they are constantly in contact with the object that arouses them. A shoe fetishist is a good example. A man with this condition is sexually stimulated by the sight, smell, and touch of women's shoes and often by women's feet as well. If he gets a job in a ladies' shoe store, he is getting paid for doing the same things he would gladly pay for. During working hours, he constantly touches women's feet and handles shoes. In the beginning it can be overwhelming. Lester has been a foot man for about nine years. He is thirty-one and just started working in a fashionable shoe store for women. At first he couldn't believe it.

Before that he had gone out with girls but when the kissing began he tried to nonchalantly work his way down to their feet. Most of the time they had other ideas and he had a hard time getting all the way down. He considered the evening a smashing success if he found a young lady who would let him masturbate against her bare toes. Obviously it didn't happen very often. In the shoe store things were different:

"That first day I almost went out of my mind. To another guy it probably would have been like working in a room full of naked girls. I couldn't believe it. Dozens of women asking me to touch their feet! I had an erection from the minute I came in that morning until the last time I masturbated just before I went home. I must've gone in the back to relieve myself about a dozen times. Did you ever try to wait on two or three women with a good firm erection? I was afraid the boss was going to fire me but later I found out he digs feet too."

Men who sell ladies' underwear are sometimes also attached to their product. They make the best salesmen because their hearts are in their work. At least that's the way they describe it.

What are some other objects fetishists are attracted to?

There is really no limit to the number of items which may receive sexual attention. Hair, odour (both pleasant and unpleasant), hands, jewellery, even the voice.

How do men make a fetish out of a voice?

Chaps who make obscene telephone calls are generally voice fetishists. They are sexually stimulated by the voice and vocal reactions of their victims. This is the usual pattern:

Late in the evening, the telephone rings. When the woman answers, there is a moment of silence, followed by an obscene monologue. Typically this consists of descriptions of sexual intercourse, promises to engage in sexual relations with the recipient of the call (promises that are never fulfilled), and sometimes recitations of obscene words. The woman must react emotionally—otherwise the caller is disappointed, hangs up, and calls someone else. Most women give him what he is after—not sex, but shouting. It may go like this:

Telephone rings, and woman answers.

> VICTIM: Hello?
> OBSCENE CALLER: (heavy breathing).
> V.: Who is this? Who's calling?
> O.C.: That doesn't matter. How would you like to get laid?
> V.: (Screams) You must be out of your mind!
> O.C.: No, I'm not. I'm just going to come over and get into you.
> V.: (Screaming) Leave me alone! What do you want? What do you want?
> O.C.: All I want is to get my hands in your pants—that's all!
>   (Heavy breathing)
> V.: (Hysterical) My God! My God! (Hangs up).

The caller usually masturbates during the entire conversation. A big part of his stimulation is from the shock and indignation of the victim. Unless she cooperates, he can't have any fun.

Cooperates? How does the woman cooperate?

By listening and responding. If she isn't interested in his wares, she has only to hang up. Every man with a sexual problem needs a woman who is willing to play a complementary role, however small it may be. A woman who doesn't want to be an answering service for fetishists can put out their fires fast. All she has to do is hang up. The gentleman cannot converse with the vast silences of a disconnected line.

What if they call back?

Hang up again. It's more work for them to dial than for the woman to disconnect. For the persistent caller, a short message may solve the problem with finality:

> VICTIM: Hello?
> OBSCENE CALLER: Listen, do you know what I'm going to do to you?
> V.: Now you listen to me. You're sick! You need a psychiatrist! If you take my advice . . .
> O.C.: (Hangs up.)

No mere man can stand up to a woman for persistence on the telephone anyway.

Do fetishists do other things?

Fetishism branches out in all directions and frequently merges with other sexual variations. Leather fetishists are an example. They collect objects, clothing, and equipment made of leather. Leather shirts, pants, skirts, stockings, boots, helmets, whips, handcuffs, bras, straitjackets, and other items are fascinating to them. Some objects have utilitarian value as well, like whips.

Sadism and masochism begin to enter the picture. A fetishist who likes to wear the leather clothes from his collection while he is whipped by a girl who subsequently performs fellatio on him has crossed into new territory. He is a fully-fledged sexual masochist. If he ties up the girl in leather and then *forces* her to perform fellatio, he is a sadist.

Aren't these dangerous people?

Hardly. They are like timid children playing games. Since they cannot obtain gratification from grown-up sex, they get their stimulation from the trimmings. Generally they are harmless folks who have fun with each other. In spite of the whips, belts, ropes, and leg irons, it is rare for anyone to get hurt. If they did, they wouldn't come back next week for more games.

There are exceptions. Some persons with severe mental illness may act out sexually, killing and mutilating their victims. These are the rapist-murderers who get big headlines in the evening papers. These unfortunates are psychotic and have no relationship emotionally to the part-time, weekend sadist/masochist.

Why sadist/masochist?

Because they frequently switch roles back and forth. This week's vicious sadist can be next week's cringing masochist. It is all for fun, although the participants tend to take themselves very seriously. Homosexual fetishists are also a mixture of several types.

In what way?

They are sexual variants who use their fetish objects. Their collection is like a hobby related to their prime interest, homosexuality. They collect things like worn-out men's workshoes, athletic supporters, and men's underwear. In contrast to regular fetishism, the objects are used sexually.

Is there a difference between someone who collects things and a fetishist?

It may be hard to tell sometimes. Their activities may appear almost identical. A man who collects ladies' panties may obtain them as trophies from his sexual conquests. Another man may have purchased the same kind of collection to masturbate with. The first chap is a small-time fetishist—his collection is incidental to his major sexual activity. The one who has to buy his lingerie is a primary fetishist.

Occasionally it can be confusing. Like the woman who tearfully complained to her doctor that her husband was a pervert. After twenty-two years of marriage she discovered his gigantic collection of old boots, both ladies' and men's. He had rented a large room downtown to store them—he had over 400—and would spend one or two evenings a week there, alone, going over his collection.

> WIFE: But doctor, I never imagined he was like that! After all these years to suddenly find out!
> DOCTOR: Didn't you suspect there was something going on when he left you all alone two nights a week?
> WIFE: That's just it—he told me right from the start! He said he was going to spend the evening going over his old boots!
> DOCTOR: Why did it take you so long to get upset?
> WIFE: That's just it! For twenty-two years I thought he was saying "old books"!

Are people who collect pornography fetishists, too?

Not necessarily. Representations of sexual activity are as old as man himself. The word pornography has its mind made up already anyhow. It comes from two Greek words, *pornos*, meaning dirty, or obscene and *graphos*, meaning writing. Thus, pornography equals dirty-writing. But representations of sexual behaviour are not dirty—they just depict some of the things that people do. The idea of pornography didn't even exist until about 300 years ago.

How come?

Until then sexual drawings and writings were considered entertaining, like any other form of literature or graphic art. In most of the world, it's still that way.

In China, Japan, India, Africa, the Middle East, and many parts of Europe, there is nothing obscene about depicting men and women going about their sexual business. What we would consider pornographic plays an important role in their social and religious lives.

In their social and religious lives?

Yes. In Japan every newly-wed couple is given a richly illustrated book showing every imaginable variation of sexual activity. It is considered an honour to be the one who offers this gift and it is traditionally placed under the couple's pillow to assure a memorable wedding night.

What about the religious part?

In India, there is the Sun Temple of Konarak, an architectural masterpiece. The outside walls are covered with life-size statues of men and women having sexual relations in every conceivable way. Cunnilingus and fellatio and everything else are amply and dramatically represented. One of the Hindu religious concepts is the maximum enjoyment of earthly life, and sex is part of that enjoyment. Of course they also do a big business hauling pious foreign tourists back and forth to see the "dirty statues."

Why do some countries ban sexual literature?

Probably moral indignation. Some people, including those who make the laws and the ones who make them make the laws, believe pornography is bad. But they also make it good for those who sell pornography.

A picture of a woman that wouldn't bring a penny if she had her clothes on may sell for a pound if she is naked and displaying her sexual apparatus. The same holds true for all the other forms of pornography.

Recently, in Denmark, all restrictions on depicting sexual scenes were lifted. The sales of such material fell about forty per cent. Maybe it was more attractive when it was forbidden.

Pornography has kept up with the technical advances of our civilization. Starting with drawings, it moved forward dramatically with the invention of the photograph. Some of the early daguerreotypes were well-composed pornography. Moving pictures made dirty pictures move, too. Since sex is basically a dynamic activity, the enjoyment of observing it on film was enhanced by seeing action. Then came sound, technicolour, wide screen, and stereo sound. The pornographers kept up to date. The next advance on the horizon is feelies, movies where the audience actually touches, smells, and tastes the action. That will probably mean the doom of pornography as we know it. The process will have come full circle—right back to sexual intercourse.

What is pornography really like?

Most pornography can be divided into two categories, visual and literary. These days most visual pornography consists of photos, all basically the same. The beginner's collection shows naked women with emphasis on the breasts and genitalia. Since all females have identical equipment, if you see one, you've seen them all. Once the dramatic revelation that woman have a clitoris, vagina, labia, and breasts sinks in, there are no more surprises.

The next category of visual pornography is men and women having sexual intercourse. These pictures bring home emphatically the fact that penis and vagina somehow go together. The complete collection of this group of "dirty pictures" constitutes ninety-six separate positions, most of which are unfeasible except for circus acrobats.

When the customer tires of peering at shots of naked gymnasts, views of heterosexual fellatio and cunnilingus may provide further diversion. That's about it. Since human anatomy is well standardized, pornography quickly becomes boring and monotonous. Two-dimensional snapshots lack the vitality of real live human beings.

What about literary pornography?

It suffers from the same fatal disease as photographs—dullness. The enthusiastic descriptions of a gigantic penis descending into a bottomless vagina, of males with limitless vigour endlessly servicing insatiable females, begin to wear a little thin after three chapters. Since pornographic material is written for a special purpose, it has trouble standing on its literary merit.

What is the purpose of pornography?

Pornography is primarily a substitute for sexual activity. Those who are unwilling or unable to organize sexual activities with others turn to a world of fantasy, of photos and stories of the exploits of those who are sexually more intrepid. At least ninety-nine per cent of pornography is used as a prelude to masturbation; men are the major consumers but women are also involved. The other one per cent is utilized heterosexually or homosexually as a prelude to sexual intercourse.

Isn't pornography harmful?

It is very difficult to see how. Pornography simply represents people as they really are, sexual organs and all. They are shown doing what they really do: using these organs. Everybody has genitals and everybody uses them, one way or another.

Doesn't it encourage sex crimes?

There has never been an authenticated case of anyone being motivated to commit a sex crime as a result of pornography. Occasionally someone is apprehended after a particularly grue-some sexual murder and pornography is found in the room. A dictionary, a telephone directory, and occasionally a Bible may be lying around there, too. Many psychiatrists, police officials, and police solicitors feel that pornography is a useful and desirable safety valve that drains off the sexual tensions of potential sex criminals and prevents them from acting out their sexual fanta-sies with others.

Is pornography good for children?

Probably not. But it doesn't have to be bad for them either. If their entire knowledge of sex comes from the somewhat exagger-ated accounts of the pornographers, they are going to have trouble. If they are already sexually well educated, pornography can't do them any harm.

How do they get sexually well educated?

Ideally, from their parents. Continuous sexual enlightenment and guidance from understanding and sympathetic parents is the ideal form of sex education. Unfortunately most mothers and fathers are unable to provide this. Their own lack of sexual knowledge and their own uneasiness about discussing sexual matters prevent them from helping their children as much as they would like. The burden is then shifted to the schools who are further handicapped —they cannot tailor the information to the needs of the individual student and are tied to the prevailing moral code of the culture which is usually about thirty years behind current sexual practices.

What's the answer?

Educate the parents. If the average parent knew as little about eating as he does about sex he would quickly starve to death. Yet an unwise nutritional diet does not have nearly the potential for producing unhappiness as does foolish and unrealistic sexual behaviour.

11

PROSTITUTION

When did prostitution begin?

In one form or another, prostitution has been around a long time. "Harlots" are mentioned forty-four times in the Bible, "whores" and "whoremongers" are featured fifty-three times, and "committing whoredoms" is mentioned eight times. Obviously love for money was well established by 2000 B.C. From its origin until relatively recently, prostitution has been a more or less respectable profession.

How can that be?

The ancient Hebrews were the first to condemn whores. Most of their complaints were directed against Hebrew women who took up the trade, however. Foreign prostitutes were relatively well tolerated among them. The New Testament began where the Old Testament left off and commenced a religious campaign against prostitution which took on all the attributes of a Crusade and which continues with its original fervour even today in certain countries (including the United States).

Things were not always that way. Among the ancient Chinese, Greeks, Armenians, Syrians, and Cypriots (to name only a few), prostitution was considered a noble calling and played a role in many religious ceremonies. Nearly every temple had its official prostitutes; intercourse with them (for a small fee) was considered an acceptable form of worship. Many of these ladies were volunteers in the sense that they only worked for a year or so, donating all the proceeds of their labours to the church. This was considered the equivalent of modern missionary work and brought with it great religious rewards. When their time was up, the part-time prostitutes returned home to their husbands and families with greatly enhanced prestige.

Among certain groups, sacred prostitution has a more practical twist. The early Armenians and Cypriots encouraged their daughters to earn their dowries by working as freelance prostitutes before marriage.

Even through the Middle Ages prostitution was accepted as a way of life and the more elegant whores moved freely in upper-class society. Under the euphemism of courtesans, they consorted with royalty. Among the lower classes, the prostitute's life was harder, but not necessarily unrespectable.

What about in modern times?

Prostitution has remained a socially acceptable if somewhat expedient way of earning a living in many parts of the world right up to the present time. After the Communists took control in Eastern Europe following World War II, prostitution was outlawed. Suppression of ladies of the evening was instituted subsequently in France, Italy, Belgium, and Japan. Moreover, whore is still not a nasty word in many parts of the world. Most of Asia recognizes legal prostitution as do large segments of the Arab world. Latin America, with certain exceptions, allows unrestricted prostitution. Mexico has considered prostitutes legal for a long time.

Isn't prostitution a terrible thing?

A lot of people seem to think so, but the facts don't necessarily bear out their emotions. The major objections to professional prostitution usually fall into the following categories:

    1. Prostitution spreads venereal disease.
    2. Prostitution increases sex crimes.
    3. Prostitution corrupts young people.
    4. Prostitution is morally degrading.

Based on the facts available, none of these criticisms seem to hold up. In the United States, which suppresses prostitution as vigorously as any country in the world, the rate of venereal disease hits new highs every week. In Mexico, the incidence of VD is much lower per capita in spite of—or perhaps because of—legal prostitution. Contrary to popular folklore, prostitutes are not nearly the source of venereal disease they are supposed to be.

But aren't most prostitutes infected with syphilis or gonorrhoea?

That's the way the story goes. Ministers and moral educators who couldn't be further removed from practical knowledge of the subject if they lived on the moon, have insisted that prostitutes are racked with terrible disease. Ostensibly the threat of infection will keep their flocks in line. Prostitutes obviously have some drawbacks as a source of sexual satisfaction, but risk of venereal disease is not one of them. In a survey done in New York City in 1966, 4,700 women arrested for prostitution were carefully examined for venereal disease. Of the group 1,313 had positive blood tests for syphilis. When the story hit the papers, it emphasized that twenty-eight per cent of the ladies were infected with syphilis. Nothing could have been further from the truth. Actually only four had syphilis, an incidence of about 0·8 per cent. The other 1,309 had a biological false positive test for syphilis—

they either had the flu, an allergy, a bad cold, or a recent case of the measles, all of which make the blood test for syphilis come out wrong. (None of these is particularly lethal to customers.) Gonorrhoea was found in 619 of the girls, a rate of about thirteen per cent. Considering that only the lowest category of prostitute —the street girls and bar girls—usually fall into the hands of the police, an evening with a high-class girl carries negligible risk of infection. If plying their trade were not a crime, perhaps the 619 with gonorrhoea would have gone to a public health clinic to get their penicillin.

Doesn't prostitution increase sex crimes?

It doesn't seem likely. In countries where the trade is legal, sex crimes are almost non-existent. If a dollar or so buys a willing companion, raping a stranger doesn't make sense. Peeping, exhibitionism, child molestation, incest, all feed on undischarged sexual tensions. In countries where prostitution is tolerated, these crimes hardly exist.

How about the corruption of young people?

Corruption is a loaded word. If it means that prostitution encourages them to engage in sexual intercourse before society approves, then they are probably corrupted. Judging from the countries where prostitutes are freely available, the moral fibre of the nation doesn't seem to be adversely affected. In the United States, where the majority of college students regularly take drugs, prostitution might even be considered as the lesser of two evils. If the choice is a night with a prostitute or a trip on drugs, most rational parents would reluctantly opt for the young lady—at least an evening in bed leaves the brain intact.

But isn't prostitution degrading?

Definitely. We make it that way. By looking down on those who sell their sexual favours, by making them criminals, by shutting them off from the rest of society, we succeed in alienating them completely. Some of the bitterness and contempt rubs off on the customers who are more than willing to pass it on to the lady of the evening.

Prostitution is a fact of life. In itself it is neither good nor bad. Indiscriminate sexual intercourse for money goes against our moral grain because we have been indoctrinated that way. Instead of complaining bitterly about the result of the problem, it might make more sense to go to the source. Like the old saying, "If there wasn't the demand, there wouldn't be the supply."

What causes the "demand"?

Let one of the girls tell her theory. Bonnie is twenty-seven; she has been playing for pay in America since she was nineteen.

"The only thing that keeps us in business is the American wife, God bless her. Those overfed, overdressed smug little bitches help me buy a new mink coat every other year. If all the wives woke up at once and gave their husbands what they wanted, I'd have to go back to waiting on tables in a beer joint. But I'm not too worried—business gets better every month. As long as the average woman thinks she has a golden vagina I'll be in good shape."

Like most prostitutes Bonnie needs to justify her way of life, but she obviously has a point. Most of her customers, like those of every other prostitute, are married. Theoretically they have access to complete sexual gratification with their wives. Realistically, if they did, they wouldn't need Bonnie. A tabulation of the services customers demand from the girls is revealing.

What do they want?

The activity men most often seek from professional prostitutes is fellatio. At least seventy-five to eighty-five per cent of the clients want to have their penises sucked. Most of them feel compelled to explain to the girl that the only reason they like it is that their wives refuse to do it.

How do the girls feel about it?

They love it. Not because it is their idea of ecstasy (no prostitute is in the business for sexual pleasure anyway), but because it is a lot more profitable than anything else. A blow job, as it is known in the trade, is fast, easy, and clean. No linen to change, no washing up to do (except for a swish of antiseptic mouthwash), and if the girl is crafty, she doesn't even have to get undressed. As one lady who should know puts it, "I could do B.J.s all day without working up a sweat."

The next most popular activity with the gents is cunnilingus. The girls don't like that so well. Laurie tells how it is:

"I always charge them extra if they want to work on me down there. It takes such a long time and then they want a regular fuck too. In this line you got to please the customers, but a girl still has to make a living. I usually charge an extra ten bucks for it at least."

What does "trick" mean?

Prostitutes have their own private language. It gives them a feeling of togetherness and helps keep the customers in the dark (or even more in the dark than they already are). Some of the trade lingo is original with the girls, some is appropriated from carnivals, the underworld, and narcotics addicts. Since many prostitutes served an apprenticeship in these fields, they come by the slang naturally.

This form of expression is fluid and constantly changing—these examples can only be considered representative.

TRICK: male customer

JOHN: the same as a trick

JANE: lesbian customer

IN THE LIFE: on the game; working as a prostitute

GIRL: prostitute, sometimes specifically a call girl

WHORE: disparaging term used by a prostitute; means a low-class prostitute

HOOKER: any kind of female prostitute

TURN A TRICK: perform sexual intercourse with a john

BALLING: the same as turning a trick

SLAM-BAM-THANKY-MA'M: fast intercourse, usually at the customer's request

B.J.: fellatio or blow job

GET BURNED: perform intercourse without getting paid; prostitutes hate this

K.U.'D: knocked-up or made pregnant by a customer; prostitutes hate this even worse

FREAK: a customer with bizarre tastes (prostitutes worry about these johns, and with good reason—many of them are sadists, and bruises are bad for business)

TURNED OUT: to be worked over by a freak; this is one of the many occupational hazards of prostitution

AROUND THE WORLD: to perform fellatio, anilingus, and regular intercourse with a customer in addition to licking his body from head to toe

HALFWAY AROUND THE WORLD: fellatio, anilingus, and copulation without the licking

THREE-WAY GIRL: a prostitute who is equally at home with a vaginal and anal intercourse and cunnilingus; she commands extra fees but ranks low on the social scale

DYKE: prostitute who is a lesbian with masculine characteristics

BULL DYKE: a dyke, but even more masculine

BUTCH: same as dyke

FEMME: feminine-appearing lesbian prostitute

LEZZ: any lesbian prostitute or female customer

GO DOWN ON: perform active fellatio

How does a girl get started as a prostitute?

Fortunately the terrifying tales of white slavery exist only in grade-B films. "Helpless young virgins forced into degrading submission against their will" went over big at the Saturday matinee, but real-life prostitution is a different story.

Most girls become prostitutes because they like it. The transition from a "straight" girl to a straight "girl" is usually a gradual one. It starts with run-of-the-mill promiscuity, maybe a divorce or two, then a job in a night club as a waitress or barmaid. Freelance sex with customers for gifts plus association with full-time professional hustlers who hang around the club often prompt a girl to put the pieces together and get in the life. Ronda tells how she got started:

"First of all, don't think I'm making excuses. I know what I'm doing and I like it—I could quit any time. I started screwing when I was fourteen. In the crummy hick town where I grew up there wasn't anything else to do. By the time I was seventeen I'd laid every john in the county. I wasn't a hustler then—I mean I'd let 'em take me out to dinner and all that, but I just did it for kicks. I got married when I was eighteen and we moved to the city—boy, what a jerk he was! After six months, I left him and got a job in a bar. There wasn't much to do so I started screwing around again. We had a couple of hookers working the bar and I got friendly with them. One day they said to me, 'Jesus, what're you giving it away for? You want to put us out of business?' After closing time that night we went out for a few drinks together and they laid it out for me. I tried it a couple of times with guys they sent over and it wasn't so bad. I mean, I get paid for what I was throwing away before and the johns get what they want, so everybody's happy."

Unfortunately Ronda missed one point: in prostitution, nobody's happy.

How come?

Prostitution is a hard life. The average call girl turns about fifteen to twenty tricks a night. Some nights the fast jobs are few and far between. A freaky evening can be mighty hard on a young lady.

Some men have original ideas. It is not unusual for a man to pay a girl to watch while he masturbates in front of her slowly and deliberately. Sometimes he keeps up a running conversation, sometimes he has the girl do the talking according to his script. Some men like to masturbate while the prostitute urinates (or, rarely, defecates) on them. Sadism can be time-consuming and risky—occasionally what started out as a friendly whipping ends with a trip to the hospital for the hooker—without workmen's compensation. Masochistic males who like to be tied up and B.J.'d can also waste a lot of time on a busy night. A diversified girl has to be ready for anything. Some men like (and are willing to pay for) two girls at once.

What can a man do with two girls at the same time?

Obviously most of the gratification is emotional—one penis can't be in two vaginas simultaneously. Some men seem to enjoy this form of conspicuous consumption—others are attracted by the allure of doing something forbidden. It usually amounts to variations on a theme. Sometimes the man has regular intercourse with one of the girls while he performs cunnilingus on the other. He may also have the unoccupied girl titillate him anally while he is working on her partner.

Occasionally these little parties can get crowded. A prostitute may team up with a male assistant (usually a homosexual) for a special customer. The girl and her associate have sexual intercourse and variations thereof while the john watches. When he gets tired of watching he has his choice of further fun with either one—or both. The ultimate in this type of scene is the three-decker: the customer has vaginal intercourse with the prostitute while the other man has anal intercourse with the customer.

Sometimes it's the other way around. Three (or more) men hire a three-way girl. They have oral, anal, and vaginal intercourse with her simultaneously. It's great for the girl who usually charges triple her usual fee plus as much more as she can get.

Of course three-way girls have to charge more—they wear out faster.

Why do people do these kinds of things?

Men who pay for this sort of sexual caper often have emotional problems. Cunnilingus and fellatio are relatively routine these days, and if the johns could arrange it with their wives, the girls would probably lose the business. But the triple-decker, three-way girl, and the two-gents-one-lady-routine are clearly homosexual.

The chap who pays to see two ladies perform homosexually also has his problems, as do the father and son who patronize the same hustler. Whether she realizes it or not, the prostitute frequently functions as a sexual safety-valve. The exhibitionist who masturbates in front of a hooker makes a better choice than masturbating in front of the ladies in the supermarket. It is probably preferable for the gents who like their sex in groups to let their friendly neighbourhood hustler set it up rather than relying on willing but indiscreet amateurs.

How much do the girls make?

Prostitutes have high gross incomes while they are working, but their expenses eat up most of the profit. For the average high-class girl, the balance sheet might run something like this: Nineteen working days per month: fifteen customers at an average of £10 per customer = £2,850 per month gross income. (The girls have to set aside an average of seven days a month for menstruation; while it is possible for them to work freaks during their periods, few of them like to do it.)

They also take about four days off a month to relax—they perform, in a sense, manual labour and need some time off to recuperate.

Upper bracket hustlers must have a place to take customers from time to time and nice apartments cost money. Including maintenance and linen service (thirty sheets a day), it can run to £160–200 a month.

Clothes, shoes, cosmetics, hair-dos, and other "front" expenses range up to £400 a month. Prostitutes usually pay more for their clothes, hair-styling, and everything else. Everyone they deal with knows they make a lot of money and charges them accordingly. As long as the money comes in from the johns, the hookers are willing to pay.

A girl who is expensively dressed in the latest fashions with every aspect of her personal appearance at its best brings in the customers. No one wants to rent a dumpy looking hustler.

What else do they have to pay for?

Probably the biggest item for the average big-time prostitute is pay-offs and tips. Prostitutes are in a strange position. Their livelihood depends upon their availability to the greatest possible number of men. Yet their activities are illegal. The hustler has to pay for referrals—from cab drivers, bartenders, bell hops, and other contacts. According to the girls, everyone else has a hand-out, too.

Smart hookers spend a lot on doctors and drugs—infections are bad for business. Those at the top of the profession get a medical check-up every week and take antibiotics regularly.

Many successful hookers have their own answering service. This makes life easier in many ways. First, it helps to insulate her from the police, cutting down but not eliminating one of the big risks of her trade. Second, it increases her availability to customers. Third, it saves time—when she finishes with one john, all she does is call in for the location and time of her next "appointment."

In these fast-moving days a girl needs transportation. If she drives, she can't pull up to the client's apartment in a jalopy. Girls who are just starting out lean to mini cars but successful hookers like to go first class.

Do they have to pay taxes?

Not yet. However, the ubiquitous tax collector is beginning to cast his eye in the direction of the last charming bastions of free enterprise. These gents are just beginning to make professional calls on hustlers (their profession, not the girls') to collect their share of the take.

As one of the girls complained: "So I told him, 'What the hell do you guys want me to do, put a taxi-meter between my legs?' He just shook his head and walked out."

If prostitutes don't wind up with so much money, then why do they do it?

Virtually every prostitute is in the life because she wants to be. Obviously any woman who chooses to rent her vagina to a dozen men a day has a serious emotional problem. These are the ones who find prostitution glamorous, exciting, and strangely gratifying. One of the hustlers explains it this way:

"I know some people think it's terrible to be in the racket—but they don't understand what it's really like. Always knowing that men are running after you, knowing that they leave their own wives just to make it with you, controlling them just with your sex—there's nothing else that can make a girl feel so powerful."

Another hustler is more direct:

"I love to see them beg for it. They act just like babies, pleading for a B.J. or whatever they have to have. I get a kick out of taking their money. Twenty bucks for fifteen minutes work—I never had it so good!"

All prostitutes have at least one thing in common—they hate men.

Why is that?

The full answer is a complicated one related to the deep underlying emotional problems that drove them into the game.

Basically, prostitution is an ironic form of revenge against all men, acted out on the johns. An expensive hooker in Hollywood sums it up this way:

"They think they're screwing me, but that's all wrong. I'm the one who screws them. Oh, I put on a big show but take it from me, I never feel a thing. None of these 'great lovers' ever made a dent in me."

Why don't prostitutes get pregnant all the time?

The risk of pregnancy is never as high as it seems. Many hustlers have contracted gonorrhoea early in their careers and ended up sterile from sealed Fallopian tubes. A lot of customers don't do things to a girl to make her pregnant, which is one reason fellatio and cunnilingus are fine with every hooker. Some girls have tried to use diaphragms or douches, but these devices just weren't designed for mass production sex. Ninety-nine per cent of johns refuse to wear a condom—as far as they are concerned, if the girl gets pregnant, that's her problem.

The birth control pills have changed everything. Nowadays it is rare for a hooker to get pregnant unless she wants to. Most of them aren't interested.

If prostitutes have sexual intercourse as often as twenty times a day, doesn't it affect their sexual organs?

It doesn't seem to have much effect. The lining of the vagina is composed of mucous membrane, almost identical with the lining of the mouth. If the girls are careful to use adequate lubrication (natural or artificial), friction is kept to a minimum and the amount of wear is insignificant.

Occasionally a problem does come up when a girl has had a great deal of stimulation in the course of an evening resulting in congestion of the clitoris and labia which tends to linger after working hours. An experienced hooker clears this up quickly with a masturbation-induced orgasm.

Since most of the girls are conscientious about attending to minor irritations and vaginal infections, their genitals are usually in better condition than those of the average woman.

Don't prostitutes enjoy sex?

Not with their customers. Only in the rarest situations does the hustler experience any sexual feeling, much less sexual gratification. The customer, however, insists that the girl have an orgasm —or a reasonable facsimile—and is willing to pay for it.

Why do men want the prostitute to have an orgasm?

A lot of wives never reach orgasm during sexual intercourse with their husbands and some of them complain about it. In some men this breeds the nagging fear that they may be inadequate sexually —that their wives don't reach a climax because the husbands aren't doing it right. Often the husband seeks out a prostitute to prove he can do it. He pays, the hooker plays the role of the passionate woman he never married, and everybody wins—or loses, depending on how you look at it.

Doesn't the customer realize that the girl is just pretending?

If the customer thought too hard—if he really analysed the situation, he would probably jump up, put on his clothes, and go home. In addition to leasing her anatomy, the good hooker also sells some fantasy; the grinding, moaning, and clutching that she substitutes for an orgasm are all part of the illusion that sexual intercourse is taking place.

But isn't it sexual intercourse?

Not in the real sense. Masturbation in a vagina is probably a more accurate description. Besides, the hooker and the john are really adversaries. He wants to make it last as long as possible to get his money's worth. She wants to speed it up so she can get another penis working for her. He wants her to feel something; she wants to protect herself against any emotional relationship with him. The outcome is usually a dismal compromise. He despises her but needs the use of her vagina; she hates him but likes his money. Prostitution is a hard life in other ways.

What makes it hard?

Let Daphne tell about it. She is twenty-six and works in a major West Coast city; she has been in the racket for about six years. As she sits in a doctor's office, she looks like a young actress or a fashion model—actually she has worked as both. Tall, slender, long blonde hair, bright blue eyes, she has the look of a well-scrubbed teenager.

"Well, doctor, my line of work is not exactly ideal. Of course it's a lot better than trudging around to the casting offices all day. I had to give away plenty to get a job when I was in films. The funny part of it is, I'm still laying the same crummy studio guys, but now they're paying for it. Anyhow I get up about noon and I'm ready for the first trick about two in the afternoon. That's when the phone starts ringing on good days. I get what I call the breakfast club. These are guys who are so afraid of their wives they can't come up with an alibi for being out at night so they come over in the afternoon for a quick one. I don't mind them—it breaks up the day. But I always get some jerks who want a discount because it's still the afternoon. Sometimes I get mad and tell them off. Yesterday I told one, 'Look man, what do you think this is, the kiddie matinee? You can come over for half price but you only get half a screw!' When business is slow I even take those jerks on for a fast one—it's better than nothing.

"Anyhow, about six I get ready to go out—I usually try to line up a dinner date. If no one calls, I get on the phone myself and fix something up before five o'clock."

Do girls call customers?

Yes. Prostitutes are in business and when things are slow they have to promote, just like any other businessman. The old days of standing under the lamp post with a slit skirt are gone forever, except for what the girls call street whores.

What's a street whore?

Usually an over-age hustler, an alcoholic hooker, or one that's on narcotics. They have become so dilapidated that they are willing to go for the price of a drink, a fix, or a cheap hotel room. They don't last long and are swept up by the police.

Another class of prostitute works the bars; these hustlers are carefully segregated by the class of bar they frequent. The neighbourhood girls hang around cheap corner bars; the club girls make themselves available at selected night spots. The more expensive hookers choose the more expensive cocktail lounges in the fashionable hotels and motels.

If business is bad, the call girl (like Daphne) may work as a bar girl. Call girls don't like to cruise the bars—they consider it degrading, but as one of them said, with a wink, "A girl has to eat to live!"

What's a call girl?

A call girl is a prostitute who makes most of her arrangements with customers over the telephone. They usually contact her through her answering service, though in certain cases she may call them. As Daphne was saying, on a slow day (or night), she calls around to see who wants a little action. Some girls carry the personal approach a little further—they may send Christmas cards and even birthday cards to valued customers. Occasionally a hustler with a sense of humour has business cards printed—

under her name, the line referring to her work often reads *Public Relations*. Rarely, the relationship gets even closer.

When a good customer separates from his wife he may receive a sympathetic call from his favourite hooker and sometimes even a trick on the house to console him for his loss. Even rarer is romance between hustler and john. Every so often an unfortunate man with fantasies of rescuing a girl from life as a prostitute talks her into marrying him. Their chances for happiness are microscopic. The hookers themselves have a saying—"Once a hooker, always a hooker, and once a john, always a john." Sadly, unless some dramatic change like psychiatric treatment intervenes, that's usually the way it is.

What's a call girl's routine like?

Back to Daphne and her typical day:

"So I go for a dinner date—but I like to keep it short. Most nights I have tricks waiting. I check in with my answering service during dinner and if I have some other guys lined up, I tell the john we have to get on with it. I'm usually pretty busy from then until about two a.m. Things slow down unless there's a convention in town, and then it's wild. That's all those convention guys can think of—making it with a girl. You'd think they never get any at home.

"When I finish up, sometimes I meet a few of the other girls and we have coffee and then it's home to bed after another thrilling night. What nobody understands, doctor, is that it's hard work to hustle. Letting fifteen guys lay you every night is like digging ditches—unless you're in top shape, it gets to you after awhile. Sometimes I'm glad when my period comes on—at least I get a rest."

In many ways prostitution is just like any other business.

How is that?

The better prostitutes have their own informal code of ethics. If it were ever written down, it might go something like this:

1. Never recognize a customer in public unless he greets you first.
2. Never reveal the identities of your customers in a way which might embarrass them.
3. Never steal another girl's johns (she might do the same thing to you).
4. Help a "sister" out if she is in trouble (if you don't risk anything by doing so).
5. Never help the cops.

Are there male prostitutes?

Yes. In every large city there are dozens of tall, athletic young men whose sexual service are for hire. Urbane, sophisticated, well dressed, they can be had for an hour, an evening, or a month. They are skilled in every possible sexual nuance—they will engage in every type of sexual intercourse except one.

What form of intercourse won't they perform?

Intercourse with women. Virtually every male prostitute is a homosexual. Mirror images of their sisters in many ways, they cater to the small army of homosexual men who want a penis for hire. There are, however, certain important differences.

Every gay hustler is a four-way boy; fellatio, active and passive, and anal intercourse, active and passive, and whatever else a customer can think of. In one way, the gay hooker's life is easier. Since male homosexuals rarely make a pretence of romance, there is no time wasted on counterfeit love. Every transaction is cash and carry and things go a lot faster. An enterprising gay guy can service twice the customers a female hooker can. Of course his capacity for orgasm is limited but there are ingenious ways to overcome that. Niki, one of the busier hustlers in his part of town, tells how he does it:

"Well, I'm only twenty-two, so I can still go pretty good, but what's the use of throwing it away if I don't have to? For the first job in the afternoon I try to let the man go down on me. It kind of gets me warmed up for the rest of the night. For the next five or six tricks I always schedule old guys—you know, senior citizens. They pay better—they have to—and they always want a blow job because they can't come any other way. What do I care?

"I work in a few 'rips' (active anal intercourse) after that because I'm a little tender around the mouth by then. Just before dinner I look for the guys who like to 'brown' (be active in anal intercourse). I don't have to do anything but lie there and groan like I'm feeling something big, if you know what I mean.

"After dinner the prices go up, and I have to do whatever the customer wants. But I'm not rough trade (coarse or tough homosexual prostitute) and I keep away from the S and Ms. I do mostly B.J.s until midnight unless I'm working an orgy. (Homosexual orgies are just like their heterosexual equivalents.) Those damn orgies really wear a guy out and they don't pay that much. Those queens want you to spend all night with them. They think they're doing you a favour—they don't realize that I'm in business. A guy's got to make a living."

Gay hustlers have a couple of other distinctions. The rate of venereal disease among trade is about ten times higher than among female prostitutes. Male hustlers have a lot more customers to catch things from and strangely enough, they just don't seem to care. Another factor of course is that most men are anxious to blow the whistle on a girl who gave them VD—few men want to explain to the Health Department how they picked up their gonorrhoea from another man.

Male homosexuals only have one real professional advantage over female prostitutes—so far no gay guy has ever become pregnant.

Are there any male prostitutes who cater to women?

In spite of the adolescent fantasies of being pursued by hordes of beautiful girls willing to pay for a night of passion, male hustlers have never caught on with women. Few ladies have any trouble finding willing partners at the corner cocktail lounge—if they are so inclined. Most women recognize intuitively the basic absurdity of sex for hire and insist on at least the illusion of emotional involvement in their sexual encounters. Even the enterprising young gigolo who is hired on a long-term basis by his menopausal mistress has to go through the motions of love. If he allows his true feelings to peek through, he finds himself looking for a new matron to make up to. The middle-aged lady and her handsome young companion are about the closest thing to male heterosexual prostitution in our society.

What about female homosexual prostitutes?

Among the hookers this is not a recognized speciality. Most hustlers will take on anyone, women included. Since the majority of prostitutes are female homosexuals in their private lives anyway, making it with another girl is like a busman's holiday.

What do female homosexuals do with each other?

Like their male counterparts, lesbians are handicapped by having only half the pieces in the anatomical jigsaw puzzle. Just as one penis plus one penis equals nothing, one vagina plus another vagina still equals zero.

The most common lesbian sexual activity is mutual masturbation. They caress each other's clitoris and labia until sexual excitation and orgasm occurs. Many different techniques are used but the effect is basically the same. Occasionally they use the third or index finger to massage the vagina, and, rarely, lesbians

EAS—H

lean to the Italian three-fingered method. In this variation of masturbation, the thumb is on the clitoris, the index finger is in the vagina, and the middle finger works on the anus. The effect is something like a do-it-yourself three-way girl.

Some female homosexuals lean toward tribadism. This calls for one woman to lie atop the other while the pubic areas are rubbed together—faster and faster as the sexual excitement increases. Pressure and friction on the clitoris finally brings on orgasm. Some "tribads" almost accomplish an equivalent of heterosexual intercourse.

How is that?

Occasionally a woman may have an unusually large clitoris which reaches as much as two or more inches in length when erect. If she happens to be a lesbian and her partner spreads her legs widely, the clitoris may just penetrate the vagina. What would be a disgrace to a man is a delight to a woman. Lesbians with this anatomical quirk are in great demand.

For homosexual women with average endowments, the dildoe may be useful. These sponge rubber or plastic penises can be held in place with an elastic harness and an unreasonable facsimile of heterosexual intercourse is possible.

(This is of course the curse of the homosexual, male or female. No matter how ingenious they are, their sexual practices must always be some sort of imitation of heterosexual intercourse.)

Some women simply take turns using the dildoe to masturbate each other. Often this tends to be too exciting for the lady who is waiting her turn to be copulated with the artificial penis and too dull for the one who has already had her turn. About 200 years ago, an anonymous Japanese genius came up with the solution. It is known in Japan as the "harigata." It is a long, flexible dildoe with two heads. Each woman inserts one end into her respective vagina, and both of them get what they are looking for. The unanswered question at this point then becomes why they need each other. If they snip the harigata in the middle, both girls can go home and enjoy themselves at leisure.

What else do lesbians do?

Another common lesbian technique is mutual cunnilingus. Some girls consider themselves experts and prolong this form of intercourse for hours. Mary Anne, a twenty-seven-year-old hustler, tells about it:

"Sure I'm a lezz and I'm not ashamed of it. I've been in love with girls since I was fourteen—I only hustle so I can take care of my lover-girl. I hate men and I don't try to hide it. Only a woman knows how to make love to another woman. I can do more for a girl with my tongue in fifteen minutes than a man can do for her in fifteen years. I should know—I've let 50,000 men lay me since I started and I wouldn't trade one of my girls for all of them!"

There are some other differences between gay guys and lesbians.

What are they?

The girls make out much more than the boys. Kissing on the lips, kissing and fondling the breasts, hugging and squeezing, are popular with the girls. This is probably a reflection for the female desire for at least the illusion of romance in sexual involvement. Most gay guys just want to hurry up and get down to the business of masturbation. Female homosexual relationships also seem to last a little longer than the male equivalent, but their course is no less stormy; the girls betray and deceive each other with monotonous regularity.

Anal activity is not quite so popular with lesbians—most of their attention is focussed on the vagina and clitoris. But basically all homosexuals are alike—looking for love where there can be no love and looking for sexual satisfaction where there can be no lasting satisfaction.

Aren't some prostitutes heterosexual in their personal lives?

Yes, but not in the usual way. First of all, for obvious reasons, husband and family are out of the question. Imagine an over-worked hooker rushing to get the kids off to school and husband off to work so she could get some sleep in time to catch the first bargain hunters of the afternoon. After making it with fifteen to twenty johns a day, few girls even feel like going out on a date. The hustlers who are heterosexual manage to find a solution to their own sexual problems. Most of them live with pimps.

Isn't a pimp a man who finds customers for a prostitute?

In popular slang, that's what he's called, but in the lingo of the hustlers a pimp is the man who lives with and from a hooker. These days most girls have their established clientele expanded by referrals from cab drivers, bartenders, and other key people. Besides, most modern johns know what they want and where to find it—procuring as a trade has been made obsolete by updated communications, improved merchandising, and greater consumer sophistication.

But no one can replace the pimp. He is the only man a girl can talk to. When she comes home in the wee hours of the morning after drawing three freaks in a row, after being burned, and in general having a bad night, it's her pimp who understands. If she feels like sex (she doesn't really consider her professional activities sex), the pimp is ready to oblige. If she is arrested, he is there with bail and a lawyer and sympathy. Her pimp is her own private boy friend who provides her with what little emotional warmth he is capable of.

What does the pimp get out of it?

For his services he takes a big cut of the girl's earnings. Out of the average hooker's net, the pimp may cut himself in for 50 per cent or more. In spite of his promises, if a girl falls on hard times, her pimp may simply find himself another girl who is doing better. In a grim form of poetic justice, the hustler hustles the john and the pimp hustles the hustler. (Another hustler inevitably hustles the pimp and everything comes out even.)

Most hustlers have a hard time making the transition from john to pimp. Their professional frigidity carries over into their personal lives; few prostitutes achieve orgasm even in the privacy of their own bedrooms.

Do prostitutes ever have orgasms?

Certainly, but they are few and far between. On one occasion as a detective was interrogating a girl who had just been arrested in a raid, more for his own curiosity than anything else, he asked her:

"Say, do you girls ever really make it with a customer?"

The girl gave him that look that hustlers reserve for policemen and answered:

"Do you cops ever get parking tickets?"

Occasionally hookers begin to have regular orgasms with the johns—for them it is bad news.

How come?

Prostitutes know that orgasm means emotional involvement, and getting hung up with their customers to them is a sign of the beginning of the end. From their own experience hookers know that orgasms at work often are the first sign of an impending nervous breakdown. Every hooker can tell a story about some-one she knows who committed suicide or started on drugs shortly after letting the tricks make her. When it starts happening, they take a long vacation until things cool off. If that doesn't help, sometimes they get worried enough to see a psychiatrist.

Do many prostitutes take drugs?

Not the girls at the top. They know from their own observations that drugs are the first step on the way down. Many female drug users turn to prostitution to pay for their habit, but these are the ones the hookers refer to as whores—the real professionals feel that addicts give the life a bad name. Occasionally a hustler may take some pep pills or amphetamines to keep going during a convention or a party, but they try to keep away from everything else. Juanita explains why:

"Look, with me it's a job. A truck driver doesn't drink while he's driving and I don't pop pills while I'm hustling. I got enough to worry about without getting turned on. Lately I've noticed some of the johns blowing pot but that's crazy—you can get in trouble that way!"

Juanita is referring to the interesting legal point that prostitution is generally a misdemeanour while possession or use of marijuana is a felony. Any girl can stand a misdemeanour or two, but a felony is very bad for business.

What happens to prostitutes when they get old?

That's when things get tough for the girls. Some of the lucky ones have managed to save enough out of their earnings to go into a small business. One of the favourite lines is a ladies' ready-to-wear shop supplying fashionable clothes and fancy underwear to other hookers. A few hustlers retire into the straight world by getting married. They usually marry men who are unaware of their previous line of work; the girls are in no hurry to confess their past. As one of them said, "How do you think my husband would like it if he knew I was screwed by 25,000 other men before he came along?"

Less often they marry johns, and even more uncommon is a wedding between hooker and pimp; as they say, "We know too much about the life to ever trust each other."

Contrary to popular folklore, ex-hookers do not make ideal wives. Their underlying hatred of men always breaks through and makes trouble for both partners. Some of them just can't resist the temptation to turn a few tricks on the side. Alice is one of those and her explanation summarizes the basic problem that hustlers run into when they try to settle down and live like the squares:

"Well, after putting in my fifteen years, I thought it was time for me to live a nice respectable life—you know, work in the kitchen instead of the bedroom. Was I wrong! After six months I thought I'd go out of my mind! Everything was screwy. After spending half a year watching housewives stab each other in the back trying to make it with each other's husbands, I'll take a nice honest bunch of whores any day! And talk about dull— the biggest thing in their crummy world was which band was playing at the country club that weekend! Remember, I used to go out every night with guys who thought spending a hundred bucks was just warming up! So I got bored and just for something to do, I turned a few tricks—just a couple of fast ones, and when my husband found out about it, that was that. I got mad and told him what he could do about it and here I am back in business again. It was a lousy life anyhow."

How about the girls who don't get married?

Some of the hookers who can't make it as call girls any more move down in the social scale and work the houses. The number of houses of prostitution have declined a lot since World War II. In most big cities, they have all but disappeared. The exception is the poorer neighbourhoods which can support sexual discount houses.

In these joints a customer can still get what he wants cheaper if he isn't too particular. To make any money at all, the girls have to service up to fifty johns a day—they don't last too long at that rate.

Small towns and rural areas are the last hold-outs of such these days—they are tolerated by the police for practical reasons. Even though the local police are not sociologists, they have observed that sex crimes increase when the houses are shut down and virtually disappear when the joints are running full blast. Some of these institutions have served their purpose so well that two American states—Nevada and Arizona—never felt it was necessary to outlaw prostitution in houses.

What's a typical house of prostitution like?

A house in a small farming town in America is set up something like this: at the end of one of the main streets there is a rambling fifteen-room frame mansion. It is well kept and from the outside looks the same as any other house in town except maybe a little nicer. The customer enters and gives his hat and coat to a middle-aged lady at the door who invites him into a large living room. A juke box is playing quietly and drinks are available. There are three or four girls sitting around in bathing suits.

Why bathing suits?

Local customs differ. In some towns the girls wear simple dresses, others wear slacks, others swim-suits—whatever seems to go over best. In any event after a drink or two the john chooses a girl and they go up to her room. She closes the door, hands him a soapy washcloth, slips out of her bathing suit, and lies on the bed with her legs apart. The john is expected to wash his genitals (a social gesture at best) and then pay cash. The girl deposits the note into a slot in the top of her bedside table—the customer makes his own deposit in another opening. If he isn't on his way in fifteen minutes there is a knock on the door to let him know his time is up.

What about customers who make trouble?

In small towns they are few and far between. Most of the johns are solid local citizens and don't want trouble. If things get out of hand, the girl has a buzzer at the bedside and one of the town police (picking up some extra cash in his spare time) is there in a moment to quiet things down. Most rural houses have few problems in this area—if a customer is blacklisted, he has nowhere else to go. The fear of enforced celibacy keeps most johns in line.

What if a girl can't get a job in a house?

Maybe she can work parties. One of the great talents of American business is knowing what the customer wants and giving it to him. If the customer is a purchasing agent or other big buyer and he wants sex, the company who wants to sell its product keeps him well supplied. Slightly ageing hookers are available for £40 a night—dinner, party, and leave-in-the-morning. The customer doesn't care since he doesn't have to pay, the hooker is happy to be working, and the company charges the whole thing off as a business expense—which it is.

If the girl can't make it on the party circuit, the next step down is exhibitions.

What's an exhibition?

The popular term is stag show. Most of them take place in hired halls packed to the rafters. They start with pornographic movies and work up to a grand finale. The show may begin with a strip tease and some go-go dancing. Then one of the girls may have intercourse with a dog. As the pace accelerates, two girls simulate homosexual intercourse with each other—usually mutual cunnilingus. (The girls never really do it. They are homosexuals and are unwilling to show their true feelings in front of men. The customers never know the difference.)

As a climax, one of the girls has intercourse on stage with a volunteer from the audience while the other goes home as a door prize to the holder of the winning ticket. Few human beings can hold up under this sort of thing very long.

What happens to them then?

They may try to get along with occasional jobs—acting in pornographic movies, posing for pornographic photos, and taking whatever else comes along. (Unfortunately for them most of this work is being taken over by talented amateurs who perform just for kicks.) The most common solution is the one chosen by Tina —she describes it:

"Well, I'm forty-two now and I've put on about thirty pounds —there's not exactly a demand for overweight hookers. I tried some of the other angles but it was too much of a comedown. I used to be right up there when I was in the racket. So I figured I got started waiting on tables and I might as well go back there. It's regular hours, I'm building up Social Security—which is one thing I never got in the racket—so I work standing up instead of lying down, so what? For me it's the best way out."

A lot of other girls finish their careers by coming full circle— they go back to work as barmaids, hostesses, and waitresses. For them it is probably the best way out too.

12

BIRTH CONTROL

What is birth control?

Birth control refers to the hundreds of methods that have been employed to separate the act of copulation from the act of reproduction. Since the earliest stages of civilization men have sought ways to deliver sperm into the vagina and no farther. Regrettably these little creatures have a compulsion to swim upstream and unite with an expectant egg; they stubbornly resist any effort to impede their progress.

The spectre of unwanted pregnancy has always cast its shadow over sexual enjoyment. The prospect that each act of intercourse might result in a new addition to the family has dulled the sexual appetites of untold husbands and wives. The possibility that sexual intercourse might start a family has ruined the fun of a lot of people who aren't married. Some of the saddest lines ever spoken during sexual relations are these:

"Don't stop, Roger, but this is the wrong time of the month."

"Now, Alice, are you sure your period will start tomorrow?"

"I was just thinking, Milt. What will my husband do if I get pregnant while he's away?"

"We might as well go ahead; I'm three weeks late already."

Of course some people in this world never give a thought to birth control.

Why is that?

Certain primitive tribes don't realize there is any connection between sex and pregnancy. While they are as enthusiastic about sex as their distant cousins in say, Chelsea (maybe more so), they think pregnancy is a magical event resulting from prayers and animal sacrifices. Sex is for fun and babies come by themselves. Actually they are lucky they don't know any better. Lack of sanitation and rampant disease claim so many of their infants that constant reproduction barely keeps the tribe intact. Other tribes are a little more sophisticated.

How is that?

They know that sex brings babies. They even try to control reproduction by a crude technique of birth control. A split-second before ejaculation the man jerks his penis out of the vagina. He squirts the seminal fluid all around, on his girl friend, or on himself, depending on his aim and degree of self-control. If his self-control is substandard, he squirts it in the vagina. He hopes that one doesn't count.

Does it work?

No, not really. The withdrawal method goes against human nature and the laws of physics. At the moment of greatest sexual excitement, it requires a cool head and good aim. As far as physics is concerned, it compels the man to go backward when he wants to plunge forward, to stop when he wants to really get started, and to subtract when he wants to add. It also makes the woman feel left out. At the moment of impending orgasm she is jolted back to reality as five or six jets of hot semen are sprayed on her tummy. Not exactly ecstasy.

Another point against withdrawal is the risk of pregnancy—very great. Even before ejaculation there are always a few drops of secretions in the penis; each drop contains about 50,000 sperm. If they leak into the vagina, one drop is more than enough to make an egg into a baby.

Sometimes there are more than a few drops. Imagine how a man feels if in spite of solemnly resolving to withdraw his penis at the ultimate moment, his reflexes get the best of him and he delivers 100 per cent of his ejaculation deep into the vagina. Then imagine how his girl friend feels.

If the withdrawal method is so bad, why does anyone use it?

It is one of the few techniques of birth control that doesn't require any equipment. Two teenagers parked in a lover's lane at one a.m. who get carried away with mutual masturbation don't have much choice. The chemists are closed, they were supposed to have been home an hour ago, and their pulsating genitals won't wait until next Saturday night. They do the best they can.

Other people just don't know the odds. They don't realize that each ejaculation can contain 4,000,000,000 sperm—that is 3,999,999,999 over the amount needed to get pregnant. Most of the people who rely on withdrawal for contraception consider it better than nothing. It is better than nothing—but not much better.

Is the rhythm method more reliable?

A little bit more reliable. It depends on the physiological fact that fertilization is more likely to occur as a result of intercourse a day or two before (or after) ovulation. The couple assumes that ovulation takes place about the midpoint of the menstrual cycle; they avoid intercourse during this time. Theoretically it works fine. In actual practice it is reproductive roulette—the house has all the odds.

The big problem is that ovulation generally occurs fourteen days before the first day of the next menstrual period. If the woman can predict for sure when her next period will start, she wins. However, if she can consistently predict future events like that, she should be able to pick the winner of the Irish Sweepstakes.

There is one other little detail. Ovulation can actually occur on any day of the menstrual cycle, even during menstruation itself. Rhythm? That mischievous little egg doesn't have any rhythm. There are some other crude methods which are more dependable.

What are they?

The chastity belt is one. Originally used during the Middle Ages by knights who wanted to defend their wives' honour while they were defending the honour of their country, it was a sort of armoured bikini. There was a screen in front to allow urination and an inch of iron between the vagina and temptation. The whole business was fastened with a large padlock. Even in those days love laughed at locksmiths (and padlocks) and many a knight returned to find his wife with a virtuous look on her face and a two-month pregnancy under her cast-iron underwear. The only thing to be said for the chastity belt is that used conscientiously it will prevent conception (and everything else).

A somewhat more direct (and drastic) process is known as infindibulation. This was common in African cultures and was a favourite of departing husbands. The man of the house had an elderly female relative sew his wife's vagina shut with a big needle and stout thread. The procedure was so painful that the wife rarely had any interest in transgressing. Once home, the husband removed the sutures and began where he left off. This method has nothing to recommend it.

Is there anything like infindibulation for men?

Yes, in a way. It is called posterior urethral compression and amounts to temporary infindibulation. In the final stages of intercourse, when orgasm is imminent, the man tells his partner. She reaches down and swiftly squeezes his penis at the base, tightly. Her iron grip shuts off the urethra completely and prevents any seminal fluid from leaving the penis at ejaculation.

Where does it go?

Back where it came from. Under the tremendous pumping pressure of orgasm, the semen is forced back into the prostate gland and seminal vesicles. It is a painful experience and eventually damages these delicate structures. Some men, especially in Europe, are used to it and don't mind. In America it is primarily used by prostitutes as a means of revenge to get even with customers who forget to pay. Next time they remember.

Aren't there some techniques women can use themselves?

Since it is the ladies who have to carry the burden of unwanted pregnancy, for thousands of years women have been searching for methods they can control themselves. The techniques range from the incredibly crude to the amazingly complex. Sometimes the women in the most technically advanced cultures use the crudest methods; the primitive women occasionally utilize extremely sophisticated means of contraception.

Peasant women in Eastern Europe and parts of Asia have a method that could be taken right out of the scientific laboratory. After intercourse they immediately squat on the floor and insert an index finger into the vagina. By then the semen has begun to coagulate and has the consistency of thick mucus. The woman makes a rapid swirling motion with her finger and suddenly jerks it out of the vagina. The semen spins out in one gob, almost as if it had been extracted with a laboratory centrifuge, a device that spins solids out of solution at high speed. The centrifuge approach is inexpensive, can be used anywhere, and requires no equipment. However, it is messy, relatively unreliable, and requires rapid disengagement immediately after ejaculation if it is going to have any chance of success. It has most of the drawbacks of the douche.

How does the douche work?

The douche is probably the most common means of contraception used by modern women. In effectiveness it is only one bare notch above the human centrifuge. As in the other technique, time is of the essence. Immediately after ejaculation, the woman must rush to the bathroom and wash out the vagina with a solution designed to inactivate sperm. Generally she uses a douche bag, a small rubber sac connected to a long plastic nozzle. The nozzle fits into the vagina, and by squeezing the rubber bag, she can pump solution throughout the vagina.

What kind of solution is best?

It's hard to say. Over the hundreds of years in which this method has been used, thousands of substances have been advocated to destroy sperm. Every chemist has at least a dozen varieties on the shelves and perhaps two dozen more gathering dust in the back. Fashions change in this line, too. At one time clear solutions with a small amount of carbolic acid were popular. Then deep blue mercuric mixtures took over. In the 1950s chlorophyll captured the douche market briefly. What will be next is anybody's guess.

Actually they are all about the same; their primary effect depends on washing the sperm out of the vagina. The liquid of choice, with one exception, is just plain water. Cheap, sanitary, harmless, it is as effective as any of the others.

What's the one exception?

Coca-Cola. Long a favourite soft drink, it is, coincidentally, the best douche available. A Coke contains carbonic acid which kills the sperm and sugar which explodes the sperm cells. The carbonation forces it into the vagina under pressure and helps penetrate every tiny crevice of vaginal lining. It is inexpensive, universally available, and comes in a disposable applicator.

How is it used?

After intercourse, the woman doesn't even have to get out of bed. She merely reaches over to the table, picks up a bottle of warm Coke, uncaps it, places her thumb over the top, shakes vigorously, and inserts the neck of the bottle into the vagina. A bowl under her hips to catch the overflow helps. Instantly she has an effervescent douche. The six-ounce bottle is just the right size for one application.

Are douches effective?

Not really. All of them, including Coca-Cola, suffer from the defects of too much and too late; too much trouble and too late to do any good. Leaping up to rinse the vagina immediately after orgasm is too acrobatic for the full enjoyment of sex.

Any method applied after intercourse is too late. By the time the douche is started, 100,000 or so microscopic wigglers are probably swimming around inside the uterus where no douche in the world can reach them. They probably won't even hear the rushing waters.

How about vaginal suppositories?

These are little waxy bullets designed to be inserted into the vagina just before intercourse. They are a kind of solid-state douche that theoretically should work. At body temperature the wax melts, releasing any one of a number of chemicals to incapacitate sperm. Since the suppository is in place at the start of intercourse, there is no rush to pump in a solution. Suppositories are also a little neater.

The only drawback is that they don't work. Sometimes they don't even melt. Even if they dissolve, the semen whizzes through the vagina so fast on its way to the uterus (and the egg), that it doesn't spend much time in contact with suppository. Suppositories do have one real advantage over douching—the waxy substance keeps the tissues of the vagina smooth and pliable.

Aren't some disinfectants good for killing sperm?

Some women do use a solution of household disinfectant as a contraceptive solution. It is not much of an idea. Since the companies who make these chemicals brag about their ability to kill germs, women frequently assume the same power against sperm. This can lead to complications. Any solution strong enough to kill germs will eat away the vaginal lining—it has happened occasionally. Disinfectants belong inside sinks, not inside people.

Is there a substance that can be used inside the vagina that is safe and effective?

Yes. Some of the newer vaginal foams are pretty good. An aerosol can of foam, like shaving cream, is used to fill a plastic applicator. The applicator is pushed into the vagina and the foam forced out with a plunger. Unlike creams, there is no overflow and the chemicals are probably about ninety per cent effective. There are some disadvantages. The little plastic rod has to probe the vagina before each copulation, which some ladies find distracting. If the user tries to apply the foam directly from the can, the results are catastrophic—foam for miles around. Another question mark is the ability of the user to understand instructions clearly. Foams were used at one time in birth control clinics, but the results were not entirely satisfactory. It sometimes went like this:

DOCTOR: Well, Mrs. Brown, are you using your foam?
MRS. BROWN: Yes sir, doctor. I take it every night.
DOCTOR: Don't you feel better now that you don't have to worry about having any more children?
MRS. BROWN: Well, to tell you the truth, doctor, I'm thinking about having another one. I'd rather get pregnant than have to eat that little tube of foam every night—it tastes so awfully bitter!

Mrs. Brown didn't have to worry about having another one. By the time her doctor cleared up the misunderstanding she was pregnant again.

How about the diaphragm? Isn't that a good method?

The vaginal diaphragm, until recently, was probably the most popular method of birth control in America. Crude, expensive, and somewhat unpredictable, it was the best available.

This device consists of a rubber-covered metal ring surrounding a thin rubber dome-shaped membrane. It resembles a rubber skull cap. A lump of contraceptive jelly is placed inside to cover the dome and rim, and the diaphragm compressed to the size and shape of a slice of melon. It is slid into the vagina and rocked into place with the upper edge against the pubic bone, the lower edge beneath the cervix, and the rubber dome between the cervix and the onslaught of sperm. Since rubber is waterproof (and spermproof), a diaphragm should be 100 per cent effective. It isn't.

Unless it is put in place precisely and remains there throughout the inner turmoil of copulation, it merely serves to guide billions of little surfers into the cervix. Even with the diaphragm properly in place, a pinhole in the membrane is like a wide-open door to a sperm.

The diaphragm does have one advantage—it can be inserted long before intercourse and thus avoids interruptions at delicate moments. It is nearly ninety per cent effective in preventing pregnancy; good statistically but bad realistically if you are one of the unlucky ten per cent. At one time an attempt was made to overcome some of the diaphragm's disadvantages by modifying it into a cervical cap.

What is a cervical cap?

As the name implies, it is a sort of rubber shower cap that fits tightly over the cervix and keeps sperm out. Unfortunately, cervical caps never fitted tightly enough and were often found at the mouth of the vagina the morning after. This sort of internal condom just didn't work out.

What about the condom?

The condom was the first big technical breakthrough in the birth control field. Known by its many aliases: French letter, safety, *preservativo* (Spanish), *capote* (French), it is the most common method in use in the civilized world. Originated in the fifteenth century as protection against syphilis, the first model was made of linen saturated with a mercury solution. In the form of a little linen stocking, it fitted loosely over the penis. The early condoms broke frequently: they were patched with glue and reused again and again. The glue quickly dissolved under the stress and strain of penile thrusting and the device frequently disintegrated just when it was needed the most.

New designs appeared rapidly including condoms of fish bladder and lamb gut. While these improvements held up better, no one really liked them.

The same complaints hold true for the modern condom, though the design is much improved. The latest models are of very thin latex rubber and give a skin-tight fit over the penis. Dozens of different varieties are offered. There are transparent condoms for the natural look, opaque condoms for those who are modest, red condoms for festive occasions, condoms with eyes, nose, and mouth painted on the tip for the whimsical, and condoms with fluttering fringes for the flamboyant. For men with super-potency there are condoms with reservoirs at the end to hold the flood of sperm. They are all basically the same. These rubber raincoats keeps the uterus from getting caught in a sudden shower of sperm. Unless something goes wrong.

What can go wrong?

Too many things. Since they are basically balloons, condoms can break. There are few sights more spine-chilling than that of a penis being withdrawn after ejaculation with the tattered remnants of a condom waving in the breeze. Sometimes the product is defective, sometimes it just can't take the friction. Sometimes the couple make the mistake of using petroleum jelly for lubrication.

What's wrong with petroleum jelly?

Nothing in itself. But it energetically attacks rubber and dissolves it. In the process it may also dissolve friendships, marriages, and bank balances. Water-soluble surgical jelly is a better idea.

Problems can also come up at the other end. The condom is held on the penis by a rubber band at the base. During erection it is held tightly; after ejaculation, it loosens up and sperm may spill over the top in a frightening cascade. Prompt withdrawal after orgasm minimize this risk.

Condoms, like diaphragms, can develop pinhole leaks. Distending them with air or water before use prevents unpleasant surprises.

Is the condom safe?

Most of the time. About eighty-five per cent reliability is the best it can offer. Odds like that mean that couples who rely on the condom exclusively will eventually be disappointed.

Notwithstanding, many people continue to use it. It is inexpensive, fast, simple, and available. It also has the bonus of giving some protection against venereal disease, both to men and women.

Is rubber the only material used in modern condoms?

No. A small percentage of condoms are made from the large intestines of lambs. They are processed to make them soft and transparent; they are known as skins. Some users prefer them, claiming they give a better feel, but their primary advantage is that they are non-allergenic. For a man who is allergic to rubber, dermatitis of the penis can take the fun out of sex. Skins solve this problem. There are also home-made condoms of various materials.

Why should anyone make his own condom?

A man on a camping trip with his wife, a fellow suddenly finding himself in a motel room at one a.m. with his girl friend, a college student in the back seat of a car—if they have not been foresighted —may find themselves ill-equipped for a night of love. Human ingenuity being what it is, they make do with the materials at hand. A motel room has plenty to offer. Those plastic bags they wrap the drinking glasses in give some protection. They may be a little wide and a little short but they are better than nothing. After an evening's celebration, many a couple has kept sperm and egg apart with a hastily-inflated party balloon. Even the kitchen can occasionally save the day (or the night). A housewife describes it:

"Well, I told Joe he was running low on protectors but he didn't believe me. We were in bed last night and all set to make love. He opened the drawer on the bedside table—that's where he keeps them—and all he had was an empty box. I wasn't going to be let down again! I got up, went to the kitchen and started looking around. The first thing I saw was a box of poly-wrap. Well, I tore some off, got Joe to wrap it around his organ and we went right ahead. In the ads it says, 'Keeps things from spoiling!' Well, it worked—it kept Joe from spoiling my evening!"

Aren't there some operations for birth control?

Yes. The ultimate in birth control is sterilization. By surgically blocking the natural pathway of the egg and sperm, fertilization becomes impossible. A more exact term might be egg control and sperm control.

Many women are sterilized as a by-product of another operation. A partial hysterectomy or removal of the uterus leaves the other reproductive organs intact and effectively prevents pregnancy. Some patients refer to this as taking away the baby carriage but leaving the play pen.

The operation specifically designed for sterilizing women is the tubal ligation. In this procedure the Fallopian tubes are cut and tied. Everything continues as before but after ovulation sperm cannot get to the egg and the egg cannot get to the sperm. Tubal ligation is easy to do, fast, and has few complications. It is, however, expensive and fickle.

Fickle?

Yes. Occasionally women change their minds (sometimes after changing their husbands) and want to get pregnant again. In a very delicate and complex procedure, the doctor may try to fasten the cut ends of the tubes together. It is roughly comparable to sewing two pieces of soggy macaroni while someone is pulling at each end. Usually it doesn't work.

On the other hand, years after they have parted company, the severed ends of the Fallopian tubes may find each other in the vast wilderness of the pelvis and reunite. Another reunion, sperm and egg, follows swiftly.

What is the operation for men?

The male equivalent of tubal ligation is called vasectomy. The small tube leading from the testicle to the penis is called the vas deferens. (Vas means duct.) If this section of tubing is sealed off, hardly anything changes except sperm cannot get out of the testicle into the penis, out of the penis into the vagina, and thence to the Fallopian tubes to keep an appointment with an egg.

The operation takes no more than ten minutes, can be done in the doctor's office under local anaesthetic, and is about ninety-nine per cent dependable. It even has the advantage of sometimes being reversible to allow for second thoughts later on. If the man wants to be a father, a splint of plastic tubing brings the ends of the duct back together again. The chances of success range up to forty per cent. Occasionally a mechanically inclined patient suggests that the doctor insert a shut-off valve to control the flow of sperm. Such a device could solve a lot of problems if clearly labelled, "Make sure valve is in proper position before commencing operations." While it is technically feasible, there are still emotional obstacles to its acceptance.

The routine vasectomy is an excellent method of birth control and has wide acceptance, especially in countries like India.

Why is it so popular in India?

In that country, the government pays a bounty for these little ducts. Any man who submits to the operation gets his choice of cash or a transistor radio. (Most men take the radio.) India is a poor country with a nearly hopeless population problem. Most of the usual methods of birth control are too expensive or too complex to be successful. Vasectomy is ideal. Clinics are set up in vacant stores, tents, and even busy railroad stations.

A good Indian doctor can do fifteen vasectomies an hour and cut the potential birth rate by ten to twenty for each patient.

Regrettably, most of the advantage is an illusion since one well-motivated Indian with his vas intact can fertilize up to 365 (or more) women each year.

Do Western Men like the operation?

No. The first problem is that no one gives them transistor radios. Vasectomies have also gained a bad reputation they don't really deserve. Some men have had the operation and two weeks later impregnated their wives (or girl friends). Somebody should have told them that living sperm remain in the duct for about six weeks after surgery. They must be flushed out by ejaculations over that period of time. A sperm test, just to be sure, is a good idea too.

Probably the biggest objection to cutting the vas is the feeling of insecurity it causes. The incision is at the upper part of the testicle and starts off just like castration. No man even like to think of that! The idea of someone cutting on his private parts goes against the grain. As a result, most men who are vasectomized only submit to please an insistent wife. As one reluctant fellow said:

"You might as well cut it, doc. My wife says if I don't let you, I'm not going to have any use for it anyhow."

What is the best method of birth control?

That, like the perfect martini, has not been concocted yet. There are two recent techniques that have some outstanding advantages. The first one is the "Intra-Uterine Contraceptive Device," or IUD (pronounced "yood").

The IUD has been in use for about 2,500 years. Arab camel drivers in that era were faced with a difficult problem. The voyages of their caravans often lasted two years and involved many intermediate stops where several camels would be dropped off with their loads. The voyages were marred by a quirk of camel psychology—a pregnant camel refuses under any circumstances to leave the caravan. At stops their burdens would have to be shifted to other camels and the whole caravan rearranged. The camel drivers could not eliminate the female camels since they carried heavier loads and had more endurance.

One day, an anonymous Arab genius thought of implanting an apricot stone in the uterus of a camel. This foreign body effectively prevented pregnancy and was the perfect camel contraceptive. From that time on, every female camel (except those used for breeding) was equipped with her personal apricot stone. Even today camel caravans are protected this way.

Aristotle knew this technique and mentioned it in his writings. Apparently no one paid much attention until almost twenty centuries had passed. About fifty years ago a German doctor, von Graff, decided to try the same approach in human beings. He fashioned a coil of silver wire which he inserted through the vagina directly into the uterus. More elegant and more sanitary than an apricot stone, it worked as well. The pregnancy rate dropped dramatically in the women who used them. He later refined the appliance into the form of a wishbone made of silver, gold, or platinum. The two wings of the wishbone were compressed and pushed into the uterus; the base partially covered the cervix.

While women who used it didn't get pregnant, they did get other things—like cancer. This IUD got bad reviews, which it probably deserved, and was abandoned.

In the early 1950s, an Israeli physician, Dr. Margolis, revived the von Graff IUD. This time he made it of polyethylene plastic. Plastic doesn't react with body tissues as much, and the risk of cancer is considered much less. The modern IUD looks like a thin strand of white spaghetti. It comes in imaginative shapes ranging from a spiral coil to a snappy bow tie. The shape really doesn't make any difference—a IUD in the form of the user's monogram would probably work just as well (and be the ultimate status symbol). What does matter is that the plastic seems to be harmless to the body.

The doctor pops the IUD into the uterus with a device that

looks like an olive stoner—a push on the plunger and that's it. The entire process hardly takes ninety seconds. To avoid anxious moments, a small thread with a few beads on it hangs out of the cervix; the woman can always reassure herself that the coil hasn't gone anywhere else. Only one shape, the bow tie, tended to wriggle out of the uterus. It has now been almost completely replaced by less migratory styles.

Does the IUD work well?

It's only fair. The rate of protection is about ninety per cent. This is compensated for by the convenience—no chemicals, no condoms, no diaphragm. However, for those who might be inconvenienced by pregnancy, the IUD has its limitations. There are stories of babies being born clutching the plastic coil in their little hands.

There are other difficulties. Some women cannot tolerate the loop. Vaginal bleeding, abdominal cramping, and pelvic discomfort dictate its removal. Other women expel the IUD spontaneously—their bodies just don't like it. It would seem to be an ideal device for a country like India except the Indian ladies don't like it very well either. The IUD is probably just a step along the way in the search for better ways of birth control.

Is the pill better?

In some ways. The principle behind chemical control of conception has been known for many years and was successfully used in animals. In 1956 a formulation for human beings was developed. The original pill was a combination of two female sex hormones, oestrogen and progesterone. All subsequent oral contraceptives are basically the same, though the ratio of oestrogen to progesterone may vary. These tablets prevent conception by preventing ovulation. They alter the hormone balance of the body and interfere with the normal operation of the ovary. No ovulation, no egg. No egg, no baby. The one outstanding advantage of this method is its reliability. If taken correctly, the protection is virtually 100 per cent.

How are the birth control pills taken?

To be dependable they must be synchronized with the menstrual cycle. On the fifth day after menstruation begins the woman takes the first pill. She then takes one pill a day for the next nineteen days. When all twenty are consumed, she waits for the onset of her next period—usually three to five days later, and begins the routine again.

This is one of the problems with oral contraception. The woman must start on time, finish on time, and take all the pills each month. Twenty is a funny number—it doesn't fit into any easy-to-remember schedule. Some companies have tried to overcome this by putting up their tablets in packs of twenty-one— three weeks taking pills, one week without pills. Other systems have the woman take a pill every day of the month. She is given a packet of thirty identical pills; twenty contain hormones, the rest are imitations. Unfortunately if she doesn't take them in the right order the baby she has will be genuine.

In backward countries, oral contraceptives can go far to help solve overpopulation problems. That is, if the women can be educated to take their pills the right way. Pakistan is a good example.

Although the Pakistanis were amply supplied with the tablets (by the United States), their women just couldn't seem to keep track of those five days from the beginning of menstruation. As a result they were not taking their pills on time. The medicine was being wasted, a lot of money was being spent, and the birth rate was rising. A distinguished American doctor was dispatched to see what he could do. He immediately recognized the difficulty— most of the women didn't know how to count. He suggested that each woman be told at the time she was given her pills to synchronize her medication with the moon.

Now in Pakistan, when the new moon appears in the night sky, thousands of Pakistani women reach for their birth control pills. A few minor kinks still have to be worked out, however. Since they all start together, they all finish together—most of the women in Pakistan menstruate simultaneously. The thousands who are Hindus wash themselves in the sacred rivers at this time. It can be a problem.

Are nuns allowed to take birth control pills?

Only under certain unusual circumstances. In the early 1960s when the Belgian Congo was given its independence, things got a little ugly. Bands of terrorists swarmed over the country killing, looting, and raping. It was the raping part that particularly disturbed the Catholic Church. Many hundreds of nuns manned Catholic missions there and they were the rapist's primary targets. Several hundred half-breed children fathered by black terrorists and borne by white nuns was an appalling possibility. The Church ordered a special dispensation and birth control pills were distributed to the nuns. They took them obediently.

Isn't there another kind of oral contraceptive that combines two kinds of pills?

Some drug companies have introduced a new twist in contraceptive tablets. These are the sequential pills. They were developed to overcome one of the drawbacks of the original tablets, breakthrough bleeding. About the middle of the menstrual cycle, certain women taking oral contraceptives develop a bloody vaginal discharge which can drag on until the next period. The ladies don't like it since they have to wear a vaginal pad or tampon all month and their husbands are understandably dismayed.

The sequential tablet is actually a combination of two tablets. The first fifteen pills are pure oestrogen; the last five are a combination of oestrogen and progesterone. This is an attempt to duplicate the natural hormone mix of the body. (The name, sequential, was coined because the tablets are taken in sequence.) If sequentials come closer to producing the natural hormone feature of the body, they also come closer to producing another natural function as well—pregnancy. Women taking these combination contraceptives have a significantly higher pregnancy rate than those who take the original two-in-one-tablets. In Britain the sequential pill is considered a health risk.

Are there any disadvantages to birth control tablets?

The most common difficulty is breakthrough bleeding, usually controlled by increasing the dose of the drug, and fluid retention, which usually responds to diuretic tablets.

There is one other problem. A careful study of a substantial number of British women who took oral contraceptives for extended periods revealed some unpleasant facts. This survey, reported in April 1968, showed that users of birth control tablets had a death rate from blood clots seven to ten times higher than comparable women who did not take the tablets. The rate of illness due to blood clots among users was almost ten times as great. Those who died usually succumbed to blood clots of the brain or lungs. The women who got sick had various illnesses resulting from blood clots ranging from leg cramps to total blindness. As a result, all contraceptive pill advertising directed at doctors carries a 1,200-word warning that states these facts and lists the following conditions "which are known to occur in patients receiving oral contraceptives":

"Nausea, vomiting, oedema, breast changes, change in weight, suppression of lactation, jaundice, migraine, allergic rash, mental depression."

The warning also points out that there is a significant association between the use of the pill and blood clots of the veins and lungs.

Then should women continue to take oral contraceptives?

That is a matter for the woman and her doctor to decide together. If they are willing to take the risks involved and if no other method of birth control is satisfactory, the pill might be the answer. Apparently for a lot of British women, it wasn't.

Isn't there something as reliable as pills without the risk?

Not yet. A new injectable contraceptive, requiring one injection per month, is in the final stages of testing. It is a long-acting form of progesterone and is said to be as effective as the tablets. Its safety remains to be established.

A male contraceptive that is given the same way is also under development. This monthly injection would render men temporarily sterile for the next thirty days. Birth control applied to the male has never been particularly successful; motivation is lacking. Unfortunately the ideal contraceptive has yet to be developed.

What would the ideal pill be?

One which is adapted to human nature. In sexual matters men and woman usually act first and think afterwards. Once the sperm have been launched, there is no calling them back. The process of reproduction proceeds relentlessly to its inevitable conclusion nine months later. If the lady forgets her pill, once the egg and sperm unite a thousand pills won't send them back where they came from.

What is needed is a retrospective method of conception control. In Japan, where birth control pills are not available, legal abortion fulfills that need. Modern biochemistry is struggling to come up with an easier way. The ideal drug is the morning-after pill. Taken anytime up to a week or so after intercourse, it would prevent implantation in the uterus of the fertilized egg. With seven days to think it over, reason might prevail, parents might be a little happier, the children who are born might be loved a little more, and the world might be a little less crowded.

13

ABORTION*

What is abortion?

Abortion is simply the interruption of a pregnancy. It can happen either of two ways—accidentally or on purpose.

Most abortions happen on purpose. The exceptions, accidental abortions, result from physical defects of the mother or the child, sometimes both. They are called spontaneous abortions, to distinguish them from the non-accidental kind, which are given the rather dramatic title of Criminal Abortions. This is confusing since some allegedly criminal abortions are undertaken rather spontaneously. It would be better to call these events deliberate abortions.

What causes an accidental abortion?

This type of abortion is probably nature's way of saying no. About half of these result from product defects. The sperm or

*See publishers note in preliminary pages.

EAS—I

ovum is imperfect and produces an imperfect embryo. Such abortions, regretted as they may be by the prospective parents, are literally a blessing in disguise. The baby they have lost is actually being thrown away by a vigilant reproductive defence mechanism. Virtually all such embryos are monstrosities. A twist of biological fate has rendered them unprepared for earthly life. Careful examination of the products of accidental abortion reveals a lilliputian chamber of horrors. There are babies with no heads and those with two heads. Some have heads but no brains, others have gigantic hollow brains bursting through their skulls. There is no reason to regret the loss of these genetic mistakes.

What causes the other half of accidental abortions?

The remainder are determined in the brief moments of implantation when the fertilized egg is being attached to the lining of the uterus. Sometimes there is a lapse at the critical moment when the circulatory system of the mother is connected to the infant's blood supply. If this falters, the pregnancy must falter, either then or later.

Are deliberate abortions more common than accidental abortions?

Yes. Accidental abortions, delicately referred to as miscarriages, occur at the rate of about one million a year in the United States. Deliberate abortions of the so-called criminal variety probably exceed two million yearly. If therapeutic abortions are added to the list the proportion is even higher.

Therapeutic abortions? What's a therapeutic abortion?

A therapeutic abortion is an abortion done in a hospital, by a doctor.

The deliberate mechanical termination of a viable pregnancy done for a good reason—that is for the health of the mother or child—is called a therapeutic abortion. It may not be immediately apparent how such a procedure can be beneficial to the health of the aborted embryo, but it can work that way.

How can abortion be good for the child who is aborted?

German measles or rubella is a mild virus disease. If a child gets it at the age of six years, it keeps him out of school about a week. If he gets it at the age of minus six months (three months after conception) it keeps him out of life.

How can he catch German measles in the uterus?

From his mother. If a woman contracts the infection in the first three months of pregnancy it is likely that her child will be born defective. In the unborn, the mild disease of childhood becomes a sadistic ravager of innocents. If the pregnancy is allowed to continue the foetus may emerge at birth blind, deaf, mentally retarded, with a defective heart. This is poor preparation for a competitive world.

For this reason, physicians agree that German measles in the mother is an absolute justification for concluding the pregnancy.

Then every woman who gets German measles while pregnant is entitled to an abortion?

Oh, no. Physicians don't make the abortion laws. They are made by politicians with the help of ministers, teachers, priests, police officers, and philosophers. Sometimes these laws make it impossible for any woman to obtain an abortion legally under any circumstances. It can get pretty gruesome. There have been instances where a doctor has diagnosed German measles in the early weeks of pregnancy, informed the parents, got their consent to the abortion, but could not obtain permission from the authorities. The mother then was condemned to wait out the months of gestation not knowing (but vividly imagining) what kind of monster she was growing inside her. She was compelled to go through all the risks of pregnancy and delivery for the sake of producing a distorted lump of quivering protoplasm instead of a human being.

There are few places as tragic as rubella baby farms. In these institutions scores of shrunken goblins grow up together. Only it's not growing up. There is nothing to grow up to. Seeing, hearing, thinking, in the usual sense, are denied to them. They are even more pathetic than the phocomelia babies.

What are the phocomelia babies?

A German drug company some years ago introduced a new drug for insomnia. It was called thalidomide. It differed from the usual sleeping tablets in certain ways and had some real advantages. It worked fast, wore off quickly, and was not habit forming. It also had a disadvantage: mothers who took it during pregnancy gave birth to unfinished children. The head and body were okay —it was just that the arms and legs didn't turn out right. The hands were attached directly to the shoulders like flippers and the feet were hooked right onto the hips. It made them look like baby seals—thus the name: phocomelia or seal limbs.

Many European women found out about the effects in time and had therapeutic abortions. A number of American women also took the drug. They found out about it in time, too, but they weren't allowed to have the abortions. Some of them did anyhow. Some of them didn't. They wished they had.

The sight of a dozen or so bright healthy youngsters playing in the school yard, cheerfully flipping their flippers, totally unaware that all children aren't that way, is hard to take. Some day they will have to leave their special school and face a world full of arms and legs.

Are German measles and phocomelia the only reasons for a therapeutic abortion?

No. Most doctors feel that any condition that has an overwhelming chance of producing a hopelessly deformed or defective child is ample justification for such an operation.

What kind of operation is done to produce an abortion?

The procedure is identical to the one which is done a dozen times a day in hospitals all over the country on non-pregnant women. It is called Dilatation and Curettage, or D and C for short. This is how it goes:

The pubic hair is shaved and the entire vulvar area is prepared antiseptically. An instrument, called a speculum, is inserted into the vagina to distend the walls and provide access to the cervix. The opening into the cervix, normally about the diameter of a pencil lead, is dilated with another instrument. After it widens enough to admit about two fingers, a curette is introduced directly into the uterus. The curette is a special instrument consisting of a wide smooth loop of surgical steel on a large handle. Deftly, the surgeon scrapes the inside of the uterus with the curette. His goal is to dislodge the embryo from its attachment on the uterine wall. If he succeeds, the embryo is removed, a moderate amount of bleeding occurs, the vagina is filled with cotton packing, and the woman goes home. In a few days she is back to normal.

If the operation is done under sterile conditions the risk of complications is less than one per cent. With good anaesthesia and suitable drugs for pain there is little subsequent discomfort. The woman is back to household activities in a few days, back to sexual intercourse in a few weeks.

What if the mother just doesn't want the child?

That's when things get complicated. It depends on what her reasons are, where she lives, who she is, and the size of her bank balance.

In some areas of the country a pregnancy that endangers the mother's life qualifies her for a deliberate abortion. Of course it's not quite that simple. Usually she must find two or three doctors willing to confirm that she qualifies. She must also be able to afford the assorted medical fees and hospital costs. The whole package runs about a thousand dollars.

What if the woman doesn't really have anything wrong with her but just wants to end the pregnancy?

If she can find the required number of doctors to make the required diagnosis and comes up with the fee, she qualifies. Practically speaking, few wealthy women are denied an abortion whenever they desire one.

Jeannette, the wife of the president of a large bank, tells a typical story:

"Well, when I found out I was pregnant, I just couldn't stand the idea. Our children are both away in college and Harry and I were just starting to have fun again. It's not that I don't love children, but when you have our position in the community they can be such a bother."

She shrugged her mink jacket off her shoulders and lit another cigarette. "Well, then I told Charles. He's my gynaecologist. We've been friends for ever so many years and he and Harry play golf together every week.

"Well, Charles was a little stuffy at first but when Harry called him from the bank and emphasized how important it was to us, he came around. He asked me how long I had the bleeding. I told him, 'Don't be silly, I don't have any bleeding—I'm pregnant!' I should have known but he explained it.

"He went into all those silly old laws—I'm sure they weren't made for people like us. He told me if I said I had vaginal bleeding and didn't tell anyone I had missed my period they'd have to do a D and C to find out what was causing it. By the time they found out they were wrong, I wouldn't be pregnant any more. He said they would need two other doctors to approve the operation and that it would be a little expensive. After all, what's money for?"

Jeannette's solution was an easy one—all she needed was a wealthy husband and a doctor who agreed that a child should be spared a mother like Jeannette and a father like Harry. Sometimes it's even simpler.

Simpler than that?

Yes. If the woman lives in a "good" state the process is more direct. A woman living in one of the few areas where danger to the life or health of the mother is reason enough simply goes to her family doctor and tells her story. If another doctor or two agree, she appears before a group of three or four other doctors usually known as the Abortion Board. If they also agree, she may be unpregnant within the hour.

The cost is still high—and there are a lot of bureaucratic requirements to contend with. But she does solve her most urgent problem.

What if she doesn't live in a "good" state?

Then, in America, she has to do a little travelling. The easiest plan is simply to fly to one of the liberal states and have her abortion done there. California, Colorado, Georgia, and Maryland currently have the most liberal abortion laws; Michigan and Virginia may follow soon.

While these areas are somewhat reluctant to do out-of-state abortions, it is still possible, particularly if she has relatives or friends living there. The cost remains high.

If she can't get what she wants there, she needs a passport and an airline ticket. She can go to the "legal" countries or the "illegal" ones depending on her tastes in travel. The most popular illegal lands are Mexico and Puerto Rico. Both have strong statutes against abortion—both do a big business in illegal operations. The quality of the D and C runs all the way from first class to unimaginable. It is strictly a matter of price.

Which are the legal countries?

The legal countries most in fashion these days are Britain, Japan and Sweden. There the operation is just like any other, with the best doctors willing to perform it. Their fees are low, the hospital accommodations good, and the results satisfactory.

What about the woman who can't afford that kind of money?

That unfortunate lady must then travel around the corner into the Dark Ages. Society has turned its back on her and everything she does from that moment on will be a crime. If her doctor suggests an abortion, he stands to lose his license. If the chemist sells her some mixture to bring on an abortion, he is a criminal. If a neighbour tries to find someone to help her out, he can go to jail. In some parts of the country, she herself can be prosecuted for seeking a solution to her problems.

If she is married and has an understanding husband anxious to help her, it is still tough. If she is unmarried and her boy friend has taken wing it is terrible. If she has been impregnated by rape or incest, it is impossible. Imagine the state of mind of a young girl fertilized by a drunken rapist. What can she look forward to? What can the child look forward to?

What can a girl do in a situation like that?

Listen to her tell it. Ginny is twenty-three. She is a typist in an insurance office. Mike was an insurance salesman whose paper work she used to type up. They had been going out about six months when she found out she was pregnant. She told Mike about her predicament Thursday night over dinner. Friday he didn't show up at work. He never showed up at all after that. His apartment was empty, his phone disconnected; he just disappeared.

'I thought I was going to go out of my mind. I kept saying, 'This can't be happening to me! It just can't!' Well, it was, and after three or four days I stopped crying and tried to figure out something to do.

"I couldn't tell my parents—they're in their seventies and senile. They weren't much help even when they had all their buttons."

She managed a wry smile. Brushing her long blonde hair out of her eyes, she went on, "Well, I started asking around and I got the usual advice. All the girls knew something that would 'start your period.' 'Just take some of this and it'll bring you around.' God, I spent a fortune on that garbage! Later I threw up the last awful dose!"

Nearly every pharmacy has shelves loaded with dozens of preparations guaranteed to bring on delayed menstruation. They all work provided the delay is caused by a minor irregularity in the menstrual cycle. If the girl is pregnant they merely bring on fat balances for the manufacturer.

Ginny continued, "Then I started the work-outs. They said 'hot baths' so I took hot baths. I looked and felt like a lobster—a pregnant one. No good. Then they said exercise. So I exercised. I lifted the heaviest damn things I could find. I hoisted the sofa, the refrigerator, the television set. I would've picked up my car if my back hadn't been killing me by then."

Unfortunately for Ginny, lifting heavy objects rarely brings on an abortion. If not overdone, exercise, like hot baths, promotes a general feeling of well-being, unless of course you're pregnant and desperate.

"That's what affected me the most—I was so tremendously

depressed. I kept thinking, 'I'm going to lose my job and everything. Just for one lousy night I'm stuck with a kid I don't want
from a guy that I hate.' Every morning I woke up wishing I was
dead.

"About that time I got so I didn't care about anything. I was
already resigned to losing my job so I wasn't afraid to tell my
problem to Eleanor, the office manager. I figured, 'What the hell,
she's been married five times so she must've been in this spot at
least once or twice!' I was right."

Ginny went to the right person, in one sense. The overwhelming majority of deliberate abortions occur in married
women, usually those who have already had children. In another
way, her choice of Eleanor didn't work out so well.

"She was real nice. She said, 'Don't worry, honey, I been down
this road a couple of times myself.' She took me out to lunch that
day. I would've been better off if I'd stayed home. I was sick to my
stomach. I couldn't eat anything. She told me about this doctor,
anyway he used to be a doctor, who really wanted to help girls in
trouble. It sounded good to me then—if I'd only known.

"Anyway she made an appointment for me that Saturday afternoon. I had to come up with cash so I sold my car. I would've
sold anything to get the money. I met her in the office parking lot
just after noon—we went in her car. She drove all the way across
town to this crummy neighbourhood. We went upstairs into
what must be the filthiest 'surgery' of all time—you wouldn't
believe it! I was feeling bad by then but when I saw the doctor
who was going to work on me, I wanted to run away—only I had
no place to run. It was that or nothing.

"So this creep told me to take off my skirt and panties and
climb up on the table. I was half afraid he was going to rape me
but the way I felt it didn't matter.

"Then he asked for the money. That was the one thing I hadn't
expected. I started crying. Then he said if I would put on this old
pair of hip boots and walk around the office while he watched,
he'd do it cheaper! I must've flipped at that point—the whole

thing was so crazy! I remember I kept thinking, over and over, 'How did this ever happen to *me?* To *me?* To *me?*'

"I didn't care about anything by then. I just slid off that table half-naked, put on those crazy boots and started walking around. I noticed Eleanor was starting to pull up her skirt and then I passed out. When I woke up I was in my apartment all full of blood and I felt like my insides were falling out."

Ginny got the works. She fell into the hands of a psychopathic abortionist who gave her the full treatment: abortion, extortion, and sexual perversion, no extra charge. This one was a fetishist who was sexually aroused by girls in hip boots. After Ginny passed out, he had a little fun with Eleanor, who was his "salesman" and assistant. Then he went to work on Ginny. The exact order was really extortion, perversion, and abortion.

He was about average for his category of abortionist. Actually he had been a dentist who lost his license after a narcotics conviction. He was still addicted to drugs, which explained his filthy office in spite of his high prices.

In a certain sense, Ginny was lucky. She had her abortion and she got over her infection. Since Eleanor had taken a liking to her, she washed the instruments in the sink with soap and water. (Most customers took them the way they were.) That kept Ginny from getting a bad infection. In about a month she was feeling great.

Ginny was lucky in another way. She paid for a horrendous version of an operation that would have cost a Swedish or Japanese girl about £10—with a well-trained doctor in a spotless modern hospital. It could have been a lot worse.

Worse? How could it have been worse?

Well, Eleanor might not have washed the instruments. Most abortionists don't bother with such finicky little details. Their patients always get infected, though few of them die. They frequently end up in the emergency room of the County Hospital at midnight with a temperature of 105. Their stories are sometimes masterpieces—

"I don't know what happened, doctor. I must have been in an automobile accident."

Sometimes they are unconscious and there is no story. It could happen another way. The dentist, so far away from familiar territory, might have made a little mistake. Curetting a uterus under the best conditions is no easy job. It is roughly like trying to peel an apple with one hand—with both the hand and the apple in your back pocket.

During pregnancy, the uterus becomes soft, like an over-ripe pear. One slip and the instrument goes through the uterine wall into the abdominal cavity. Often it goes into the intestine too. That is a real surgical emergency and requires an immediate operation, an operation that no abortionist is willing or able to do.

If a girl is pregnant, wouldn't she be better off without one of these abortionists?

Sometimes it doesn't make any difference. A self-induced abortion can be just as dangerous. The traditional do-it-yourself method hasn't changed in the past ten thousand years. The primitive tribes in Africa use the same technique as the most up-to-date swinger. Only the instrument is different. The disconsolate African housewife uses her abortion stick. It may be an intricately carved family heirloom or just a sharpened branch she pulled from a tree. It doesn't matter because she only needs it for a moment.

She squats in front of her hut, pushes aside her bark-cloth skirt, and slides the stick into her vagina. She then guides it more or less carefully through the cervix and into the uterine cavity. Then she pushes it around vigorously, pulls it out and hopes for the best.

Eight thousand miles away her light-skinned sister is sprawled on her queen-sized bed. She brushes aside her expensive nylon underwear, spreads her carefully shaved and powdered legs and with the aid of her cherished magnifying mirror guides her abortion stick toward its final goal. Only she uses a coat hanger.

Both ladies have the same chance of infection—very good. Both have the same chance of perforating the uterus—very good. The white woman will probably pull through with antibiotics. The African lady may go to her great reward. There should be a better way.

Is there a better way?

Not in the abortion-at-home field. It only gets worse. A girl who's been through it tells it best:

Marge is twenty-eight and works in an insurance company. Her husband is in the Navy. Six weeks ago he left on a year's tour of duty to Japan. Two weeks after his ship sailed, Marge found out she was pregnant. She already has two children and just about makes it. An old car, a used TV, and a crummy apartment are all they can manage. When her husband gets the next promotion, things will be different. But she's pregnant now.

"When I came back from the OB clinic I said to myself, 'You just can't have another kid. If I stop working now the three of us will starve to death; even if I work the whole nine months I can't have the baby in the office. Besides, we just can't afford another kid.'

"So I was crying about this to the lady next door one Sunday morning and she told me about a friend of hers who fixes people up. I'll tell you, I was willing to do anything about that time."

One thing that women who consult abortionists have in common is desperation. They have come to the end of their rope and are willing to try anything. Under these circumstances, they will submit to the wildest and most bizarre manipulations. Let Marge continue:

"So the next night we went over to her house and she was nice. She didn't even ask for any money. We all sat down and had a couple of beers. If I knew what was going to happen I would've drunk *ten* beers. Then she showed me the stuff she used. It was a long rubber tube about as thick as your finger. I said, 'You ain't goin' to put that up me!' She said, still friendly, 'Well, you want to get rid of it, don't you?' She was right. So I lay down on the couch, pulled off my pants, and closed my eyes. It wasn't as bad as I thought it was going to be—at least not then.

"So I was laying there on the couch with this long rubber tube hanging out and I says, 'How long does it take?'

"Then this dame started laughing and said, 'It ain't that easy —now get up and start walking around.' "

Marge was getting some free lessons in abortion technique— although she was not really an eager pupil. That piece of rubber tubing is called a catheter and is available at most chemists— no prescription needed. Inserting it into the uterus is not enough. The abortee has to walk around and exercise vigorously to rub the tubing against the inside of the uterus. The aim is to tear the embryo away from its attachment.

"So I started walking around. I felt pretty damn silly—in about five minutes that piece of rubber fell out. Then they put me back on the couch and this time they put a coat hanger inside that damn tube and bent it so it couldn't fall out. They shoved it up and made me start walking. In about half an hour, I started bleeding, passed some chunks of stuff, and she said I was finished. Maybe she was finished but I kept bleeding for six weeks. I was so dumb I thought it was supposed to happen that way."

Our old friend the coat hanger makes another appearance. After lying on the cupboard floor with muddy shoes for a year or two it does not exactly make the ideal surgical instrument. But among abortionists, who cares? Actually this abortion solved Marge's problems—some of them anyway. What she passed was part of the embryo; the rest stayed inside. That's what caused the bleeding. As long as there is tissue remaining within the uterus the blood vessels cannot close and bleeding ensues. By the sixth week Marge had lost so much blood she had to see the doctor.

His diagnosis was "Incomplete abortion with secondary infection."

It was the last part that relieved Marge of her problems. The uterus, ovaries, and Fallopian tubes were so infected the only possible treatment was to remove them all. Marge will never have to worry about getting pregnant again. Of course, she is looking for another job now, she has started the change of life after losing her ovaries, and she is going to have a lot of explaining to do when her husband comes home. But all in all she got off pretty easily.

Pretty easily?

Yes. Most abortionists don't realize the uterus is a part of the inside of the body like the heart or lungs. Shoving a wire hanger down a person's throat would set off a series of reflexes—sweating, gagging, increased heart rate. These are designed to protect the body from the attack but sometimes they work the other way. When that ubiquitous bit of wire enters the uterus, the body's reflex control centre goes wild. Occasionally in the confusion the wrong buttons get pushed and pregnancy suddenly becomes a minor problem by comparison. The most feared accident is cardiac arrest. The reflex nerve impulses get going in the wrong direction, the heart stops, and the pregnancy is finished. The mother is finished, everything is finished. It would have been better to have the baby.

But cardiac arrest is pretty rare, isn't it?

Not to the person who gets it. The other possibilities are not exactly attractive either. If it is a do-it-yourself project the poor prospective mother works under many handicaps. She is frightened, depressed, unfamiliar with her own anatomy, and works with trembling hands. None of this contributes to the success of a surgical procedure. Sometimes she gets a knitting needle into the vagina and then pokes it up into the bladder. Wounds like this take years to heal and in the meantime every time she urinates, the urine trickles out the vagina too. If she lunges downward with the weapon it perforates the rectum and makes a more-or-less permanent connection between that area and the vagina. Every bowel movement is now detoured partially through the vaginal cavity.

Can't those perforations be sewn up?

Yes. The operations are complex, painful, expensive, and undependable. It is much better to avoid the extra passage in the first place.

What else can happen?

Another of the possibilities seldom appears out in the open. It has to be pieced together from newspaper stories and police files. The news item usually reads something like this:

"The nude body of Carol Ann Pratt, a young blonde divorcee, was found early this afternoon in her apartment by police. They had been alerted by her employer when she failed to report for work today. No signs of violence were evident; a complete investigation is under way."

The coroner's autopsy report read, in part:

" . . . twenty-seven year old white female approximately nine weeks pregnant. Vagina and uterine cavity contained small amount of weak solution of hydrogen peroxide; full lab analysis pending . . . examination of the brain revealed multiple areas of haemorrhage. Apparent cause of death: air embolism of brain."

The police report:

"The subject's nude body was found in the empty bathtub. No signs of struggle, violent entry, or trauma were noted. A douche bag containing a few drops of clear fluid was found on the bathroom floor nearby. A rubber catheter was noted in the sink."

These three short paragraphs constitute a young lady's epitaph.

This is probably what happened:

At bedtime the previous night Carol Ann finally decided it was time to get rid of the pregnancy. Taking the advice of one of her friends, she made up a weak solution of hair bleach and poured it into the rubber douche bag. She then slipped the end of the catheter over the small douche nozzle, undressed, climbed into the empty bathtub, inserted the catheter tip into the uterus, and squeezed the bag. From that moment on, she was doomed.

During pregnancy, the veins that supply the uterine lining are dilated and close to the surface, especially near the embryo. If air is injected into the uterus under pressure it will probably enter these veins. It then travels quickly to the brain where it causes coagulation of blood within the small blood vessels. Death occurs within a few moments. Carol Ann lived long enough to take the catheter out, stand up, and put it in the sink. Then she slumped back into the tub and died. Not much of a way for a pretty blonde to go.

If a girl just gets an infection from an abortion she usually gets over it, doesn't she?

Of course. Usually. It depends what kind of bacteria lived on the end of the umbrella rib that she forced into the warm, moist uterus. If they are the wrong kind, the tale has a different ending. Gas gangrene, for instance.

What's gas gangrene?

It is a rare condition seen primarily in wounded soldiers and badly botched abortions. Once introduced into a friendly environment like the uterus, a particular kind of bacteria multiply prodigiously, often at the rate of a billion a day. As they grow, they dissolve the tissues of their host, the young lady, and turn it into gas. The odour is unbearable, the destruction unbelievable, the result unthinkable.

As the tissues are consumed by the germs, the red pigments of the blood are separated and released into the circulation. This gives the skin an overall deep mahogany hue, like an old piano. The gas swells the organs grotesquely until they are gigantic. What was once a slender, attractive young girl now lies in a hospital bed with a tiny shrunken face, a horribly bloated belly, and a sun tan that looks like six weeks on the Riviera. There must be a better way.

Isn't there some medicine a woman can take to bring on an abortion?

Yes. There are a certain number of drugs which effectively kill the embryo and cause it to be expelled. Many of them are 100 per cent dependable in that respect.

Then why aren't they used by doctors?

Two reasons. One, it is illegal for a doctor to give a patient a drug to cause an abortion. Two, in killing the embryo, the drug frequently kills the mother.

All abortion drugs are poisons. The trick is to give just enough to poison the child without harming the mother. It is like shooting an apple off a woman's head with a cannon. A little too much, even a drop or two, and a simple abortion becomes suicide and murder.

The list of drugs that have been used is almost endless. Quinine, ergot, tansy, pennyroyal, aloes, are popular plant remedies dating back hundreds of years. They don't really work. In desperation some women have even tried Spanish fly—maybe with the theory that like cures like.

Metallic substances are more poisonous and thus potentially more lethal for both mother and child. Arsenic, mercury, lead, have all been used. If they kill the baby they usually kill the mother. In the days when matches were made of white phosphorus, women would occasionally eat match heads to solve their problems. This chemical causes atrophy of the liver—a long, lingering, painful death.

Then there is no drug that will cause an abortion without probably killing the mother as well?

Actually there is one class of drug that might do the job. This is the group known as anti-metabolites. They are used commonly in the treatment of leukaemia and certain types of cancer. They selectively kill certain blood cells and other types of tissues. If used during pregnancy, there is a chance they will kill the embryo without killing the mother. On the other hand they sometimes don't kill the embryo at all—they simply convert it into a nightmarish monster. Some of the anti-metabolite babies are born with a giant head and a tiny body. Others have a perfect head but no eyes. Others have the brain perfectly developed, but outside the skull. And so on. It gets to be a game of reproductive Russian Roulette. Pull the trigger by taking the medicine and eight months later you see the results—if you can bear to look at them. The other possibility is that the drug just kills the mother.

Isn't there a way to prevent all this terrible suffering?

There should be. Physicians, who are dedicated to alleviate human misery, are powerless to help the most helpless members of our society when they need help the most. Because the guardians of public morals, few of whom have ever been pregnant themselves, have decreed that abortion is a sin, millions of women each year are sentenced to terrible danger, crippling illness, and financial ruin, and the bungling incompetent abortion butchers are able to ply their trade. With rats one needs cats; thousands of police officers, prosecutors, and judges are tied up disposing of these vermin instead of constructively improving our society.

The women who lack the courage or the fear to descend into the abyss of illegal abortion give birth to hundreds of thousands of unwanted, unloved children. Our social planners in their omnipotence have decided that quantity not quality counts. Better ten urchins to languish on welfare than two loved and wanted children to enrich the world.

What about birth control?

Birth control via pills and gadgets will be a perfect method of controlling conception when there are perfect people. Human nature being what it is, men and women take sexual intercourse as they find it. Family planning is no match for throbbing genitals. Abortion is always an afterthought. It is retroactive birth control. Denying abortion is denying an individual the chance to correct his mistakes.

But shouldn't people be made to take the responsibility for their actions?

Unquestionably. Should a newborn child be propelled into a world that doesn't want him because his mother and father, on the one occasion they met each other, had too many drinks? Should a woman who fulfils her biological destiny by copulating pay for each sexual act with another pregnancy? By making deliberate abortion freely available the responsibility is placed upon the one who acts—not upon the innocent child resulting from that action.

Wouldn't making abortions easy encourage immorality?

Making abortions almost impossibly difficult hasn't kept anyone moral. It has only made law-abiding citizens into criminals and criminals into wealthier criminals.

In an era when man is transplanting organs, exploring distant planets, and manipulating living molecular structures, it is incredible that he is not allowed to control his own reproduction.

14

VENEREAL DISEASE

Why are syphilis and gonorrhoea called venereal diseases?

Venereal refers to Venus, the goddess of love. This makes the term especially inappropriate. You don't give diseases like this to someone you love, and you certainly don't love someone who gives them to you—that is once you realize what you've got.

Actually the expression has come to mean any disease transmitted by sexual contact.

What are some of the other venereal diseases?

Although most people think of syphilis and gonorrhoea when VD is mentioned, there are three lesser-known but serious venereal infections. They might be considered underground diseases—not only are they unknown to the average person, but even the victim is rarely aware of what is happening to him.

The conditions are insidious in onset, progress relentlessly, and cause widespread damage to the genitals. The sexual organs are riddled with holes, eaten away slowly, or distorted into shapeless monstrosities. The destruction is far more dramatic and immediate than anything produced by syphilis and gonorrhoea.

To make matters worse, in spite of the sophistication of modern medicine, for one of these diseases, no specific treatment exists. The victims are on their own.

If these diseases are so terrible, why aren't they better known?

It is rare for a heterosexual to be stricken. Up to now those who come down with the underground diseases rarely have spread it outside of their own group.

Syphilis and gonorrhoea can strike the mayor's daughter, the bank manager, solid citizens in general. The underground diseases afflict the errand boy, the homosexual prostitute, the call girl. These people never get into the newspaper, at least not on the society page. Nobody organizes fund drives for their nasty little infections. Not much happens until they start spreading it to "nice" people. That hasn't happened—yet.

Is there any chance that it will happen—that these underground infections will become widespread?

It is probably only a matter of time. As sexual activity in our society becomes more free, the rate of all types of VD increases astronomically.

Inevitably the mayor's daughter will come in contact with one of these infected victims. After that it may take only a month or so for the infection to diffuse to the bank manager.

That sounds impossible. How could something like that happen?

The recipe goes something like this: Take a sexually vigorous young lady of twenty-two, add birth control pills and maybe a little marijuana. Stir in some false confidence in penicillin, a dash of hippie philosophy, and a lot of immaturity.

Put all ingredients into a snappy new car that goes into some swinging neighbourhoods, and mix thoroughly. Incubate for ten days and the infection that results will be astounding.

What about the mayor's daughter and the call girl?

A variation of the same recipe. Let's say the call girl has a customer, maybe a shoe store manager whose wife doesn't understand him. He gets one of the underground diseases from her. A month later he spends the night in a motel with one of his customers, the young wife of a law student whose husband doesn't understand her. Now she comes down with it. Obviously her quest for understanding doesn't stop with the gent from the shoe store. Six weeks later at a party she pairs off with one of her husband's friends from school, a nice boy who's just had too much to drink. Guess who he is engaged to?

Two months after the party the mayor's nineteen-year-old daughter notices a vaginal discharge and a lump in her groin. With a few detours, it only took six months for the infection to get from the vagina of a call girl to the vagina of a debutante. Where else it has gone in the meantime is anybody's guess.

How about the bank manager?

His infection could be a dividend from the shoe store manager. Maybe the manager's secretary gets her shoes there and a little something else at the same time. When the boss's wife is absent visiting her mother, the boss is visiting his secretary. Two weeks later he notices a funny-looking sore on his penis. He never associates with call girls, at least not socially, but he associated with one sexually, if only by proxy.

As this sort of activity intensifies, it won't be long before everyone is exposed to these little-known but devastating venereal diseases.

What are these diseases anyway?

To start with the mildest first: chancroid. Chancroid is caused by bacteria that get into the skin of the genitals and form little pus-filled blisters. These rapidly break down into painful ulcers which spread over the entire pubic and genital area. The ulcers are particularly vicious since they attack the victim two ways. One type burrows deep into the skin; in men it may penetrate through the penis into the urethra so that urine leaks out uncontrollably. The other type of ulcer spreads rapidly over the skin surface to cover the stomach, groin, and thighs.

Fortunately, chancroid responds well to sulpha drugs once it is diagnosed—but that's the problem. It is extremely difficult to make a positive diagnosis in a specific patient. Effective control of this disease awaits improved diagnostic techniques. Further progress in research can be anticipated when more prominent people get the disease.

If that's the mildest, what are the others like?

Next on the list is granuloma inguinale. Like chancroid, it is caused by bacteria. Little bumps slowly break out over the surface of the genitals. Gradually they turn into raw oozing masses of tissue and spread out over the penis, labia, clitoris, and anus. Soon a pungent, overpowering stench develops. Once in a while the penis, clitoris, or scrotum become permanently and outlandishly enlarged. If the patient happens to develop a resistant case, the entire lower half of the body becomes ulcerated, the patient rapidly loses weight *and dies*.

Two other aspects make granuloma inguinale dangerous. The early manifestations are painless, encouraging victims to postpone treatment until the condition is well advanced. In addition, three months must elapse between exposure and the first sign of infection, by which time the original carrier of the disease may have infected scores of others.

On the bright side, if the disease is treated early and if it responds to antibiotics, good results can be expected.

How could anything be worse than that?

That brings us to Lymphogranuloma Venereum, or LGV for short. About three weeks after exposure the usual small bump appears on the sexual organs. Two weeks later another lump the size of an egg appears in the groin. Then the trouble really begins.

LGV is entirely different from all other venereal diseases. It is the only one caused by a virus. (The others originate from bacteria.) Bacteria respond to antibiotics—viruses don't. To make matters worse, it is the only venereal disease that has a pronounced effect on the entire body. The sufferer usually feels sick. Fever, chills, and joint pain are common. Unfortunately they are nothing in comparison with what happens later on.

The most humiliating and disabling changes occur when the infection spreads from lymph glands in the groin to those around the anus. At that point anal stricture occurs, and scar tissue completely obstructs the anus. Defecation becomes first painful, then impossible. The only hope is constant dilatation of the rectum—for a lifetime. In a desperate attempt to keep the vital passage open, the sufferer pays a weekly visit to his doctor who inserts a gloved and lubricated finger into the rectum and vigorously stretches the opening.

More and more LGV is being spread from one homosexual to another via anal intercourse. Rectal stricture is rapid and intense, but for obvious reasons is less disabling among homosexuals.

Another curse of LGV results from swollen lymph nodes breaking through the skin at dozens of different points. This pus drains through the openings constantly, particularly in the area between the genitals and the anus; this area is known as the perineum. Because the pus flows from a dozen or more tiny holes simultaneously the patient is said to have a "sprinkling-can perineum." Unfortunately it is an accurate description.

Treatment? A typical medical textbook says: "Unfortunately no specific treatment for Lymphogranuloma Venereum exists at the present time."

But aren't syphilis and gonorrhoea much more serious than the other venereal diseases?

In the years since syphilis became established in Europe (about the fifteenth century), the disease has acquired a fearsome reputation. It is depicted as The Great Destroyer, ravaging the innocent and not-so-innocent indiscriminately, filling mental hospitals, and leaving a trail of eroded bodies and warped minds. Once a person is exposed, he must become infected. Once infected, he succumbs helplessly as the malady progresses. Nothing could be further from the truth.

Obviously syphilis and gonorrhoea are serious infectious diseases and as such deserve the attention due any hazard to public health. However, when viewed objectively, some interesting facts emerge about their effects on human beings.

Take syphilis for example: it is often presented as a dramatic example of a dread disease. Moralists frequently cite syphilis to illustrate the wages of sin. If so, sin comes pretty cheap these days.

The truth is that if 100 people contract syphilis on the same day, fifty of them will never experience any ill effects whatsoever. In other words, half of all the people infected with this "terrible disease" will never show any symptoms or even know they have it.

Another twenty-five will have some minor symptoms without any disability. The remaining twenty-five can expect serious symptoms, including disability and death. These statistics are based on the assumption that none of the 100 receive any treatment. If they are treated promptly, virtually 100 out of 100 will be completely free of the disease.

Gonorrhoea offers even better odds. About fifty per cent of men are naturally resistant to gonorrhoea. Even if they are massively exposed to the infection, they will not succumb. The other half of the male population, even if infected, still comes out pretty well. Only ten per cent of those, or five per cent of the total, will have serious problems. That unlucky five per cent may take some consolation in knowing that serious disability or death from gonorrhoea is almost unknown. The disease responds quickly and completely to simple, inexpensive drugs.

Those are still terrible chances to take, aren't they?

Certainly: No matter how the odds are quoted, if you get the infection it might as well be a million to one against you. Nobody pretends that coming down with either of these conditions is much fun.

Isn't it possible to get syphilis without having sex, like say from a toilet seat?

Certainly if you're an acrobat. If you customarily occupy the toilet seat so that your sexual organs are pressed firmly against it, you have a good chance of picking up syphilis—provided of course that the person who used the toilet seat just before you was also an acrobat infected with the disease.

So these conditions are always transmitted by sexual contact?

Not always. Rarely, physicians and nurses who are in contact with syphilis contract the infection. If they are careless in handling bloody instruments and needles from syphilitics, they run a significant risk of being infected. Of course doctors and nurses can get it the regular way, too.

How does syphilis start?

The first sign of syphilis appears about two weeks after exposure. It consists of a small painless sore at the site of infection.

At the site of infection? What does that mean?

Depending on who you are, it may mean a lot. Just as Sherlock Holmes could tell a man's occupation by the calluses on his hands, the doctor can tell the patient's sexual inclinations by the location of his syphilitic sore.

In the average man a syphilitic ulcer occurs on the penis. In the average woman, it can be found on the labia minora. In those with an inquiring mind, the sore can appear on the fingertip. The female breast is also a common location. Lips come in for their share of infection. In homosexuals, the sore can be found on the mucous membranes of the anus. Once in a while an adventurous gentleman turns up with syphilis of the tonsils.

What happens to the sore?

Disarmingly, it goes away. All by itself, without treatment, it disappears.

As a matter of fact in the days before modern therapy of syphilis evolved, a basic knowledge of the natural history of the disease allowed faith healers and other quacks to reap fortunes. These crooks guaranteed to cure the French Pox, as syphilis was known in England (or the English Pox, as it was known in France). They advertised in houses of prostitution, employed runners to spread the word, even offered their services on the stage curtain of cheap music halls.

When the newly infected customer appeared (after paying cash in advance), he was given a bottle of worthless grease and told to rub it on his sore, and was assured that his disease would disappear within sixty days.

The swindlers weren't really taking any chances. Ninety per cent of syphilitic ulcers clear spontaneously in that period of time. There was also a fringe benefit for the phonies: even though the ulcer goes away, the victim continues to spread the disease to all comers. Every customer netted a bumper crop of new suckers.

Then syphilis always starts with an ulcer somewhere on the body?

Not always. Half of the women infected and one-third of the men never develop an ulcer at all. They may have no symptoms whatsoever, or two or three months later so-called secondary symptoms may develop. These take the form of a mild skin rash, inflamed patches on the mucous membranes of the mouth or sexual organs, or small flat warts around the vagina or anus.

In some cases, the unfortunate infectee has to stay for a double feature—he gets both the primary ulcer and the secondary skin involvement. If he happened to be treated by these crooks, he might be rightfully indignant.

How does gonorrhoea act?

Any time from two days to two weeks after exposure, a man with gonorrhoea notices burning on urination, coupled with a white discharge. The inflammation hangs on for awhile and then goes away.

Is that all there is to it?

Not quite. If he is going to be one of the unlucky few, months or years later he wakes up one morning with a full bladder, goes to the bathroom as usual, and tries to urinate. Nothing happens. At first the poor fellow is surprised. As he continues to strain with no results, he becomes concerned. After an hour of squeezing with no effect, and a painfully distended bladder, he is panic-stricken.

What happened?

A simple little plumbing emergency. The smouldering gonorrhoeal infection has slowly deposited scar tissue in the urethra, that is, the little channel that runs from the urinary bladder through the penis to the outside. No matter how hard he tries the poor man just can't get the urine out. Eventually of course the bladder will empty itself by rupturing and spilling its contents inside the body, but that only makes his problem worse.

What's the solution?

As mentioned, it is simply a plumbing problem. The doctor takes a stainless steel rod about the diameter of the little finger and gently forces it up the urethra. (Unfortunately the patient doesn't consider it to be gentle.) This reams out the tubing and allows the urine to drain. Then the doctor replaces the rod with a rubber hose of the same diameter (called a catheter) which allows the urine to continue to drain.

Is this the way the patient has to urinate from then on?

Not so long ago that was the way it worked. Before the late 1930s (before an effective treatment for gonorrhoea existed), men with chronic cases carried these sixteen-inch rubber catheters with them at all times. Inside the hat band was often a convenient place. When the time came to urinate they simply reached into their hats, pulled out the catheter, slipped it up the urethra and drained the bladder. Back into the hat until next time. Almost every doctor had his faithful patients who came weekly to have the urethra reamed out so that their plumbing wouldn't clog.

Does that still happen?

Fortunately about the time that men's hats went out of fashion, so did catheters. When the sulpha drugs came into common use, about 1938, everything changed. The treatment of gonorrhoea became fast and reliable and most complications were avoided. As penicillin was introduced, the results were even better.

Urethral obstruction from gonorrhoea is now almost a medical rarity.

What happens to women with gonorrhoea?

That is not such a cheerful situation. Since obvious signs of infection are so rare in women, gonorrhoea is much harder to diagnose. The infection may fulminate in the uterus, ovaries, and Fallopian tubes, causing serious damage. Eventually the tubes are sealed off—permanent sterility results. Of course this outcome is not necessarily a bad one.

How can sterility not be bad?

If you're talking about a prostitute, it's not bad. Gonorrhoea is sometimes known among professionals as "the hooker's friend." To a lady of the evening pregnancy is embarrassing, inconvenient, and expensive. Before birth control pills, the risk was much higher. Gonorrhoea helped bring down the odds.

Doesn't gonorrhoea prevent every prostitute from getting pregnant?

The world of biology is full of surprises and one of them is that many prostitutes are immune to gonorrhoea. No one knows why —the best guess is that massive and prolonged exposure to the condition may build up their resistance.

Then gonorrhoea is not really such a dangerous disease after all?

Correct, with two exceptions. First, arthritis. As mentioned, about five per cent of untreated infections later develop gonorrhoea of the joints. Without treatment the results can be pretty awful. With treatment almost everyone gets better.

The second exception is one of those rare situations where passing a law can virtually eliminate a disease. In nearly every state in America it is mandatory for newborn babies to have silver nitrate solution or penicillin ointment applied to their eyes at birth. Usually this is done within seconds of delivery. This treatment is substantially 100 per cent effective in preventing gonorrhoea of the eyes. Previously, if the mother had gonorrhoea, the child's eyes were infected as he passed through the vagina. Without treatment, permanent blindness was certain to result. The only cases seen now are in babies delivered outside hospitals to women with gonorrhoea.

If it's so easy to eliminate gonorrhoea of the eyes, why can't gonorrhoea of the penis and vagina be eliminated the same way?

From a scientific point of view, gonorrhoea could be wiped out rapidly and effectively. As a bonus, at no extra cost in time or money, syphilis could be made a thing of the past.

Both these conditions are well understood by doctors, easily diagnosed by inexpensive, dependable laboratory tests, and absurdly simple to treat.

Has anything like this ever been done before?

Medical history is full of precedents. Typhoid fever is a good example. Once a serious threat in this country, even before the condition was fully understood by doctors, it was virtually eliminated without drugs or effective laboratory tests.

Then what's holding up the war on venereal diseases?

The real barrier appears to be the psychological one. For a long time venereal disease was considered punishment for sins. Bad people who did bad things with their genitals got punished by big sores on the bad organs. Apparently the bad folks never understood the moral lesson because they continued to go around giving other bad people the same sores on their bad organs.

The great awakening came during World War II when it looked as if the entire American army was going to get VD. The guardians of morality swung into action with their usual fervour and the War Department made it a serious offence for a soldier to get VD. Condoms were supplied freely and penicillin was given before and after sexual contact.

As a result VD among the troops was almost eliminated. After the war the same enthusiasm carried over into public health work and the phoney moral barriers collapsed. The campaign in America was conducted via radio, TV, magazines, matchbook covers—even by skywriting. It paid off—the diseases were almost knocked out.

Almost knocked out?

As usual America won the war and lost the peace. The word got around that nobody had to worry about VD any more because of penicillin. So everybody forgot to worry. They also forgot about penicillin.

The bacteria that cause VD are primitive organisms—they neither remember nor forget—they just keep spreading. And spread they did.

There were a few other unfortunate coincidences that came along about that time. Birth control pills appeared on the scene and removed the last barrier to fearless fornication. Without the risk of VD or pregnancy, how bad could it get?

During that period homosexuality took a great leap forward. Whatever the reason, the incidence of sexual contacts between male homosexuals multiplied tenfold. This was a special complication since promiscuity among homosexuals makes even the greatest Don Juan look anaemic by comparison. Furthermore, homosexual encounters are so casual that often the participants don't even see each others' faces. Such informality makes it impossible to trace the spread of infection.

The final event is probably the most tragic. When teen-age

hippies made the scene the last chance of controlling VD by traditional methods went out of the window.

These young people are a set of kids who are out for a good time at any cost, no holds barred. They will do anything any time with anyone. (Some cynics say they're just following the example of their parents.) In this twelve- to seventeen-year-old group, sex is the order of the day. Any kind of sex—without experience and without restraint. Most teenage hippies will take on all comers— receiving infections and dispensing them freely.

The tragic part is this—because of their tender years they rarely even know the symptoms of the sexual diseases. Even if they do suspect infection it's tough for them to get treatment. No doctor can treat a minor without the parent's consent and no teenie wants mum and dad to know they picked up the clap. The other problem is finding mum and dad. They're usually out bopping on their own—separately.

If things are that bad, how can we stop VD?

The answer has been staring us in the face for twenty years: penicillin. At a cost of less than £1, every infected individual in the entire country could be cured of syphilis and gonorrhoea completely by a single injection of penicillin. Those who were about to come down with the diseases would be protected—it would never develop. Everyone treated would be unable to transmit or contract the conditions for the next fifteen to thirty days. For a few pence a head, these vicious venereal diseases could be sent the way of typhoid, measles, polio, and the bubonic plague.

Then why hasn't it been done?

One of the biggest obstacles to destroying these diseases once and for all is lack of money. The single most important requirement for combating any health problem is sufficient finances to support research, drug development, and prevention.

Unfortunately these conditions don't lend themselves to fund drives and heart-rending publicity campaigns. Can you imagine a little girl ringing the doorbell imploring you to give money to fight syphilis? What aspiring beauty queen looks forward to being crowned Miss Gonorrhoea? Would anyone buy a couple of tickets to the Annual Venereal Disease Ball? Who would respond to a television appeal picturing a sweating, red-faced truck driver as a victim of VD?

Yet each of these techniques has been used to sell the fund-raising campaigns for children's diseases. These emotionally charged appeals don't work with venereal diseases. Nobody thinks of babies getting syphilis, but they do.

Babies get syphilis?

Yes. In infants and children syphilis is devastating. The children are ruined both physically and mentally—if they live. About twenty-five per cent of infants infected in the uterus die before birth. Another twenty-five per cent die in the first few weeks of life. The rest might be better off dead.

The survivors are divided into two groups. One set has a grab bag of deformities including collapse of the bridge of the nose (making the nose flat and saddle-shaped), shrivelled, notched teeth with giant spaces between them, distorted leg bones ("sabre shins"), blindness, and deafness. The lucky ones only develop gummas. A gumma is a chronic low-grade infection of a part of the body which may persist for years. The tissues break down, are replaced by scar tissue, break down again, and so on, intermittently. This variation affects primarily the skin, liver, bones, testicles, and larynx.

Can't children's syphilis be cured as easily as the adult form?

Except for the fifty per cent who die before or after birth, most children respond well to treatment. But no drug can restore their teeth and bones. No drug can make them see and hear again. The destruction of innocent children is probably the most compelling argument for an all-out victory against venereal diseases.

Is it really possible to finish with VD once and for all?

There is a way it can be done. Simply, cheaply, effectively. Let us proclaim one day as Victory Over VD Day. With appropriate support from religious leaders, well-known athletes, movie stars, and other influential people and pre-publicity from our gigantic communications network everyone is prepared emotionally. On that day, everyone in the age group where sexual intercourse is possible receives one injection of penicillin. That's it. Virtually all those who are infected with syphilis or gonorrhoea on that day will be cured. Those who have been exposed will never come down with the diseases. What is most important, the gigantic reservoir of infection, that festering pool of disease in millions of penises and vaginas, will be eliminated. It is like getting a new lease on life. From a public health point of view the slate will be wiped clean and these destroyers will be cut down to peanut size.

But wouldn't it cost too much?

Assuming the cost would be a couple of shillings per patient, and that 100,000,000 people would be injected, the expense would be £10,000,000. This sum is pocket money compared with national expenditure on war and welfare.

What about those allergic to penicillin?

They could be given an alternate antibiotic at the same cost.

Why are these infections common among homosexuals?

Homosexuals are capable of prodigious promiscuity. Simply by the laws of probability, sooner or later a wide-ranging, infected homosexual will come in contact with another, similarly inclined but "clean". The infection then passes to both their partners and their partner's partners and their partner's partner's partners and so on.

What about the underground diseases, LGV, granuloma inguinale, and chancroid? Would this plan cure them, too?

Unfortunately not. But these are the neglected diseases anyway. Once syphilis and gonorrhoea are out of the way, much more money and time would be available for them.

Would this programme really cure syphilis and gonorrhoea?

Not in the usual sense. It would reduce the number of cases drastically, break the chain of infection, and dramatically underscore both the problem and the simplicity of the solution. Existing public health facilities could be zeroed in on high-exposure groups such as prostitutes and homosexuals. Victory Over VD Day might even be celebrated annually for awhile until the diseases finally succumb.

Isn't there an easier way to do the job?

If there is, it must be a well-kept secret. The rate of infection among all categories of Americans and Britons is soaring. In Haiti, for example, it is estimated that ninety per cent of the population suffers from some form of veneral disease. Haiti is a backward country, but in this case our progress works against us. Mobility, leisure time, affluence, and freedom combine to create a perfect climate for VD.

The fact is that the VD rate is increasing faster in the United States than in any other country in the world.

Today, in England and Wales 1 in 200 of the population attends a V.D. clinic every year. In the last few years V.D. among women has increased rapidly. Today it is 1 woman to 1·8 men, almost the "level" record of the sexes in Sweden.

15

MENOPAUSE

What is the menopause?

Technically, the menopause is that time in a woman's sexual development when her menstrual periods stop. Actually, it is one of the most critical moments of her entire life. Cessation of menstruation is only the superficial manifestation of the profound changes under way, changes that are critical to her future happiness. Another name for the menopause is the change of life.

What causes the change of life, anyway?

A defect in the evolution of human beings. About 500,000 years ago, people were constructed with economy in mind. The average life expectancy was thirty to thirty-five years and most of the organs were designed to last about that long. (Vital parts such as the heart and brain were built a little better.) Then modern medicine entered the picture and made people live much longer than they had ever been intended to. Once upon a time a woman expired before her hormones did. Today her body lives on for thirty or more years after the ovaries have died.

Do the ovaries actually die?

For all practical purposes, they do. As the fortieth year approaches, the blood supply to those small egg-shaped glands gradually decreases. Cell by cell, the organ withers away and is gradually replaced by scar tissue. By the time the menopause is well advanced the ovaries have as much life as a fingernail or a lock of hair.

Does it make any difference if the ovaries stop working?

Only if you are a woman and they happen to be your ovaries. The entire basis for femininity is the hormone produced by the ovaries, oestrogen. This is the stuff that makes girls different from boys. Secreted into the bloodstream drop by drop, this clear liquid is distributed through the entire body. At the time of puberty it causes the breasts to develop, lays down deposits of subcutaneous fat at the hips, thighs, and buttocks, and keeps the complexion soft and hairless. It also triggers development of the labia and clitoris as well as the uterus and vagina. It works under the direct supervision of the pituitary gland which regulates the ovary by its own hormone, gonadotropin.

Oestrogen is also responsible for that strange mystical phenomenon, the feminine state of mind. It makes girls think like girls. It makes girls act like girls, especially when it comes to sex. Oestrogen rules women sexually—the word itself comes from the Greek word *oistros*, or mad desire. It is the ebb and flow of oestrogenic hormone during the menstrual cycle that is primarily responsible for the variations in female sexual desire. Once the ovaries stop, the very essence of being a woman stops.

Oestrogen is responsible for all the physical female sexual functions. It brings on sexual development, menstruation, ovulation, and plays an important role in pregnancy. It also affects the way women think sexually. Normal men and normal women both have a mature and realistic approach to sex. However, they arrive at it from different points of view. During the menstrual cycle, the amount of oestrogen in the body tends to rise and fall. When there is more oestrogen available, the women tend to feel contented and confident. As the oestrogen declines, she becomes restless and even aggressive. One of the important reasons why women are more changeable than men is that every thirty days their oestrogen level goes from near zero to a very high level and back to zero again. Most women tolerate this admirably. If men had their sex hormones taken away and given back twice a month, they probably would have made a worse mess of this world than they have with their hormones intact.

How does it happen?

Let a woman describe it.

Irene is forty-eight. She manages a small dress shop to keep busy since her children have married and moved away. Her menopause started two years ago.

"Doctor, if I didn't know better, I would think I was being turned into a man. At first when my periods stopped, I thought, 'Thank goodness that's over. No more pains, no more nuisance.' Now I'm not so sure. At least when I was having periods, I felt like a woman."

"What changes have you noticed?"

"The first thing I noticed was that my body was changing. It was as if everything were falling down. My breasts began to sag, the upper part of my body got thinner and all the fat went to my hips, abdomen, and lower legs. I'm not very happy about that.

"Then my skin and hair got terribly dry and I began to wrinkle up. I've become ten years older in the past two years. If that wasn't enough, everything I eat seems to go to fat. Gaining fifteen pounds in six months just isn't like me. And the hot flashes —I feel like I'm standing in front of an oven."

What's a hot flash?

An unbearable sensation of heat that menopausal women experience. It is probably the most common symptom of "the change." Caused by dilatation of blood vessels at the surface of the skin, most women describe it in dramatic terms:

"I felt like I was standing in front of a blast furnace!"

"Now I know what it feels like to go to hell!"

"I wake up at two a.m. on fire—I want to go out and roll in the snow!"

These thermal reactions can occur as often as every ten minutes, day and night. The usual quota, fortunately, is about four a day.

Do all women have these changes at the menopause?

Irene was noticing the general changes from oestrogen starvation. Weight gain, shifting of fat deposits, increased wrinkling of the skin, and dryness of the hair are annoying. There are worse things to come:

"But this is the reason I'm here, doctor. In the last few months I've started to grow hair on my face. And my voice is getting deeper. But that's not all . . ."

Irene began to sound embarrassed.

"I can't even have relations with my husband any more."

"Why is that? What seems to be the trouble?"

"I don't know. I can't seem to describe it. My—my—it just isn't—he can't even——"

She was gritting her teeth.

Patient questioning by the doctor revealed Irene was trying to tell him her vagina was shrinking. The atrophy had progressed to the point where the vaginal opening would no longer admit her husband's penis. Irene's sexual desire had vanished more than a year before and intercourse was a monthly event. On the most recent occasion, it was as if the vagina had vanished. Combined with the other body changes, this dramatic event caused a panicky reaction.

Her description was accurate. Without oestrogen, the quality of being female gradually disappears. The vagina begins to shrivel, the uterus gets smaller, the breasts atrophy, sexual desire often disappears, and the woman becomes completely desexualized. Actually it is a little worse than that.

What could be worse?

As the oestrogen is shut off, a woman comes as close as she can to being a man. Increased facial hair, deepened voice, obesity, and the decline of breasts and female genitalia all contribute to a masculine appearance. Coarsened features, enlargement of the clitoris, and gradual baldness complete the tragic picture. Not really a man but no longer a functional woman, these individuals live in the world of intersex. Many of them are emotionally marooned as well. Their children have departed, their relationships with their husbands have declined, and sex no longer interests them. Sometimes the husband suffers as keenly. This is how one of them, Harry, tells it:

"It's like some kind of bad dream, doc! Up until last year Peggy was a perfect wife."

"A perfect wife?"

"Well, we've had our little disagreements but nothing like this. Now it's crazy! No sex, no fun, nothing! Every time I turn around she's complaining about something else. 'Why don't we go out more? Why don't I pay more attention to her? How come I'm not like other husbands?' Then if I don't get down on my knees and apologize, she blows up. Starts crying and won't talk to me for a couple of days. If this doesn't stop pretty soon, I'm going to be as nutty as she is!"

Unfortunately, Harry's situation is typical. In addition to physical changes the menopause can bring a lot of mental altera-

tions, too. Depression, irritability, and insomnia become the order
of the day.

Are the mental changes from lack of oestrogen, too?

It's hard to say. When a woman sees her womanly attributes
disappearing before her eyes, she is bound to get a little depressed
and irritable. This reaction, superimposed on an oestrogen deficiency, can make plenty of trouble. At this stage the divorce rate
takes a big leap, and the unhappiness rate (which cannot be
measured statistically) goes through the roof.

To many women the menopause marks the end of their useful
life. They see it as the onset of old age, the beginning of the end.
They may be right. Having outlived their ovaries, they may have
outlived their usefulness as human beings. The remaining years
may be just marking time until they follow their glands into
oblivion. *But it doesn't have to be that way.*

Why not?

Because she has been castrated by Father Time is no reason for a
modern woman to give up the battle. She has many weapons at
her disposal, if she will only use them. If she is determined and if
her doctor is skilful, they can virtually turn back the clock.

How can they do that?

By replacing the lost hormone. No one can bring back the ovaries
but the substance they once produced in abundance can be replaced. Most of the degenerative changes resulting from lack of
oestrogen can be reversed by appropriate administration of hormone tablets or injections.

The first thing a woman notices, within a few weeks of starting
the medication, is a sudden feeling of well-being. After months or
years of depression and discouragement, the change is more than

welcome. Gradually other nice things begin to happen. The voice goes up an octave or two, facial hair diminishes and becomes downier, and the breasts become firmer. The elastic fibres of the skin regain some of their strength and wrinkles recede. The skin and hair get back their old consistency and sheen. With the help of a diet, extra pounds come off and something resembling a feminine figure returns. The effect can be dramatic: Evelyn is in her fifties. She finally got around to seeing her doctor about the menopause six months ago.

"I don't believe it! Even though it's happening to me, I don't believe it! When I went to the doctor I was so desperate I was even thinking about killing myself. Now I feel like I'm sixteen again. It's even a little embarrassing. My breasts are getting bigger and I find myself thinking more about sex."

The effect on the genitalia is striking too. As Evelyn said, it is almost like puberty. The uterus enlarges, the vagina lengthens, the vaginal lining becomes moist and receptive, the clitoris diminishes to a more feminine size, and everything feels right again.

What about women like Irene? Can they be helped, too?

Most of the time. Irene's doctor would probably do it gradually. First he would advise her to administer oestrogen directly into the vagina in the form of a cream. After a few weeks of this treatment the vaginal tissues would stretch and soften enough to admit the penis. Later, oestrogen tablets and injections would do even more, but the primary responsibility rests with Irene and her husband.

What would they have to do?

Engage in regular and frequent sexual intercourse. In the world of biology the key phrase is, "Use it or lose it!" Any structure that is not utilized regularly and vigorously withers away. The vagina is no exception. A combination of replacement hormone and conscientious copulation will preserve the genitals better than anything else.

What kind of hormone is used to replace the oestrogen produced by the ovaries?

Oestrogen from any other source. As long as the substance is oestrogenic, it doesn't seem to matter where it comes from. One common source is urine. Females with active ovaries pass a relatively large amount of oestrogen in their urine. Menopausal women have been successfully treated with hormone extracted from human urine and horse urine. They would probably do as well on penguin urine if it were available. The only thing that matters is the chemical composition of the hormone. Oestrogen has even been synthesized from soya beans.

The method of administration doesn't make much difference either. Most women take their hormones by mouth, in tablet form. Many others receive it by injection. At one time it was even given by implanting little pellets under the skin. What matters is that it enters the bloodstream and is distributed throughout the body.

Don't these hormones cause cancer?

There is no reliable evidence that oestrogens cause cancer. Researchers have been interested in that question for years and have conducted thousands of careful experiments. The only precaution is this: women who have malignant tumours of the breast or uterus should not take oestrogens since the hormone may cause the tumour to grow faster. As far as precipitating a tumour is concerned, oestrogens won't do it.

The other side of the picture is even more encouraging. It is likely that adequate amounts of oestrogen throughout life protect a woman against cancer of the breast or uterus. Hormones also protect against some other serious diseases.

What diseases do they protect against?

Oestrogenic hormones offer outstanding protection against heart attacks. It is almost unknown for a woman with the normal amounts of oestrogen to suffer a heart attack. After the menopause, women begin to die from coronary thrombosis, rarely before. Gout, with its crippling arthritis, is almost unknown in a menstruating woman, due to her oestrogen supply. Some years ago, doctors tried to apply this knowledge to men. In an attempt to protect men who had suffered a heart attack from another attack, they administered high doses of oestrogens.

Did it work?

They never really got a chance to find out. All the men developed gynaecomastia—enlargement of the breasts, and complete loss of interest in sex. Total impotence went along with the deal. The men decided they would rather run the risk of another heart attack. Oestrogens given to women after the menopause also protect them against hardening of the arteries. No woman was ever heard to complain if her breasts became a little more impressive.

There is another disease which makes the use of oestrogens in the menopause vital. This condition is seen mainly in women, in their late fifties and older. It has the impressive name of osteoporosis, and it is a grotesquely dramatic disease. If a woman is starved for hormones, the calcium and phosphorus gradually drain from her bones. The process is something like taking the mortar from between the bricks in a wall—the wall remains standing but loses its strength. Most affected are the spinal vertebrae which carry the full weight of the body. After a period of time they may collapse, one after the other, like dominoes. The process is silent and insidious and relatively painless—at most the patient may complain of a little lumbago. As the vertebrae fall in, the woman actually loses height, sometimes at the rate of a half-inch or more per year. Obviously hormones can't put the broken bones together again but they can stop further destruction. Other joint problems, from the same cause, often clear up miraculously on hormone therapy.

Isn't it true that some women don't need hormones? Don't they just get over the menopause?

It is true that a small group of doctors believe that the menopause is something women go through and eventually get over. They never give hormones or much of anything else except manly advice like, "Just get hold of yourself! Ignore your hot flashes!" This group is composed exclusively of male doctors; male doctors who have never had a hot flash, never watched their breasts wrinkle up, never had their spinal column collapse.

There is another group of physicians at the other extreme. They believe that every woman should be given hormones in the amount and variety required to keep her actively menstruating throughout her entire life. Some of these doctors are treating little ninety-five-year-old ladies who get their period regularly every month.

How do they accomplish that?

It's easy. The doctor prescribes a little progesterone with the oestrogen supply according to a fixed schedule. Each month, after the tablets are stopped, the period starts. This technique is probably harmless and may give a psychological lift to some ladies—the ninety-five-year-old is the proudest patient in her nursing home. Most experts don't feel that artificial menstruation is really necessary and don't recommend it except in special cases. Other doctors combine a little of the male sex hormone, testosterone, with the oestrogen.

Why do they do that?

Strangely enough, testosterone helps to eliminate the hot flashes. It also improves the texture of the vaginal lining.

Is it good to give male sex hormones to women?

Provided they need it, there's no reason why they shouldn't have it. Every woman has her own supply anyhow. The adrenal glands, small organs sitting atop the kidneys, produce testosterone throughout a lady's lifetime. That is one of the reasons a lack of oestrogen results in masculinization. Unopposed male hormone brings on things like clitoral hypertrophy, hairiness, and deepened voice. As the woman grows older the secretion of testosterone begins to decline as well. Since that hormone too, in appropriate amounts, is vital to her well-being, it makes sense to replace it as required. One of the most important things testosterone administration does is increase sexual interest and drive after the menopause.

Do women lose their sexual desire in the change of life?

Many of them do. With depression, hot flashes, aches and pains, and all the rest, a lot of women couldn't care less about sex. Restoration of oestrogens with a little testosterone added does wonders for this problem. On the other hand some women have a tremendous increase in sexual drive after menstruation stops. This is probably a psychological change. When fear of pregnancy diminishes, many women's sexual desires intensify. This resurgence of sexual drive may bring on two other problems.

What are they?

The first one concerns the husband. At the time when his sexual interest and ability may be slipping, his wife suddenly is rejuvenated. Her demands may be more than he can handle. The second problem is pregnancy. It is possible to become pregnant during the change of life. Menstruation may stop but ovulation occasionally goes on. For the past twenty-five years the woman has been relating pregnancy to menstruation or the lack of it—if she keeps playing by the same rules, a change of life baby may be the result.

How long is birth control necessary for a woman?

To be reasonably safe, she should continue contraception for at least one year after the last menstrual period. If another period shows up after eleven months, she needs to wait another year. Even then she is not absolutely safe—more than one woman in her fifties has become pregnant.

Can a woman take oestrogens and birth control tablets at the same time?

Certainly. Birth control tablets are just a combination of oestrogens and the other female hormone, progesterone. The dosage should be regulated by her doctor but the two medications are compatible.

Do women who start the change of life early because of surgery need hormones, too?

Women who enter the menopause surgically need oestrogens just as much (or more) than those whose ovaries give out gradually. The sudden withdrawal of hormone support requires prompt and energetic action on the part of both patient and doctor to minimize the discomfort and damage. The same applies to the small group of girls who start the menopause prematurely, at the age of thirty or even earlier.

Oestrogens don't prevent all the changes of the menopause, do they?

Regrettably not. In spite of valiant resistance, the process of ageing is relentless. But hormones keep the changes to a minimum. A woman who stops menstruating at the age of forty and lives to seventy-five may spend more than forty-five per cent of her life in the menopause. She deserves all the help she can get.

Do men have a change of life, too?

Yes. Unfortunately it is much more gradual than the female menopause.

Why unfortunately?

Because that makes it more difficult to diagnose and to treat. In women the disappearance of menstruation and the beginning of hot flashes is unmistakable. Most women, especially as they begin to feel worse and worse, do something about it. In men it works another way.

The first victim of the male menopause is that most fragile of masculine functions, the erection. The penis loses its punch. Instead of a resilient ramrod, it begins to resemble soft putty. Elevation of the penis takes longer and accomplishes less. Usually the process is so gradual that the man is barely aware of it. Glen is an example. Sales manager for a large company, he is forty-nine, but looks younger. He finally got around to seeing a doctor.

"Doc, it's the funniest damn thing. It must've been going on for about a year but I didn't even realize it. I had a little trouble now and then, but nothing big. My God, what am I saying, 'nothing big'! That's why I'm here, I've got nothing big any more!" With trembling hands, he lighted a cigarette.

The change of life is not exactly a picnic for men either. The awareness of ageing, the loss of potency, the resulting isolation from their wives, can trigger a profound depression.

After a few puffs, Glen regained his composure.

"Well, I didn't know what to think. It's a hell of a thing not to be able to do what you've been doing all your life. I wasn't getting along too well with Jane, my wife, at that time anyhow. I tried everything. I took vitamins. I tried some other pills the chemist sold me. I even thought it might be my wife's fault; she's not so young any more either. So I performed a little experiment with one of the girls at the office. I went over to her place a couple of times to see what would happen. The first shot was great and I thought I had it whipped but after that it was just the same."

Most men, like Glen, try everything. The chemist sells them pills for lost manhood, a sympathetic secretary lets them try a new copulatory environment for a while, they take vitamins by the dozens, but nothing does any good. They just get worse.

"After awhile, I couldn't do anything at all. I thought my penis had just died—I was waiting for it to fall off. I could swear it was getting smaller and even my testicles were shrinking. I really got so depressed and irritable I couldn't force myself to go to work. I thought it was time to see a doctor."

It wasn't Glen's imagination—his penis and testicles were shrinking. Testosterone, the only male sex hormone, is primarily secreted by the testicles with a secondary supply from the adrenal glands. Everything that makes a man a man originates from this substance. A few drops a day of this hormone keeps a man hairy and muscular. They keep the penis and testicles humming and maintain internal sexual structures like the prostate and seminal vesicles in working order.

What happens when the change of life begins?

About the age of forty the cells of the testicle which secrete the hormone begin to break down. They are slowly replaced by scar tissue, just as in the ovary. Very gradually the output of testosterone diminishes and male sexuality wanes. Erectile capacity suffers but there is another aspect that Glen didn't mention, probably because it hadn't dawned on him yet.

What's that?

At the same time the penis falters, the man begins to lose his interest in sex. This is often disguised by an increase in sexual activity.

Why does a man become more active sexually when he loses his desire?

Because of anxiety, he tries to prove that he can still do it like he used to. First he tries sex with his wife—when that flops, he seeks out a sympathetic third party. After failing there he looks for a fourth party, then a fifth, and so on.

Many marriages are destroyed at this stage by a combination of the husband's sexual panic and the wife's lack of understanding. Underneath everything else, the basic reason many husbands seek other women at this age is to prove that they are still capable of good-quality sexual intercourse. Tragically, if he finds another woman with whom he can function, his marriage may go down the drain.

Why tragically?

Because the menopause marches on, relentlessly. A new face and a new vagina have an aphrodisiac effect at first—actually the basis for his new success is that he is required to copulate less frequently with his new woman. When she is available every night he will probably begin to have the same problem with her.

Are there any other effects of sex hormone deficiency?

Yes. As the process continues, the manifestations become more obvious. Irritability and depression intensify and contribute to the increase in alcoholism at this age. Gradually the beard becomes thinner, the voice gets higher, and the penis and testicles atrophy even more. The man becomes bent-over and begins to lose height just like the menopausal woman. He is, in effect, becoming feminized. At the later stages, it often is hard to distinguish between the menopausal "sheman" and the "hemale." As the condition progresses men even develop enlarged breasts.

Why do the men become feminized?

Because their adrenal glands produce oestrogen, too. Typical masculinity (or femininity) depends on maintaining a balance between oestrogen and testosterone, both of which constantly circulate in normal male and female adults. When males lose their testosterone, the oestrogen takes over. It even can occur before the menopause in some men.

How does it happen?

In chronic alcoholics, severe liver damage usually occurs. Normally oestrogen produced by the adrenal glands in men is deactivated by the liver, preventing feminization. When the liver is damaged, oestrogen builds up and brings on feminine characteristics. Chronic alcoholics frequently have enlarged breasts, heavy fat deposits on the hips, and lack body hair, especially on the chest.

What is the treatment for the male menopause?

First and foremost is replacement of the waning testosterone. That part is not as easy as it sounds. Many physicians are reluctant to help their male patients through this most difficult period of their lives.

Why is that?

Some doctors don't realize that glands don't go on forever. Because many men retain the marginal ability to reproduce until well into their seventies they confuse the presence of small numbers of sperm with adequate amounts of sex hormone. On the other hand some men have had potency problems before and the doctor considers the menopausal symptoms just another episode of impotence.

Is there any way to tell the difference between the change of life and ordinary impotence?

Yes. The testicles are controlled by the master gland, the pituitary, which stimulates them by means of a hormone called gonadotropin. As the testicles dry up, the pituitary gland produces more and more gonadotropin in an attempt to urge them on to greater hormone production. It doesn't work—the testicles may be willing but they simply don't have the power. The increased gonadotropin is excreted in the urine where it can be measured chemically. If a man in his fifties has a potency problem, he should have a urinary gonadotropin test. If the reading is high, replacement of the missing testosterone may change his life. If the reading is normal, his impotence is probably an emotional problem—he needs competent psychiatric help.

What does replacement of the testosterone do?

Ideally, it puts the reproductive system back on a full-time basis. Almost all the degenerative changes are reversible. The first and most dramatic change is usually return of erectile potency. Good hard erections after moderate stimulation are common. The penis and testicles enlarge, but to the chagrin of some men, they never exceed their premenopausal size. The most important change is the emotional one. Self-confidence, determination, and optimism come rushing back. Success in the outside world breeds success in the inside world of sex. Conversely the more potent a man becomes in the bedroom, the more potent he is in business.

Let Glen finish his story:

"Ever since I've been getting these hormones, everything has changed. I didn't know a few injections could make such a difference. Jane used to complain I wasn't interested in her—now she complains that I follow her around the house like a snorting bull. But she likes it! The first two weeks I was on the hormones I guess she wasn't so sure. I had to have it at least twice a day or I couldn't go to work—those erections kept getting in the way. But that's an easier problem to solve than the other one."

By regulating the dose of hormone, the doctor can strike a balance between too much for the wife to handle and not enough for the husband to deliver.

Doesn't administration of testosterone cause the testicles to atrophy?

In a normal man, yes. It replaces his own source of the hormone. A menopausal male isn't getting much mileage out of those shrivelled testicles anyway. A little help is welcome.

Testosterone is usually administered in the form of lozenges or by injection. Ordinary tablets are destroyed by the stomach acid and are useless. Injections are inexpensive and dependable. A lozenge that allows absorption through the mucous membrane of the mouth is helpful too.

What about the other changes of the menopause; does the hormone clear them up, too?

For the most part. The beard thickens, the voice deepens, any breast enlargement dwindles, and the bones become stronger. Loss of height unfortunately cannot be reversed.

No. The sexual rehabilitation of a menopausal man requires one other ingredient—an understanding sexual partner. In some cases, in spite of continuous hormone treatment, potency still lags. This is where humanity overcomes biochemistry. A wife (or girl friend) who is sympathetic and reassuring can work wonders.

On the other hand, an impatient, petulant, degrading woman guarantees failure. No penis, hormones or not, can stand up to a nagging woman.

When Mel married Laura thirty years ago, he made a wise choice. Mel is fifty-four—he had a lot of trouble last year. His doctor gave him hormones but it just didn't seem to help. Then Laura took over. She describes it like this:

"I just couldn't stand to see it happen to him. Mel is such a wonderful man and it was tearing him apart. Sometimes he would lie awake all night trying to get an erection every half hour. Then he'd get up and pace around the house. He was in no shape to go to work the next day. The hormones helped a little but there was something missing. I tried to think if it could be anything I was doing, and when I realized my part of the problem I felt ashamed.

"I was reacting to Mel the same way I had for the past thirty years—I didn't realize that things were changing. I needed to put a little more effort into the sexual side of things than I had been. Well, it really worked. First I tried to find out what stimulated him the most. It was a lot of little things. Touching his penis was one thing—I guess I had thought it wasn't nice all those years, but anything that helped Mel now was nice enough for me. Changing positions made it more exciting for him too. The most important thing was always letting him know I wanted him sexually. That seemed to help most of all."

Mel is lucky—Laura has done for him what hormones alone couldn't accomplish.

Are there any men who shouldn't get hormones?

Yes. Those with cancer of the prostate, penis, or testicles are not eligible for testosterone therapy. Sadly, with that disease, potency is not their biggest problem.

How about homosexual men; do they have a change of life, too?

Homosexual men are no different physiologically from their heterosexual brothers. Their hormones give out, too. Replacement therapy can help them as well, but a sympathetic woman is out of the question. A homosexual partner who understands their problem and is willing to help is a rarity.

What about giving oestrogens to men in the menopause?

Under certain conditions it's a good idea. The explanation is not clear but some men seem to do better if their testosterone supplement is combined with small amounts of oestrogen. Perhaps it makes the male hormone work more smoothly. No one really knows, but the combination is worth a try in men who don't do well on testosterone alone.

How long do men and women in the menopause need to take hormones?

As long as they want to feel good. They can stop taking the hormones any time but all the symptoms will come creeping back. Nothing is ever going to bring those petrified ovaries and testicles back to life again. Once they go they are gone forever. Replacing their vital secretion can make this existence a lot more pleasant for their owners who have to stay behind.

16

SEPTEMBER SEX

When does a person get too old for sex?

Never. Because of their amazing resilience, the sexual organs just don't wear out. Though most women lose the ability to reproduce after the age of fifty or so, and men rarely become fathers after the seventh decade, sexual intercourse is feasible (and desirable) until the day one departs for a better world.

As a matter of fact, continued sexual interest and activity after the age of sixty can even be considered therapeutic.

How can sex at that age be therapeutic?

Sexual intercourse and all the events leading up to it are fascinating, stimulating, and exciting. They provide our daily life with much of its vitality and verve. Men and women who have relinquished most of their other activities such as working and raising a family need sex more, not less, than before. An elderly man who waits out his last years on the local bowls green leads a dismal existence compared to the gent who spends his days scoring in a different sort of game. A crotchety old lady rocking away the hours on her front porch might discover that time would go faster if she could look forward to breaking the monotony with a little time in bed.

This doesn't mean that older people should be transformed into sex maniacs (whatever that is) constantly looking for a way to titillate their sagging libidos. But much of the isolation and depression that accompanies old age can be forestalled by the socializing effects of searching for suitable sexual partners. If they had sex on their minds, senior citizens would not have to be prodded to get out and meet people—the problem might become getting them to come back home at night.

But isn't it a bit indecent for old people to have sex?

It's hard to understand why. If it's decent for a couple to have intercourse when they are forty-five and indecent for the same people to do the same thing in the same way with the same genitals when they are seventy-five, somebody's mixed up.

One of the problems is separating the functions of copulation and reproduction. Part of the confusion is due to the misconception, handed down through the years, that sex without reproduction is sinful. As they get older many individuals feel they no longer have a "reason" for sex. Actually they don't need one. Sexual intercourse is enough reason in itself. If reproduction is the only justification for sex, the human sexual equipment has been grossly over-designed. A man only requires, in his lifetime, enough sperm to father ten to twenty children. Actually, in one ejaculation he has about 250,000 times that amount. For reproduction purposes the human female only needs sufficient eggs to produce a family—but she has the capacity to produce about 200,000.

Sex is one of the two renewable pleasures available to human beings. Each sexual experience can be just as enjoyable as the one before—the two thousandth time can be as much fun as the second time. The other renewable pleasure is eating; a man of sixty can enjoy it as much as he did when he was sixteen—maybe even more, since he has developed taste and discrimination. Just as there is no valid reason to give up eating at an arbitrary age, there is no reason to give up sex.

Then why do some people give it up?

It may be the easy way out for men and women who never felt right about sex, anyway. When age fifty-five or sixty rolls around they are relieved to be excused from what they have considered a burden. Being too old is a socially acceptable excuse for backing away from something they never learned to enjoy. Occasionally the impetus to relinquish sexual activity comes from the children. Particularly if one of the parents has died, a daughter and son-in-law may say, "You're too old for that kind of nonsense anyhow, Pop, why don't you just settle down and forget all about that sex stuff?" Why don't the solicitous children follow their own advice and give up their own sex life if it's such a good idea? (Unfortunately some of them probably have.)

Some older people give up sex voluntarily when their partners die. After the first shock of being alone has worn off, their sexual powers and interest may have disappeared permanently. Others interrupt copulation for awhile when either husband or wife is ill. That frequently spells the end of all sex. Some couples just lose interest gradually; for others sex goes out the window when the man loses his potency. Interestingly enough there are some striking differences in the way men and women finally retreat from sex.

What are they?

The statistics reflect what everyone has probably been suspecting all along. In America, women maintain their interest in sex much longer than men do. Among the age group sixty to ninety years old, the overwhelming majority of women give up sexual intercourse only because their husbands are no longer willing or able to supply them. Of these about half the women bring their own sexual lives to a close when their husbands die. Only about one-tenth of females voluntarily choose celibacy.

On the other hand, more than half the men in this age range ring down the curtain on sexual gratification because of illness, impotence, and lack of interest.

The most important finding is that after the age of sixty, if sexual intercourse is interrupted for a period of time, usually it never starts again. This has important implications for those who are interested in preserving their sexual capabilities. As a practical matter, if a period of more than sixty days voluntarily elapses without sexual relations between husband and wife after the age of sixty (and sometimes even before) the odds are against ever taking up an active sexual relationship again.

Henry had an experience like that and it was a harrowing one. Henry is sixty-eight and a retired accountant; he tells what happened:

"Well, I was never too interested in sex, but I wasn't ready to give it up—once in awhile I really enjoyed it. I would say that my wife and I would have relations about every four weeks or so. About six months ago, back in January, Irene had a bad attack of arthritis and it made our married life pretty uncomfortable for her. So I just did without for that time. Last month she was feeling better and I tried to start again but I couldn't get sufficient strength in my organ."

What Henry means is that after six months of enforced chastity, he couldn't get an erection. At the age of sixty-eight erections don't come easily to most men, and like pigeons, once they fly away it's hard to get them back. But like most women, Irene was more practical about sexual matters than her husband. She tells what happened next:

"Well, I'm not exactly what you would call a sex fiend but I knew something was wrong with my husband. He didn't eat right and he just sat around the house brooding—he didn't even go for his walks any more like the doctor said he should And every time he tried to have relations with me and failed he just got worse. So I went out and bought some books on sex—I'd never done anything like that before but times are changing and I guess I'd fallen a little behind. One of the books said that if the wife handled her husband's organ when they had sex, it made it easier for him to have an erection. I was always taught that no decent woman did that kind of thing but I suppose things are different now. To tell the truth, I didn't really care. I love my husband and I was willing to do anything to help him be a man again. The next chance that came along I did just what the book said and it was like magic—it got harder than it used to get thirty years ago. Even more important to me, Henry was a changed man. He's much more cheerful and optimistic and even wants to look for a part-time job now. Maybe I shouldn't admit it but I enjoy our relations more than I used to. I'm even thinking of trying some of the other things I read about in that book."

Is there anything else Henry could have done to keep his potency intact?

Yes, if he could bring himself to do it. He could masturbate. As far as the body is concerned, all reflexes are equal. Physiologically speaking, the sexual reflex patterns are no different from those controlling digestion and defecation. If Henry were to refrain from eating solid foods for six months he would have a very hard time going back on a normal diet. If he avoided bowel movements for half a year, at his age, normal elimination might never return. Unless the sexual nerve patterns are constantly reinforced after the sixth decade, they may simply fade away.

The body doesn't care how this reinforcement takes place. Henry's minister may not like it if Henry brings on his own orgasms but the minister surely can't suggest a better method of preserving sexual function either. (Besides, ministers masturbate, too.) If an ageing man can understand that regular masturbation may help keep his sexual equipment functioning until his usual sexual object is again available, both husband and wife will be spared a tremendous amount of suffering.

You mean doctors recommend masturbation?

While masturbation is not the ideal form of sexual activity and certainly cannot compete with heterosexual intercourse for lasting satisfaction, it has a significant place in everyone's sexual evolution. Just as masturbation initiates sexual activity in childhood, it can perpetuate sexual function in old age. If the alternative is permanent loss of sexual powers or temporary masturbation, most normal people are likely to opt for a little masturbation. If the husband dies, it is entirely reasonable for the wife to masturbate to keep her copulatory mechanism functioning until another suitable partner comes along. Because of the delicate and evanescent nature of the erectile mechanism in older men, it is almost essential for a recent widower to exercise his orgasmic machinery literally to keep it alive.

What if the spouse can't engage in sex because of illness?

If the illness is truly one which prevents intercourse and is expected to be permanent, other sexual alternatives must be considered. Fortunately, there are relatively few physical conditions that rule out copulation completely.

One of the changes which occurs with advancing age and tends to interfere with normal intercourse is obesity. As the husband (and wife) put on weight their enlarging abdomens push the genitals farther and farther away from each other. Unfortunately the penis cannot increase in length to keep one step ahead of the tummy and the vagina ultimately gets out of range. The logical solution is for both partners to lose weight. The easiest solution is to find a way to have intercourse that detours around the protuberant abdomens. One of the most effective positions is the

"T-square" technique. The woman is in the usual position on her back with her legs spread wide apart. Her partner lies with his hips under the arch formed by her raised legs. With both abdomens safely out of the way, penis and vagina have a clear field for fun. Another simple solution is for the woman to position herself atop the man, either lying or sitting over him as he lies on his back. Once again this gives the penis and vagina a clear shot at each other.

What about people with arthritis?

As time passes, almost everyone develops occasionally aches and pains in the bones and joints. Sometimes the discomfort gets to the point where intercourse and the associated movement can cause pain. This is the worst possible reason to cut back on sexual activity. For most forms of arthritis, frequent mild exercise is beneficial. What better way is there to exercise mildly than in the comfort and privacy of one's bed with an attractive sexual partner?

But there is even a better reason than that. All the glands in the body are interconnected and ruled by the master gland, the pituitary. Since the testicles in the male and the ovaries in the female are affected by sexual activity, the message is sent back to the pituitary at the base of the brain. This stimulates, in turn, the thyroid and adrenal glands which serve to further stimulate the sexual glands themselves. Frequent sexual intercourse causes the adrenal glands to increase their production of cortisone and tends to alleviate the symptoms of arthritis.

You mean sex is good for arthritis?

In a sense, yes. For a long time doctors have known that there is much less arthritis among those who remain sexually active. They used to think that only those who somehow were spared the crippling effects of this disease were able to keep having intercourse. Now, *hormone studies have proved that it is sexual activity itself which helps protect those beyond middle age from the degenerative changes of this condition.*

Is there anything else that people with arthritis can do to make their sexual lives more enjoyable?

Certainly. Very often simply changing positions can be helpful in relieving the pressure on painful joints. There is nothing in the legal code that insists that the man has to be on top and the woman must lie on the bottom during copulation. Sensible experimentation is often indicated—any reasonable means of bringing the penis and vagina in closer proximity is worth considering. Some of the far-out techniques have their drawbacks, however. Leonard ought to know—he tried them:

"Well, you know how it is, doc, Grace and I aren't as young as we used to be. We're both in our fifties and when I saw one of those books advertised last week, *Make Your Marriage Young Again,* I just couldn't resist. It was the chapter on 'Thirty-six Exquisite Sexual Positions' that really got to me. Since Grace was willing, we tried them—not all on the same night, of course. Positions one through nine weren't too bad. Neither of us noticed anything 'exquisite' about them but they were a change from everyday. The next ones, ten through seventeen were just too much work and didn't seem worth it. Position eighteen was the one that did me in. It was called The Egyptian Grapevine, and had our arms and legs all twisted up together. It was supposed to bring on unbearable ecstasy. Well, it didn't exactly work out that way. It took about five minutes for Grace and I to get ourselves into it but when we were ready to have intercourse, we found we couldn't even move. We both started laughing so hard that I wrenched my back. I couldn't go to work for two days and I could hardly have relations for the next two weeks. I gave the book to one of the salesmen at the office—he's a bachelor. Let him see how The Egyptian Grapevine works for him. I wish him luck!"

How does sex affect the heart?

No *normal* heart was ever harmed by sexual activity. Actually a vigorous, healthy interest in sex and an active sex life is probably the best form of protection against a heart attack.

How is that?

Heart specialists agree that three of the major precipitating factors in heart attacks are lack of exercise, overweight, and nervous tension. Frequent, vigorous sexual intercourse helps to control all of these dangers.

There are few forms of physical exercise that provide the benefits of copulation. The vigorous pelvic thrusts maintain the muscles and joints of the entire spine in good condition. The circulation of the whole body is improved and deep breathing is encouraged. One of the major goals of jogging is to raise the heart rate over about 120 per minute and thereby increase cardiac reserve. During intercourse, the heart rate usually rises to about 160 per minute just before and during orgasm. In addition, the blood pressure increases, for a short time, as much as fifty per cent —this is considered beneficial. It has been calculated that the average act of intercourse consumes about 150 calories which makes it attractive to weight watchers.

A single act of intercourse is the exercise equivalent of about half an hour of jogging or forty minutes of callisthenics. For most people four times around the park on a rainy morning can't compare with once around the bed. Any man who thinks about it is bound to trade forty minutes in a sweaty gym for an hour or so in the fragrant embrace of a willing female. The other drawback of regular exercise is forgetting to keep it up. Sex is a lot harder to forget, especially if you don't have to dress for it and if there is an attractive partner who has her own way of reminding you.

An active sex life keeps the weight down in other ways, too. While some folks like their mates to be pleasingly plump, a lot of fat tends to get in the way, both mechanically and aesthetically. To maintain their sexiness most men and women have a good incentive to watch their weight.

One of the biggest burdens on the heart is our frantic society. The daily frustrations and anxieties that plague us can cause relentless damage to the heart and blood vessels. Far more effective than any tranquillizer (and far more enjoyable) is a full, loving sexual relationship. The peace and well-being that it can bring is unobtainable anywhere else—at any price. There is an added bonus: as the richness of a gratifying sexual relationship calms and relaxes the individual, the sexual experience itself becomes even more satisfying. In its best form sex can be the ideal antidote to our mixed-up world.

Doesn't sex occasionally brings on a heart attack?

Not really. If a person's cardiac status has deteriorated over the years to the point where a heart attack is about to strike, copulation may conceivably be the final stress that cuts off the blood supply to the sagging heart. That doesn't mean that sex causes heart attacks. Watching an exciting movie on television or running to catch a bus the next morning can do the same thing. Giving up sex at that point won't forestall the inevitable more than a few hours at the most. And when you get right down to it there are worse ways to leave this world.

Is sexual intercourse safe for those who have had heart attacks?

Except in unusually severe cases, the danger to the heart from sexual intercourse is insignificant. If a person can walk without heart symptoms, he can have sex. The strain on the heart of a brisk walk is probably more than that from a brisk orgasm. Copulation requires an energy consumption of about five calories a minute which is well within the capabilities of most of those who have recovered from heart attacks.

Because a heart attack does cause some immediate damage to the heart muscle itself it is sensible to wait until the first stage of healing is well under way. To be on the safe side, sexual activity should be postponed until about eight to ten weeks after the original attack. But no one can really say for sure what would happen if copulation were to begin before then. Occasionally heart patients are visited in the hospital by their husbands or wives, and have intercourse in the hospital room as early as a week or two after the heart attack without any ill effects. While this demonstrates the durability of the heart muscles as well as the durability of the human sexual instinct, it is perhaps wiser to wait a little longer.

Couldn't somebody die that way?

As far as can be determined, the number of people who die from heart attacks during sexual intercourse is very small. Two estimates suggest that about six out of every thousand people with previous heart attacks finally succumb during intercourse. As an interesting sidelight, about eighty per cent of those who cash in their chips during copulation are making it with someone other than their own husbands or wives. One possible conclusion is, for those who've had a heart attack and want to continue with sex, honesty may be the healthiest policy.

In any event, prompt resumption of sexual activities as soon as possible after a heart attack is very important.

Why is it so important?

Many of those who suffer heart attacks, both men and women, feel as if they have somehow been damaged irreparably. They often tend to consider themselves semi-invalids. Once they see that they are still effective and desirable as sexual partners they improve immediately. The wife who wants to spare her husband the strain of sex is making a mistake. It would be much better if she would stimulate him instead—tactfully. Alice handled it well:

"Jim had his heart attack about three months ago and it really hit him hard. He almost lost his business—he distributes appliances. He finally managed to get back to work slowly and got things under control. Just when I thought everything was fine, it turned out I was doing him in by trying to be considerate.

"I just didn't know better. I figured he was a sick man and that sex would be bad for him. He really used to be something before his attack—I mean sex was a big thing in his life. So when he got home from the hospital I ordered twin beds so he wouldn't get all worked up sleeping with me. The poor man thought I did it because he was all washed up. He really started to go downhill then. Fortunately I caught on fast and took him back into my bed. It was just like magic! He's even better than before—he says he appreciates it more now. His heart attack certainly didn't seem to damage any of his other organs!"

Is sex helpful in any other way to those who have had heart attacks?

Yes. Aside from the feeling of relaxation that comes from successful copulation, there is a hormonal advantage as well.

Some cardiac patients have a symptom known as angina pectoris, a medical term for pain in the chest. On exertion, after a heavy meal, or because of mental strain, the individual may develop a sudden, agonizing, crushing pain behind the breast bone. The exact cause of this symptom is unknown—it may be related to lack of blood supply to the heart muscle but the explanation is far from clear. In any event, the pain of angina pectoris is excruciating and prevents the sufferer from doing anything—sex included.

Many years ago, it was discovered that injections of testosterone, the male sex hormone, decreased (and in some cases prevented) this form of chest pain. It is also well known that regular sexual activity in men, by stimulating the testicles to produce more hormone, increases the amount of testosterone in the bloodstream. Just as in arthritis, men with angina pectoris who are sexually active seem to have less frequent attacks of pain. Though angina pectoris is five times as common in men, those unfortunate women who are afflicted with it also seem to benefit from regular sexual intercourse. In cases where chest pain tends to interfere with sex nitroglycerine tablets (a common remedy for angina) taken a few minutes before intercourse may prevent the pain from developing.

Isn't it true that sexual power in both men and women decreases with age?

Strictly speaking, the answer is yes. In men the hormone-producing cells of the testicles are gradually replaced by scar tissue. Hormone production by the testicles as well as the adrenal glands decreases slowly with age and the testicles become smaller. At the same time, the prostate gland begins to enlarge.

What is the function of the prostate gland?

The prostate is the Doctor Jekyll and Mr. Hyde of male sexuality. The organ itself is a walnut-size structure that sits astride the urethra at the entrance to the bladder. This strategic position is perfectly suited to its function of adding a powerful secretion to the seminal fluid at the moment of ejaculation which increases the activity of the sperm. For most of a man's life the prostate is a benign ally, lying dormant until the moment of orgasm when it contracts briefly and vigorously, then sinks once again into the sexual shadows. However, in some men between the ages of twenty and forty, the prostate may become inflamed and cause a chronic feeling of fullness and pain in the perineum, between the testicles and the anus. Probably one third of all men suffer from prostatitis at some time before the age of forty. There are two causes of this condition, both of them easily curable.

What are they?

The first source of prostatitis is pounding of the perineum. Cowboys, heavy equipment operators, motorcycle riders, and truck drivers, all absorb a lot of punishment in this area. Elimination of the pounding eliminates the inflammation of the gland. The other treatment is even more pleasant to undertake. Constant sexual stimulation without gratification ultimately results in a bloated tender prostate. This condition is an occupational hazard of sailors, priests, college students, and hen-pecked husbands. The treatment? Regular and frequent sexual intercourse. If copulation for some reason is impossible, regular masturbation usually relieves the pressure to a degree.

Many doctors feel that constant prostatitis leads to a much more serious problem, which goes under the misleading name of benign prostatic hypertrophy.

Why is the name misleading?

The term benign implies that the disease is relatively insignificant. Nothing could be further from the truth. (Benign in this sense only means not malignant, that is, not a form of cancer.) The consequences of BPH, as it is called by doctors, can be supremely malignant in their effects on sexual enjoyment.

After the age of forty about sixty per cent of all men suffer from enlargement of the prostate. It is not the increased size that makes the difference: it is the position of the gland. As it enlarges it progressively blocks the urethra and neck of the bladder. Ultimately the obstruction becomes complete and free urination is impossible. Sexual complications arise when the gland is engorged prior to intercourse and sudden bladder obstruction ensues. A fifty-five-year-old man who knows that sexual intercourse will make it impossible for him to pass his urine for the next eight to ten hours thinks twice about sex. Sooner or later he will only think once and the thought will be: No. Since the prostate enlarges in all directions simultaneously, other sexual structures feel the pressure and overall sexual performance declines.

What is the treatment for enlargement of the prostate?

Since the gland is non-essential, once it becomes sexually antagonistic, the best solution is to remove it. There are three ways to dispose of the prostate—each with its own advantages.

The first technique is transurethral resection or TUR for short. This operation is fast, inexpensive, and safe. A hollow stainless steel tube is inserted into the penis until it reaches the area of the prostate—just behind the testicles. A small knife is passed through the tube and used to shave away portions of the gland that block the bladder. Unfortunately the improvement is only temporary—in one to three years the tissue grows back and the operation has to be repeated. A TUR makes good sense in a seventy-four-year-old man or an individual who is suffering from some severe chronic disease in addition to his BPH.

Another possibility is the perineal approach, which requires an incision between the scrotum and the anus. While more complicated than the TUR, it is relatively easy on the patient and removes all or most of the prostate. The third surgical procedure is the supra-pubic. The surgeon makes his incision at the pubic area at the lower end of the abdomen. This operation is effective in removing the prostate but is not well adapted to elderly men.

Does removal of the prostate affect sexual performance?

Frequently it does. While the decision to operate or not is independent of a man's sexual wishes, since urinary obstruction is the major problem, there are important implications for sexuality. The one thing that can always be expected to change after prostate removal is ejaculation. During intercourse everything proceeds as usual except that no seminal fluid appears at the moment of orgasm. The man's subjective sensations are usually the same (if he is still potent) but there is something missing. One man who had the operation described it this way:

"Doc, it's the damnedest thing! We do everything just like always—I still get a good hard erection. At the right time I start to come, but then—nothing! It's a funny feeling! The first time it happened I remember thinking, 'Okay, that's fine for practice. Now next time I'll do it for real.' But after awhile I got used to it. I'll tell you one thing—I feel much better without that prostate blocking my plumbing!"

Does a prostate operation interfere with normal potency?

Most of the time it doesn't. Particularly with the supra-pubic and TUR approaches the results in this area are good. About thirty per cent of patients who are operated on have increased potency. Another thirty per cent retain their sexual capabilities pretty much as they were before the operation. Another thirty per cent find themselves impotent after the operation. Thus removal of the prostate probably causes impotence in about fifteen per cent of the cases or less.

But if thirty per cent of the men are impotent after the surgery, how can it cause impotence only fifteen per cent of the time?

Not all of the impotence after the operation is the result of the operation. For some men it is just the easy way out. The surgery may give an individual the excuse he needs to do what he was going to do anyway. Bennett's case is a good example:

Bennet is in the insurance business. He and Fay, his wife had a fair sexual relationship most of their marriage. "Nothing special," as Bennett described it. "But we got our kicks most of the time. Then when I got to be fifty-eight last year I had to have my prostate out. I guess we were having sex about twice a month at that time, and after thirty-five years of marriage, what can you expect? Neither of us really knew what to anticipate after the operation, but when I got back from the hospital Fay just concluded that was the end of fun and games for us. I suppose I kind of agreed with her and I was ready to call it quits, too. We didn't have any sexual contact for about two months. Then I tried a couple of times and there was nothing. I just retired from sex."

Under the circumstances Bennett and Fay would probably have done it the same way if Bennett had his tonsils out. Sometimes it isn't that easy to retire from sex. Bennett gradually became more depressed and irritable and his relationship with Fay began to deteriorate in other ways, too. Things got so bad finally that they went to their minister who suggested they see a psychiatrist together. Bennett can tell how it turned out:

"I just wish someone had told me about this before I had the operation. The first thing the psychiatrist asked me was how often I masturbated. I was a little ashamed but I told him the truth—twice a week. Then he explained to both of us that there was no physical reason why we couldn't have regular intercourse—he said it this way: 'If you can masturbate, you ought to be able to copulate.' Fay thought that was a little crude, but I told her that's the way these guys talk. He pointed out a lot of other things about outselves we weren't about to admit, too. We realized that the operation was just the excuse; our marriage was falling apart and we used the surgery to give it the final push. Things are different now. We have intercourse about three or four times a week, and, speaking for both of us, we enjoy it more than we ever did."

Bennett winked. "I never knew sex could be so great. If I knew it could make that much difference, I would've had that damn prostate out twenty years ago."

What about the other fifteen per cent?

Those whose impotency after surgery is on a physical basis are the unlucky ones. Most of them have had the perineal approach and fortunately are the oldest group. In any event, there is no alternative—when the gland blocks the flow of urine, it has to go. There is however some hope even for those—the same technique which helps men over the male menopause occasionally works for them.

What kind of technique is that?

A good name for it might be sexual rehabilitation. The muscles of the body lose their strength and tone if they are not exercised properly and frequently. In the same way the components of a human being which contribute to his maximum sexual enjoyment must be maintained in perfect working order if he is to get the maximum use out of them.

After the age of forty most men begin to sag. They are like wind-up clocks that have started to run down. Some of this is on a physical basis; human beings are not made of iron and steel and by the fourth decade the body begins to become less efficient. The secretions from all the glands begin to dry up, the metabolic rate lags, and more fat accumulates everywhere. In some cases the blood supply to the brain begins to decline almost imperceptibly. These changes occur to some extent in every man; it is the individual responses which differ.

How is that?

Some men, as they feel themselves getting out of shape, react with a vigorous effort to get back in condition. Others are content to let things take their course. The ones who don't fight back become the victims of the male menopause. Earl is forty-eight and is going through it now:

"I don't know what happened to me, doctor. It's as if I got old all of a sudden. First I put on ten pounds. I never got over 160 since I left college. I used to be a fanatic about it—I even made my employees keep their weight down. I'm in the drug business and we have to have a healthy image. After the first ten pounds I just didn't seem to care—I simply switched to double-breasted suits and covered it up. Then I put on twenty-five pounds more—I never weighed 195 in my life. And sex—I just don't know what happened. I haven't given it up, but I lost all interest in my wife. I don't want to hurt her—Gloria's been a good woman—but she doesn't do a thing for me sexually. I might as well tell you this if I'm going to tell you everything. For about two years now I've been sleeping with my secretary, Jean. She's twenty-four and good looking, but that's not the whole story. She respects me more than Gloria and when it comes to sex, she makes me feel important. Even if I don't do so well one night, she doesn't complain and she tries to help me. She'll do anything I want her to as far as sex is concerned—not that I ask for anything unusual—but with Gloria, it's the same old way every time or not at all. I don't know what I'd do without Jean but even with her things aren't right. I'm beginning to lose interest in my business—I just don't care what happens to me any more."

"What about drinking?"

"How did you know? Yes, that too. I wouldn't say I'm an alcoholic but every night when I get home from work I need at least two double martinis before I can face an evening with Gloria. Even when I'm over at Jean's house, I feel like a couple of drinks before I can relax. And every so often it gets away from me and I get loaded. I never thought things would turn out this way. It all seemed to hit me at once!"

Earl has described, from his own experience, most of the major symptoms of the male menopause. Depression, sexual conflict, apathy, physical decline—all these may begin to descend on the unfortunate forty-year-old.

What brings on the male menopause?

Usually it is a combination of minor defeats which gang up on the helpless victim. Each disappointment is like the slender thread of a spider's web—individually they are meaningless but as the disappointments mount up the menopausal male may feel that he is bound with chains of steel.

One of the major defeats is loss of emotional borrowing power. At the age of twenty-five, thirty, even thirty-five, a man can sustain himself with the promise of future accomplishments. The local chemist can dream of a chain of his shops, the insurance salesman can dream of his own agency. By the fortieth year, most men begin to feel they are stuck with what they have.

The feeling of being stuck sometimes extends to their wives. There is no more fantasy of exciting sex, no more prospect of something new, as far as they are concerned. As one man put it, "Just the same damn thing with the same damn wife!"

As the body begins to slow down, everything else droops even more. If a real illness like diabetes or high blood pressure appears, it is seen as another nail in the coffin.

Fortunately none of this has to happen the way it does. With a combination of enlightened medical treatment, psychiatric insight, and common sense, no modern man needs to suffer the miseries of the male menopause.

How can he avoid it?

The simplest and most direct way is an aggressive programme of sexual rehabilitation. With the assistance of a skilful doctor or psychiatrist, the results can be amazing.

The first step is to reverse the physical changes of middle-age— that is, the many changes which can be reversed. Weight reduction is the first order of the day; it serves a dual purpose. It immediately improves a man's appearance and sexual attractiveness and simultaneously augments his self-confidence. In addition it significantly benefits his health.

The next phase of rehabilitation is directed at the endocrine glands. The secretion of these tiny organs controls the inner destiny of the body. Every man at the menopause can benefit from additional testosterone, the male sex hormone. Besides controlling sexual function, this hormone literally builds stronger bones, improves digestion of protein, raises the metabolism of the body to help prevent overweight, and improves the mental outlook by infusing the individual with a feeling of well-being. Like every other hormone, unless administered under strict medical supervision it can do a great deal of harm. Hormone therapy is not a do-it-yourself project.

The next gland that needs attention is the thyroid. Considered to be the body's thermostat, the thyroid controls (among other things) the rate at which food is burned up. If the thyroid is underactive, a greater proportion of food is converted to fat. As the body ages, the cells of the thyroid gland age also, and the entire tempo of the organism slows. Apathy, sluggishness, depression, and obesity begin to appear. If these result from thyroid deficiency, small amounts of substitute hormone taken daily by mouth have a dramatic effect. The old zip comes rushing back and it is almost like the clock had run in reverse: the patient looks and feels as if he is getting younger.

In addition to the testicles and thyroid, there is another endocrine gland that merits attention during the male menopause. The adrenal gland produces a large number of hormones but the group that is most important to the man in the change of life is the corticosteroids; the best known component is cortisone. Cortisone performs many functions in the economy of the body but a few of its effects become critical at middle age.

As the years pass, every organ and tissue of the body becomes infiltrated with connective tissues or scar tissue. Essential functions decline as the heart, lungs, brain, joints, and testicles trade their working cells for fibrous masses of scar tissue. Cortisone works against scar tissue and the associated loss of function.

It is a powerful drug. In certain forms of arthritis that literally cripple the patient, a week or so of crotisone treatment can have him riding a bike or jumping rope. Cortisone must be administered cautiously; like any other drug it can have serious side effects. In small doses, taken daily by mouth, it can restore the elasticity of the joints, improve the operation of virtually every organ, and literally retard the ageing process.

In men with prostate problems, appropriate treatment is an essential part of the rehabilitation process.

The other aspect of this technique is to control any physical disease that may be present. Many common conditions such as diabetes and high blood pressure should have already improved somewhat in response to weight reduction. Attacking any residual illness as aggressively as possible completes the physical phase of sexual rehabilitation.

What about the sexual part?

The next stage is sexual rehabilitation. It begins with a frank talk with a psychiatrist. The most important aspect of sexual rehabilitation is restoring the primary sexual organ, the brain, to maximum functioning. The goal is a realistic understanding of the individual's emotional makeup as it affects his sexual life. A full-scale psychoanalysis is not required nor desirable at this stage. Sorting out some of the uncertainty and emotional contradictions that characterize this period is all that is indicated. Assuming the psychiatrist understands the goals half a dozen interviews can work wonders.

Sometimes sexual retraining can be beneficial at this stage. If the sexual reflexes have atrophied from disuse, in those cases where the man has despaired of ever having another erection and orgasm, graduated masturbation with a vibrator can be the start of restored potency.

But isn't masturbating with a vibrator wrong?

The man who is doomed to a lifetime of impotence doesn't think so. He thinks his sexual emptiness is wrong. Any reasonable treatment which can restore a human being to normal functioning can't be wrong.

Is that all there is to it?

No. That is about fifty per cent. For the method to be effective, if the man is married, his wife must be sexually rehabilitated also. In a woman, the process is similar but somewhat more extensive. It also begins with weight reduction and correction of oestrogen or female sex hormone deficiency. Thyroid and cortisone may also be required. In the sexual restoration of women, much more can be accomplished by surgery. Plastic surgery on the vagina to compensate for the stretching and tearing caused by childbirth can add tremendously to sexual enjoyment. The vaginal cavity and the vaginal opening itself can be made smaller; a woman of fifty-five can have the same vaginal feel to her husband and the same vaginal feeling herself, as a girl of nineteen. As the genital muscles lose their tone with the passage of time, the bladder may sag downward and cause leakage of urine, incomplete emptying, and frequent bladder infections. While the vagina is being remodelled, the bladder can also be put back in its original position.

It is also relatively easy to perform plastic surgery on the breasts to restore them to more youthful contours. The combination of gravity and time can cause even the most appealing breasts to lose their attraction. No matter how pendulous or enlarged the breasts may be, an adept plastic surgeon can restore them to a perfect 36. Small, shrunken breasts can be augmented to that magic dimension if desired.

Plastic surgery on the face is the dream of many women over forty. Most of them consider it only for film stars, or impossibly expensive. Yet there is nothing that restores a woman's confidence in herself and that makes her more attractive to her husband than erasing, overnight, the wrinkles and lines of the past four decades. The cost runs about £500 to £1,000. More and more people, both husbands and wives, are beginning to feel it's worthwhile.

If looking younger will make the women feel younger, if it will make her more attractive to her husband, if it will improve their sexual relationship, and if they can manage it financially, there is no reason to hold back. Few women who have had a face lift by a capable plastic surgeon were ever known to regret it later on. Not many husbands have complained about the cost of such surgery after they have seen the results.

The same psychiatric consultation and insights should of course be made available to the woman. Sexual retraining by means of the vibrator may also be indicated if sexual activity has declined significantly. There is, however, more to be done.

What else is there?

The basic reason for going through the process of sexual restoration is to increase the enjoyment of sex. In order to enjoy it, the couple has to do it. Frequent whole-hearted sexual intercourse is the most essential element in sexual rehabilitation. Once the capacity for the full enjoyment of sex has been returned (or in some cases created) it must be constantly reinforced or it will be lost.

All sex depends on a feedback mechanism. As the husband gives gratification to his wife, she stimulates him in return. That motivates him to more intensive efforts and reciprocally encourages her to respond more eagerly. The intensity of their mutual sexual pleasure then tends to increase almost without limit.

Does sexual rehabilitation work for single people, too?

Certainly. Actually it is probably more urgent in many ways for a single person to go through this process. Those who are married have more or less constant access to sexual activity (at least theoretically). Sometimes for single people it gets to be too much trouble to find a sexual partner. As sex becomes neglected, sexual interest wanes, soon to be followed by a decrease in ability.

Prompt aggressive action can restore sexual function and sexual pleasure. Look what happened to Earl:

"Actually I didn't believe it was possible. It wasn't until I lost the first twenty pounds and threw away all my double-breasted suits that I really thought it had a chance to work. I don't know whether it was the hormone shots or the thyroid tablets or the combination, but everything started to change. Even Gloria didn't look so bad. Then the next lucky break came along. When Gloria saw the difference in me she wanted the same thing for herself.

"With a new face and, let's say, a new figure, she made everything different. You know before she was so loose down there I hardly felt anything when we had relations—of course I was sort of flabby then myself. But now my erections are like a steel rail and Gloria fits tighter than Jean did. As a matter of fact I let Jean go last month—she was really a lousy secretary. I guess I just had her around to keep me from cracking up completely. I'm going to tell you something—Gloria and I went on a trip last weekend and in one day we had relations three times. How many forty-eight-year-old men can make that statement? I only wish I'd had this done years ago."

Why don't more doctors offer their patients the opportunity for sexual rehabilitation?

There are several reasons. First, most doctors are preoccupied with treating "sick" people. They may forget that the premature loss of a person's ability to enjoy sex is also an abnormal condition that deserves immediate treatment.

Second, most patients don't ask for what they want. After years of being conditioned to believe that sex is something to push into the background until the "important" things in life have been taken care of, the average individual feels guilty about asking for help with his sexual problems.

At what age is it too late for sexual rehabilitation?

It's hard to say. Provided that a person's general health has not deteriorated to the point where intercourse is physically impossible, there is no absolute age limit. Recent careful studies on elderly people (those over seventy years old) have revealed some interesting facts. It is entirely possible for a person to remain sexually active to the age of eighty and beyond provided a few minimum requirements are fulfilled. Assuming reasonably good health, the most essential ingredients are a continuing interest in sex and a cooperative partner. Obviously the more cooperative the partner, the greater the interest in sex becomes. Certain studies also revealed another significant point. In many people, after the age of seventy-five or so, the interest in sex and sexual activity increased. Other research has confirmed that especially after the age of about forty-five (particularly in women) sexual desire intensifies.

Why should sexual drive get stronger as a person gets older?

Perhaps one reason is that after the end of the fourth decade the sexual organs are liberated from the intense social pressure and inhibition. After fifty or fifty-five years have gone by most men and women are beginning to get out from under, sexually speaking. The lucky ones have disposed of most of their guilt about sex as a means of having fun. Fears of pregnancy and venereal disease fade into the background and the whole atmosphere is more relaxed. Unrealistic and magical expectations have begun to fade as many people at this age realize that full sexual satisfaction is something that has to be sought after—and is well worth the effort.

At this time of life many men and women have more leisure and they find sexual partners more accessible. There is no social pressure to conform sexually in the sense there was when they were twenty-five years old. Daniel knows how it is:

"When I think back on it, I used to worry if I would still be able to have sex when I got in my fifties. Well, I'm sixty-nine now, and to be honest I didn't realize how much I was missing when I was young. Now that I've cut down on my law practice—I only go in a couple of days a week now—I can spend more time doing important things. I never had so many girl friends and good times in my life. It used to be a big deal to spend a night in a motel with a girl—now I can go away for a week and no one seems to care. I guess if you're over sixty they think you've forgotten how to use it. Not me. No worries about pregnancy, no pressure to get married. And the thing that I like most is being appreciated. I always make a sincere effort to do my best for a girl now—that's important to me at this stage—and they seem to realize it. That makes it even better."

Benjamin Franklin, in his genial essay, "Advice to a Young Man," makes the same point. After recommending that his young friend choose an older mistress, he lists seven ways in which older women are preferable to their younger sisters. The eighth and final reason, and perhaps one of the most important, is, "They are so grateful."

Obviously the same holds true for an older man. There is an alternative to an empty, frustrating old age. A stimulating, rewarding sexual life with all its implications for happiness can give a deeper meaning to Robert Browning's words,

"Grow old along with me!
The best is yet to be."

INDEX